T0138615

The Data Protection Officer

Profession, Rules, and Role

The Data Protection Officer

Profession, Rules, and Role

Paul Lambert

CRC Press
Taylor & Francis Group
Boca Raton London New York

CRC Press is an imprint of the
Taylor & Francis Group, an **informa** business
AN AUERBACH BOOK

CRC Press
Taylor & Francis Group
6000 Broken Sound Parkway NW, Suite 300
Boca Raton, FL 33487-2742

Printed on acid-free paper
Version Date: 20161021

International Standard Book Number-13: 978-1-138-03193-7 (Hardback)

**Visit the Taylor & Francis Web site at
http://www.taylorandfrancis.com**

**and the CRC Press Web site at
http://www.crcpress.com**

Printed and bound in the United States of America
by Edwards Brothers Malloy on sustainably sourced paper.

CONTENTS

SECTION 2   THE REGULATION

SECTION 3   ROLE

SECTION 5   TOOLS OF THE DATA PROTECTION OFFICER

GUIDING POINTS FOR DATA PROTECTION OFFICERS

☐ Preparing for the New Data Protection Regime

- Consider current reporting channels, and any required amendments.

- Consider any amendments to contracts of employment.

- Consider changes required by and necessitated to the current processes and procedures of the organization.

- Spread awareness and acceptance of the new data protection regime throughout the organization.

- Consider inward-facing data protection issues, employees, and human resources (HR), as well as outward-facing issues affecting customers and users.

- Identify and consider the data held by the organization.

- Communicate the updated data protection policies and related information as appropriate within the organization, and to customers and users.

- Review the rights regime under the new GDPR, and appropriate changes that are necessitated.

- Review current access requests and consider any amendments required to the process as well as the time frame.

- Consider future deletion, takedown, forgetting, and erasure issues and requests.

- Review the personal data collected and aggregated, and the legal basis for processing such data.

- Consent issues and recordal need to be reviewed in detail in light of the new data protection regime.

- Children are expressly referred to in the new data protection regime, and the organization needs to consider if, how, and why it may seek to collect the personal data of children.

- Data breach incidents are increasingly problematic and some of the considerations for dealing with same are now encompassed in the new GDPR, including preparedness, risk, and reaction issues.

- Data protection by design and by default, and also data protection impact assessments, needs to be embraced within the organization, and will need to have appropriate information disseminated as a result.

- Transfer and international issues will be important for certain organizations, and when personal data are involved, particular additional considerations apply under the new data protection regime (in addition to issues such as the new EU-US Privacy Shield, etc.).

☐ New DPOs

New DPOs may also wish to consider the following:

- Ensure that his or her contract is compliant with the new data protection regime.

- Ensure that he or she is reporting to the appropriate level of management in accordance with his or her duties, tasks, and function, and in accordance with the new data protection regime.

- List or map out all departments within the organization.

- Identify the head or contact point within each department.

- Meet the head or contact point of each department.

- Pay particular attention to departments who interact with personal data and data protection issues more than others.

- Identify and map the categories of personal data collected, used, and stored by the organization, by which departments, for what purposes, and where the data are stored.

- Review current procedures and policies.

- Consider required amendments and updates.

- Review current access requests and other requests.

- Review data deletion policies and consider appropriateness and updates.

- Consider current issues and queries from other departments.

*Data Protection Officers (DPOs) play a fundamental role in helping to ensure a high
level of data protection.*

European Data Protection Commissioner
*EDPS website, at https://secure.edps.europa.eu/
EDPSWEB/edps/Supervision/dpo_corner*

ABBREVIATIONS

DPO   Data protection officer

DPD95 The Data Protection Directive 1995; Directive 95/46/EC of the European Parliament and of the Council of 24 October 1995 on the protection of individuals with regard to the processing of personal data and on the free movement of such data

GDPR The General Data Protection Regulation; EU Data Protection Regulation (Regulation [EU] No. 2016/679 of the European Parliament and of the Council on the protection of individuals with regard to the processing of personal data and on the free movement of such data and repealing Directive 95/46/EC (GDPR)

A New Profession

CHAPTER 1

New Role: New Impact

☐ Introduction

The newly created position of the corporate data protection officer (DPO) is empowered to ensure that the organization is compliant with all aspects of the new data protection regime. Organizations must now appoint and designate a DPO for the organization. This will be a significant appointment and will have long-term benefits for the organization. The specific definitions and building blocks of the data protection regime are enhanced by the new General Data Protection Regulation (GDPR) and therefore the new DPO will be very active in passing the message and requirements of the new data protection regime throughout the organization—including the benefits. It will also be important to highlight the potential cost of getting data protection wrong.

☐ The Parties

Organizations need to understand the concepts and parties involved in the data protection regime. The data protection regime involves a number of key parties, namely

- Individuals: Referred to as "data subjects." It is their personal information and personal data that are being protected

- Organizations: Referred to as "controllers," those who wish to collect, use, and process individuals' personal data

- Outsourced Organization: Referred to as "processors." The main controller organization has outsourced or delegated some of its processing activities to a third-party organization; for example, payroll processing regarding employees, or marketing or market research regarding current or prospective customers

In addition, organizations need to consider the following in relation to data protection compliance and data protection issues that arise, namely

- Data protection officer: The individual office holder in the organization tasked with ensuring data protection compliance, education, and so on. He or she is frequently the general point of contact within the organization for queries regarding personal data.

- Board member: Organizations should ensure that data protection compliance is prioritized at organizational board level. The DPO should regularly report to this board member.

- IT manager: Given the importance of security for personal data enshrined in the data protection regime, the information technology (IT) manager needs to be appraised and involved in assisting compliance.

☐ Personal Data Use and Compliance

Appreciation of and compliance with the data protection regime in relation to personal data is important. First, everyone has personal data relating to them. Second, every organization and entity collects and processes personal data of individuals. Sometimes, this is on a small scale. Sometimes, it is on a massive scale. Data protection compliance obligations apply to all organizations, whether small or large, commercial enterprises, official government organizations, or even charities. Obligations also apply to the primary organization involved (the "controller" organization) as well as to outsource entities such as agents, consultants, processors, and so on.

Furthermore, the instances where personal data are used are ever increasing. For example, every reservation, booking, transaction, and journey involves personal data. Every organization that one deals with, whether governmental, enterprise, or nonprofit, uses or creates data in relation to the person. The volume of such personal data collection and processing is now even more significant with the advent of digitization, social media, and e-commerce. Many commercial organizations realize the value of personal data. Increasingly, new business models are relying on personal data.

The default position is that organizations must inform individuals that they intend to collect and use their personal data, detail the purposes for which the data will be used, and obtain consent to do so. Frequently, tensions arise when organizations do not do this, or seek to do it in a manner that does not fully or transparently respect the rights of individuals. While compliance is always possible, there are many instances of organizations getting it wrong and facing the consequences of audit, penalty, prosecution, or investigation.

Personal data also need to be considered in terms of inward-facing (e.g., relating to employees) and outward-facing (e.g., relating to customers) personal data. Different mechanisms may apply to how organizations deal with personal data, depending on the type of data involved.

☐ What Data Protection Is

Data protection laws protect the personal information of individuals, that is, the personal data of and in relation to individuals. It is therefore similar, in some respects, to privacy. The data protection regime provides a regulatory protection regime around personal information, privacy, or personal data. Personal data are data or information that relate to or identify, directly or indirectly, an individual. Data protection is, in many respects, wider than privacy and confidentiality. Personal data are defined in the European Union (EU) Data Protection Directive 95/46/EC of 1995 (DPD95), the national data protection laws, and now in the new GDPR.

The data protection legal regime governs if, when, and how organizations may collect and process personal data and, where permitted, for how long.

This applies to all sorts of personal information, from general to highly confidential and sensitive. Examples of the latter include sensitive health data, sexuality data, and details of criminal offenses.

The data protection regime is twofold, in the sense of

- Providing obligations (that are *inward facing* and *outward facing*), which organizations must comply with.

- Providing individuals (or *data subjects,* as they are technically known) with various data protection rights that they, representative organizations, and/or the data protection supervisory authorities can invoke or enforce as appropriate. Significantly, the ability to invoke data protection rights on behalf of individuals by privacy groups and collective nongovernmental-type organizations is new (see the new GDPR, replacing the DPD95). The GDPR brings "comprehensive reform"[*] to the data protection regime and "will put an end to the patchwork of data protection rules that currently exists in the EU."[†]

Organizations, as part of their compliance obligations, previously had to register or notify the national supervisory authority in relation to their data processing activities (unless exempted). This compliance obligation in the national data protection laws and the DPD95 is changed in the new GDPR. Now, there is generally no need for general registration, unless coming within special categories of data protection risk activities. These activities potentially require a specific amendment to the national data protection laws to reflect the new data protection regime.

Certain sections of industry and specific activities (e.g., data transfers abroad, direct marketing [DM], etc.) have additional data protection compliance rules.

In terms of individuals, they can invoke their rights directly within organizations, with the supervisory authority, and also with the courts in legal proceedings. Now, particular requests may also be made by representative organizations on behalf of groups of individuals. Compensation can also be awarded, and injunction relief can also arise.[‡] In addition, criminal offenses can be prosecuted. Data protection compliance is therefore very important. Indeed, penalties are significantly increased under the new data protection regime.

---

[*] "In Brief," *Communications Law* (2012)(17) 3.

[†] EU Commission, Press Release, "Agreement on Commission's EU data protection reform will boost Digital Single Market," 15 December 2015, at http://europa.eu/rapid/press-release_IP-15-6321_en.htm.

[‡] Such as in Sunderland Housing; Kordowski and Microsoft v. McDonald (t/s Bizards). Sunderland Housing Company v. Baines [2006] EWHC 2359; Law Society v. Kordowski [2011] EWHC 3185; Microsoft Corp v. McDonald (t/s Bizads) [2006] EWHC 3410.

As regards the implementation of compliance frameworks, organizations must have defined structures, policies, and teams in place to ensure that they know what personal data they have and for what purposes; that they are held fairly, lawfully, and in compliance with the data protection regime; and that they are safely secured against damage, loss, and unauthorized access.

The cost of loss, and of security breach, can be financially significant, both brand-wise and publicity-wise. A 2015 IBM study estimated the cost of data breach to average $3.8 million per data breach incident. A data breach at the telecommunications company TalkTalk (in 2015) was estimated to cost £35 million. One Target (a US retail chain) data breach was estimated to cost $162 million, plus a 5.3% drop in sales. Breaches can also give rise to criminal offenses, which can be prosecuted. In addition, personal liability can be attached to organizational personnel, both separate and in addition to the organization itself.

☐ Need for Data Protection

Why do we have a data protection regime? We have a data protection regime because of the legal and political recognition that society respects the personal privacy and informational privacy of individuals. In the context of data protection, this means respect for, control of, and security in relation to informational personal data. The data protection regime protects personal data relating to individuals, which includes employees, contractors, customers, and users.

Data protection exists in order to ensure

- Protection in relation to personal information

- Consent of individuals is obtained to collect and process personal data

- Security in respect of personal information

- Protection against personal informational abuse

- Protection against personal information theft and identity theft

- Protection against unsolicited DM

- Protection for the data protection rights of individuals

- Increased protection and recognition of certain technological threats and "big data" to individuals

The threats to personal data and informational protection (and privacy) have increased as the ease with which personal data can be collected and transferred electronically increases. This has increased further with digital technology, computer processing power, Web 2.0 (i.e., the second generation of Internet websites and services), aggregation, new signals, and social media.*

☐ Growing Importance of Data Protection

Data protection compliance is important for all organizations, large and small. An example of this importance is the national supervisory authority investigation of various multinationals in relation to certain general and specific data protection issues. This example also emphasizes the significant and growing importance of data protection.† Some countries now specifically designate a minister for data protection. The budget of many national supervisory authorities has also increased. More international organizations are being approved under the EU binding corporate rules (BCR) procedure for exemption from the EU transfer ban in relation to personal data.‡

---

* Note, for example, the comments of one supervisory authority in relation to data protection by design and by default, and the report Privacy by Design at https://ico.org.uk. The GDPR refers to data protection by design and by default (DPbD) in Article 23.
† One example is LinkedIn. A facial recognition feature used by Facebook was turned off in Europe, partly as a result of the supervisory authority audit. The supervisory authority also reported that Facebook had introduced more transparent tools and preferences in relation to users' personal data, again apparently on foot of the supervisory authority audit. See audit reports at http://www.dataprotection.ie.
‡ For example, Intel is now approved under the BCR regime. The BCR procedure is one of the mechanisms by which an organization can export or transfer personal data outside of the EEA. Without the BCR (or a similar exemption mechanism), the organization would not be permitted to make such a transfer. These transfers are sometimes referred to as *transborder data flows*. The default position is that transborder data flows may not occur from the EEA to non-EEA countries, unless exempted. See supervisory authority commentary at http://www.dataprotection.ie/docs/20/1/12_Commissioner_approves_Intel_Corporation_Binding_Corp/1190.htm. Also Moerel, *Binding Corporate Rules: Corporate Self-Regulation of Global Data Transfers* (OUP, 2012).

The increasing "centralisation of information through the computerisation of various records" has made the right of privacy a fundamental concern.* Data protection is important, increasingly topical, and an issue of legally required compliance for all organizations. More importantly, it is part of management and organizational best practice. Individuals, employees, and customers expect that their personal data will be respected. They are increasingly aware of their rights, and increasingly enforce these rights. An editorial notes that "Privacy and data protection issues are never far from the horizon at the moment. There are waves of discussion in this area ... and currently that wave is riding high."† The significant attention focused on the fall-out of the EU-US Safe Harbor regime being declared void, its impact on transatlantic business, and the complex political negotiations required for the new EU-US transfer regime (entitled the EU-US Privacy Shield) highlight the mainstream significance of data protection law.

Data protection is increasing in coverage in mainstream media. This is due in part to the large number of recent data loss and data breach incidents. These have involved the loss of the personal data of millions of individuals by commercial organizations, and perhaps more worryingly, by trusted government entities.

The issue of online abuse, which involves among other things privacy and data protection, has also been hitting the headlines.‡

Data protection is also in the headlines because of national supervisory authority concerns with the damage of certain online permanent data. The Court of Justice, on foot of such concerns, issued an important decision in the *Google Spain* case and the right to be forgotten (RtbF; described later in this chapter) directing that certain personal online data had to be deleted from search engine listings.§

The Court of Justice also pronounced on the often contentious area of official data retention. This is the obligation placed by countries on Internet service providers (ISPs) to retain certain customer data in

---

* Personal Data Protection and Privacy," *Counsel of Europe*, at http://hub.coe.int/web/coe-portal/what-we-do/rule-of-law/personal-data?dynLink=true&layoutId=35&dlgroupId=10226&fromArticleId=.

† Editorial, Saxby, *Computer Law & Security Review* (2012)(28) 251.

‡ Tragically, such online abuse can and does result in and contribute to actual suicide. This is a particular concern in relation to children and teenagers. See, generally, Lambert, *Social Networking, Law, Rights and Policy* (Clarus, 2014); Lambert, *International Handbook of Social Media Laws* (Bloomsbury, 2015); and Philips, *This is Why We Can't Have Nice Things, Mapping the Relationship Between Online Trolling and Mainstream Culture* (MIT Press, 2015).

§ *See Google Spain SL, Google Inc v. Agencia Española de Protección de Datos (AEPD), Mario Costeja González*, Court of Justice (Grand Chamber), Case C 131/12, 13 May 2014.

relation to telephone calls, Internet searches, and so on, so that (certain) official agencies can ask to access or obtain copies of such data in the future. Debate frequently surrounds whether this should be permitted at all, and if so, when and under what circumstances, how long ISPs must store such data, and so on. The strongest argument for an official data retention regime may relate to the prevention or investigation of terrorism. Serious crime might come next. There are certainly legitimate concerns that the privacy and data protection costs are such that official data retention, if permitted, should not extend to "common decent crime." On one end of the spectrum is the Court of Justice decision in *Digital Rights Ireland*, striking down the EU Data Retention Directive as invalid.* By implication, this also undermined certain national measures.† It remains to be seen how challenges to new data retention legislation may transpire, and how courts and policymakers will react. The various Snowden revelations and their ripple effects lean against the data retention regime, or at least an overly broad and overreaching one. In addition to debate on legitimate data retention, there is a separate but related debate‡ on encryption, encryption by default, encryption by service providers, personal

---

* Judgment in Joined Cases C-293/12 and C-594/12, *Digital Rights Ireland and Seitlinger and Others*, Court of Justice, 8 April 2014. Directive 2006/24/EC of the European Parliament and of the Council of 15 March 2006 on the retention of data generated or processed in connection with the provision of publicly available electronic communications services or of public communications networks and amending Directive 2002/58/EC (OJ 2006 L105, p 54). Rauhofer and Mac Sithigh, "The Data Retention Directive Never Existed," *SCRIPTed* (2014)(11:1) 118.

† For example, the Regulation of Investigatory Powers Act 2000 (RIPA) in the United Kingdom. The UK government proposed a new amending regulation entitled the Data Retention and Investigatory Powers Act 2014 (DRIPA). However, two MPs (David Davis and Tom Watson), successfully challenged DRIPA in the High Court. The court held that sections 1 and 2 of DRIPA breached rights to respect for private life and communications and to the protection of personal data under Articles 7 and 8 of the EU Charter of Fundamental Rights. The decision gave the (United Kingdom) government until March 2016 to rectify the DRIPA problems. The Queen's speech has also promised a "snooper's charter," which would replace DRIPA. See Whitehead, "Google and Whatsapp will be forced to hand messages to MI5," *Telegraph*, 27 May 2015, at www.telegraph.co.uk/news/politics/queens-speech/11634567/Google-and-Whatsapp-will-be-forced-to-hand-messages-to-MI5.html. Since then, a draft of the Communications Data Bill has been issued. No doubt argument, debate, and research will ensue. In relation to data protection as a fundamental right, see for example Rodata, "Data Protection as a Fundamental Right," in Gutwirth, Poullet, de Hert, de Terwangne, and Nouwt, *Reinventing Data Protection?* (Springer, 2009) 77.

‡ Especially, but not exclusively, in the United States and the United Kingdom.

encryption, and encryption back doors for law enforcement authorities.* This remains, if anything, a contentious issue.

However, every time there is a terror-related event, and at the time of writing we are in the immediate aftermath of the Brussels, Paris, Egypt, Palestine, San Berdino, and Mali attacks, the calls and arguments for data retention/extended data retention are at their strongest.†

While the issues of *official data retention* are important, they may not be direct issues for every DPO but can be more relevant to companies in certain technology sectors.

A further reason as to why data protection is important and increasingly the focus of press attention is that organizations are increasingly using security and respect for data protection as an advantage and commercial differentiator in the marketplace. Apple has repeatedly announced that it does not operate a data-intrusive model for collecting user data. In fact, it has even criticized some of its technology competitors. Microsoft has, for many years, promoted the data protection and privacy-friendly policy of data protection by design and by default (DPbD). Post Snowden, many US technology companies have been heavily lobbying the US administration for a roll back of certain activities and practices, particularly those felt to be extrajudicial and extralegal, on the basis that it will disadvantage the US-based cloud and cloud storage industry. Many cloud companies have been highlighting that they are non-US-based. Even US companies are now promoting that they have— or are building—EU-based cloud storage facilities, and in some instances that EU data will remain located in the EU.

All organizations collect and process personal data. Whether they are big organizations or new start-ups, they need to comply with the data protection regime. Bear in mind also that even a new technology start-up can scale relatively quickly to millions of users. Many issues enhance the importance of getting the organizational data protection

---

* A Harvard study suggests, inter alia, that an encryption back door would in any event be ineffective. See Schneier, Siedel, and Vijayakumar, "A Worldwide Survey of Encryption Products," (Harvard, 11 February 2016). Also Barrett, "Bill Aims to Stop State-Level Decryption Before it Starts," *Wired*, 10 February 2016. Also note Grauer, "The Government Wants to Listen In On Your Smart Home," *Wired*, 14 February 2016, referring to connected Internet of things (IOT) devices in the home.

† Prime Minister Cameron has made statements to advance data retention proposals, in particular the UK Communications Data Bill, labeled by some as a "snooper's charter." Critics also increasingly suggest that research indicates that data retention does not demonstrate that data retention works. However, official sources in various jurisdictions refer to terror attacks being prevented, and that retained data are invaluable. The link or proof of positive effect is not necessarily specified. This debate also crosses over to issues of unauthorized access or tapping by official agencies of technology companies and their customers' data, and public and industry arguments that official access must be regulated, transparent, and proportional.

understanding and compliance model right from day one. These include legal obligations; director, board and officer obligations; investigations; fines; prosecutions; being ordered to *delete* databases; adverse publicity on the front pages of the press media; commercial imperatives; and even commercial advantages. If one also considers some of the large-scale data breach incidents, there are examples of chief technology officers as well as managing directors/chief executive officers (CEOs) losing their employment positions as a result of the incident.

In addition, organizations often fail to realize that data protection compliance is frequently an issue of dual compliance. They need to be looking at both *inward* and *outward* data processing issues.

Internally, organizations have to be data protection compliant in relation to all of their employees' (and contractors') personal data. Traditionally, this may have related to human resources (HR) files and employee contracts, but now includes issues of electronic communications, social media, Internet usage, filtering, monitoring, on-site activity, off-site activity, company devices, employee devices, vehicles, and so on. The consequences of getting it wrong are now more significant.

Separately, organizations have to be concerned about personal data relating to persons outside the organization such as current and prospective customers. Comprehensive data protection compliance is also required for those outward-facing issues. The consequences are significant for noncompliance.

Substantial fines have been imposed in a number of cases. In some instances, organizations have been ordered to delete their databases. In a new technology start-up situation, the database can be the company's most valuable asset.

Until recently, the issue of data loss was a proverbial small back-page story. However, the loss of personal data files of tens of millions of individuals in a single instance—and including from official governmental sources—makes data loss a front-page issue. There is increased scrutiny from the supervisory authorities and others, and new regulation of data security issues, preparedness, and reactivity. Organizations must look at security issues with increasing rigor. Organizations can face liability issues in breach incidents, but also in the aggravating situation where a vulnerability may have been already known and highlighted internally but was not acted on, thus contributing to the breach incident. As well as official investigation, fine, and sanction, organizations also face issues of liability to users and, in some instances, potential liability to banks and financial intermediaries. Target, for example, was sued not just by data subjects but also by financial intermediaries. Issues such as this are likely to increase. While individuals have grouped together in US cases for some time, this will likely increase in the EU as the new

GDPR expressly recognizes the possibility of data subject representative organizations.

There are enhanced obligations to report data breaches, data incidents, and data losses.* There are also enhanced financial penalties. In some instances, personal director responsibility for data loss can arise. The need for compliance is now a boardroom issue and an issue of senior corporate compliance. Proactive and complete data protection compliance is also a matter of good corporate governance, brand loyalty, and a means to ensuring user and customer goodwill.

The frequency and scale of breaches of security, such as those for LoyaltyBuild, Adobe, TalkTalk, Target, Home Depot, Sony Playstation (70 million individuals' personal data in one instance and 25 million in another†), the Sony "Interview" breach, Office of Personnel Management (OPM) (US official; 22 million individuals), the insurer Anthem (80 million individuals), the affair dating website Ashley Madison (37 million individuals, apparently), the toymaker VTech, political parties, and even the security/hacking firm Hacking Team, make the topicality and importance of data security compliance for personal data ever more relevant. Even official agencies have been involved in data loss incidents involving the personal data of millions of individuals.‡ There are many cases involving substantial fines for data protection breaches. A number of hospitals and medical facilities have been fined, including one organization that was fined £325,000.§ Zurich Insurance was fined £2.3 million for losing data in relation to 46,000 individual customers.¶

---

* Unless exempted.
† See, for example, Martin, "Sony Data Loss Biggest Ever," *Boston Herald*, 27 April 2011, at http://bostonherald.com/business/technology/general/view/2011_0427sony_data_loss_biggest_ever; Arthur, "Sony Suffers Second Data Breach With Theft of 25m More User Details", *Guardian*, 3 May 2011, at http://www.guardian.co.uk/technology/blog/2011/may/03/sony-data-breach-online-entertainment.
‡ The UK Revenue and Customs loss of discs with the names, dates of birth, and bank and address details for 25 million individuals. See, for example, "Brown Apologises for Record Loss, Prime Minister Gordon Brown has said he 'Profoundly Regrets' the Loss of 25 Million Child Benefit Records," *BBC*, 21 November 2007, at http://news.bbc.co.uk/2/hi/7104945.stm. Millions of personal details of government employees, including security personnel, were hacked in the United States in 2015.
§ The Brighton and Sussex University Hospitals NHS Trust had a fine of £325,000 imposed by the Information Commissioner's Office (ICO) in relation to a data loss incident. See, for example, "Largest Ever Fine for Data Loss Highlights Need for Audited Data Wiping," *ReturnOnIt*, at http://www.returnonit.co.uk/largest-ever-fine-for-data-loss-highlights-need-for-audited-data-wiping.php.
¶ See, for example, Oates, "UK Insurer Hit With Biggest Ever Data Loss Fine", *The Register*, 24 August 2010, at http://www.theregister.co.uk/2010/08/24/data_loss_fine/. This was imposed by the Financial Services Authority (FSA).

Text spammers are being investigated and could face fines of £500,000*, and a police authority has been fined £120,000 in relation to a data breach involving unencrypted personal data.†

Separately, a significant fine of £50,000 was issued for a nondata loss incident. A financial organization was fined for mixing up details of financial data relating to two separate individuals. This would have caused financial loss and damage for one of the individuals, as he or she was not credited with all of their payments and contributions.‡ The account details were not kept accurate and up to date. This arose despite complaint correspondence from one of the individuals over a period of time. The supervisory authority commented:

> We hope this penalty sends a message to all organisations, but particularly those in the financial sector, that adequate checks must be in place to ensure people's records are accurate. Staff should also receive adequate training on how to manage and maintain them, with any concerns fully investigated in order to ensure problems are addressed at an early stage."§

The supervisory authorities prosecute numerous breaches. This includes the prosecution of directors as well as companies. Errant outsourced private investigators have also been prosecuted. Large organizations have been prosecuted in relation to data breach incidents. Fines will increase significantly under the new GDPR to a percentage of turnover.¶

Member State data protection authorities are increasingly proactive, and undertake audits of data protection compliance as well as incidents of breaches.** Data protection supervisory authorities can also be critical of organizations, and of the data protection policies and

---

* Arthur, "Spam Text Senders Face Fines of Up To £500,000", *Guardian*, at https://www.theguardian.com/technology/2012/oct/01/spam-text-senders-fines.
† "Police Force Fines £120,000 After Theft of Unencrypted Data," *Guardian*, at http://www.guardian.co.uk/uk/2012/oct/16/police-force-fine-theft-memory-stick?INTCMP=SRCH.
‡ See "Prudential Fined £50,000 for Customer Account Confusion", ICO, 6 November 2012, at http://www.ico.gov.uk/news/latest_news/2012/prudential-fined-50000-for-customer-account-confusion-06112012.aspx.
§ Ibid.
¶ *Supra.*
** Facebook international has been audited by the Irish supervisory authority as noted previously. The audit relates to Facebook internationally, outside of the United States and Canada. See first stage of the audit report, at http://dataprotection.ie/viewdoc.asp?m=&fn=/documents/Facebook%20Report/final%20report/report.pdf. It is entitled *Facebook Ireland Limited, Report of Audit*, and was conducted by the Irish supervisory authority. Note also complaints and access requests referred to at Europe Against Facebook, at https://www.dataprotection.ie/documents/Facebook%20Report/Facebookauditreport1.pdf.

practices of an organization.* The phone hacking scandal in the United Kingdom also highlights the importance of personal data.† There has been previous criticism from one supervisory authority of the abuse of official databases by unauthorized access by police and civil servants, sometimes for personal reasons and, on other occasions, for payment by external third parties for data. In 2016, a previous minister for justice in one Member State also criticized unauthorized police access of database systems.

☐ Data Protection Regime

Personal data protection is enshrined in the data protection laws and new GDPR. The national data protection laws‡ implement the DPD95 in the Member States. (The definitions, or building blocks, of data protection are referred to in this chapter.) Now, the GDPR significantly enhances the data protection regime. The new GDPR is directly effective in Member States. However, it may require parts of the national data protection laws of Member States to be amended. DPOs should monitor any follow-on amendments to national legislation consequent to the GDPR.

☐ Outward-Facing Data Protection Compliance

The data protection regime and new GDPR create legal obligations that organizations must comply with when collecting and processing the personal data of individuals; "if someone can be distinguished from other

---

* See, for example, letter from the Article 29 Working Party (WP29) and the EU data protection commissioners to Google, at http://dataprotection.ie/docs/Home/4.htm. The UK data protection supervisory authority (the ICO) is also involved in dealing with personal data issues relating to the press phone hacking scandal, which is also the separate subject of the Leveson Inquiry (http://www.levesoninquiry. org.uk/.) The ICO investigation is called *Operation Motorman*. For more details, see "Operation Motorman—Steve Whittamore Notebooks," ICO website, at http:// www.ico.gov.uk/for_the_public/topic_specific_guides/operation_motorman. aspx.
† This resulted in the Leveson Inquiry, a large number of data subject litigation cases against newspapers as well as a separate UK Information Commissioner's office investigation.
‡ Ibid.

people, data protection legislation is applicable."* This applies to both current and prospective customers. Hence, these are *outward-facing* obligations. This can also apply to noncustomers who may be using a particular website but are not a registered customer, if their personal data are being collected.

☐ Inward-Facing Data Protection Compliance

The data protection regime also applies to an organization in its dealings regarding the personal data of its employees. Equally, where the organization is engaging third-party independent contractors but is collecting, processing, and using their personal data, the data protection regime will also apply. Hence, the data protection regime in relation to organizations is *inward facing*.

☐ A Rights-Based Regime

As well as creating legal compliance obligations for organizations, the data protection regime enshrines the rights or data protection rights of individuals in terms of ensuring their ability to know which personal data are being collected, to consent—or not consent—to the collection of their personal data, and to control the uses to which their personal data may be put. There is also a mechanism through which individuals can directly complain to controllers holding their personal data, to the supervisory authority, and to the courts.

☐ Supervisory Authority

In order to ensure that the duties are complied with and the rights of individuals vindicated, there is an official authority established in Member States to monitor and act as appropriate in relation to the efficient operation of the data protection regime. This is the national supervisory authority.

The importance of Member State data protection authorities is enhanced in the new GDPR.

---

* Costa and Poullet, "Privacy and the Regulation of 2012," *Computer Law & Security Review* (2012)(28) 254 at 256.

☐ Data Protection Issues

Controllers (i.e., the organizations that collect and process personal data; see the definitions section in this chapter) must comply with a number of data protection issues, perhaps the foremost of which relate to

- Fairness

- Transparency

- Consent

- Accuracy

- Security

- Proper and transparent purposes for processing

- Proportionality of the need and use of personal data

- Risk assessments

- Impact assessments

- Correction and deletion

The collection, use, and onward transfer of personal data must be fair, legitimate, and transparent. There are particular definitions and provisions as regards the "processing" of personal data. There are also restrictions in relation to the ability of organizations to transfer personal data, both to third-party organizations generally and also to third-party organizations outside of the EU and European Economic Area (EEA) (the latter were referred to as transborder data flows, and are now referred to as cross-border transfers under the new GDPR).

Personal data must be correct and accurate. The reason for this is that damage or harm to the individual data subject can be a consequence of inaccurately held personal data. For example, a credit rating could be adversely affected through incorrect or wrong personal data records regarding personal payment histories being recorded.

There is a general obligation in terms of safeguarding personal data. Organizations must assess and implement security measures to protect personal data. Increasingly, this is also being considered in relation to the developing cloud environment and the increasing use of processors and third parties.*

There is also an obligation on controllers to register or notify the supervisory authority regarding their high-risk data-processing activities.

If personal data are permitted to be transferred to third-party countries, they must first qualify under a specific exemption as well as under the general security conditions. No such transfer is permitted from the EEA unless explicitly exempted. The issue of the EU-US Safe Harbor Arrangement exemption mechanism is a matter of particular contention and import at this time, given that the Court of Justice has invalidated this mechanism.† The EU and United States negotiated a new arrangement, entitled the *EU-US Privacy Shield*, over an extended period. DPOs will need to monitor the implementation of the new EU-US Privacy Shield and any challenges and or changes that might apply.

Organizations have a responsibility and duty of care to individuals as regards the processing of their personal data by the organization, particularly if loss or damage arises. Injunctive relief is also possible in appropriate circumstances.

Controllers and processors have obligations in certain circumstances to have legal contracts in place between them. Processors process and deal with personal data for and on behalf of a controller in relation to specific, defined tasks including activities such as outsourced payroll, HR, marketing, market research, customer satisfaction surveys, and so on. Additional issues and considerations arise for cloud services and data protection compliance. From an organizational perspective, it is sometimes considered that organizational customers have less opportunity to negotiate clauses in cloud service provider contracts, including processor- and security-related issues. There is, therefore, greater obligation to

---

* In relation to the cloud in general, see Kuan Hon and Millard, "Data Export Cloud Computing – How Can Personal Data be Transferred Outside the EEA? The Cloud of Unknowing," SCRIPTed (2012)(9:1), at http://script-ed.org/?page_id=302; Singh and Mishra, "Cloud Computing Security and Data Protection: A Review," *International Journal of Computers & Technology* (2015)(14:7) 5887; Pfarr, Buckel, and Winkelmann, "Cloud Computing Data Protection—A Literature Review and Analysis," 2014 47th Hawaii International Conference on System Sciences (2014) 5018; and Lane, *Privacy, Big Data and the Public Good* (CUP, 2014); Millard, *Cloud Computing Law* (OUP, 2013).

† Schrems v. Commissioner, Court of Justice, Case C-362/14, 6 October 2015, at http://curia.europa.eu/juris/document/document.jsf?text=&docid=169195&pageIndex=0&doclang=en&mode=req&dir=&occ=first&part=1&cid=113326. The case was technically related to Prism and Facebook Europe and transfers to the United States. However, the wider import turned out to be the entire EU-US Safe Harbour Agreement and data transfers to the United States. As such, this is one of if not the most important cases decided by the Court of Justice to date.

be satisfied with the cloud service provider, the location of data, and the security measures and documentation available.

☐ General Criteria for Data Processing

Generally, in order to lawfully collect and process personal data, a controller should be aware that

- The individual data subject must consent to the collection and processing of their personal data.

- The data subject may object to processing or continued processing.

- Legal data protection requirements must be complied with.

- Prior information requirements, data protection principles, legitimate processing conditions, sensitive personal data legitimate processing conditions (in the case of sensitive personal data), and security obligations are required to be complied with (see the "Data Protection Overview" section).

- The rights and interests of the individual data subject must be respected and complied with, including access requests, deletion rights, and so on; risk assessment; impact assessment; risk minimization; and DPbD.

The interests of the controller can sometimes be relevant in particular instances in deciding which data processing is necessary and permitted.

☐ Data Protection Overview

The data protection laws, on foot of the DPD95 and new GDPR, set out a number of structures, obligations, rights, and implementing criteria that together form the basis of the legal data protection regime.

The main criteria and obligations to be followed, respected, and complied with in order to be able to legally collect and process personal data include

- The definitions of personal data and the data protection regime (the building blocks of data protection)

- The *data protection principles*, also known as the *data quality principles*

- The *legitimate processing conditions*

- The requirement that processing of personal data be "legitimate" under at least one of the *legitimate processing conditions*

- Recognizing the two categories of personal data covered by the data protection regime, namely, *sensitive personal data* and *nonsensitive general personal data*

- In the case of sensitive personal data, complying with the additional *sensitive personal data legitimate processing conditions*

- Ensuring that all personal data collected and processed is obtained fairly

- Taking and ensuring appropriate security measures in relation to all processing activities

- Implementing formal legal contracts when engaging or dealing with third-party processors (e.g., outsourcing data processing tasks or activities)

- Complying with the separate criteria in relation to *automated decision-making processes* or *automated decisions*

- Complying with the legal criteria for DM

- That a duty of care exists in relation to the individual data subjects whose personal data the organization is collecting and processing

- That the transfer of personal data outside of the EEA is strictly controlled. Personal data may not be transferred outside of the EEA unless specifically permitted under the data protection regime

- That access requests, or requests by individuals for copies of their personal data held by the organization, must be complied with (unless excepted)

- That registration obligations by organizations must be complied with

- Implementing internal data protection policies and terms

- Implementing outward-facing data protection policies, for example for customers

- Implementing outward-facing website privacy statements (generally a data protection policy covers organization-wide activities, whereas a website privacy statement governs only the online collection and processing of personal data)

- Implementing device, mobile phone, computer, and Internet usage policies

- Implementing data loss, data breach, incident handling, and incident reporting policies, and associated reaction plans*

- That data incidents, losses, and breaches are reported to the supervisory authority (unless exempted)

- Keeping abreast of the increasing trend toward sector-issue-specific rules, for example, spam, DM, and industry codes of conduct† in relation to personal data

- Children and personal data issues

- Data protection impact assessments and consultations

- DPbD

- Complying with new legal developments

The EEA is wider than the EU Member States and includes Iceland, Liechtenstein, and Norway. Switzerland has a similar arrangement with the EU. EU data protection law frequently refers to the EEA, generally meaning the EU Member States plus the EEA countries.

DPOs will be particularly required to fully understand the new and expanded data protection Principles and their impact on the organization. All of the relevant stakeholders in the organization will need to be updated by the DPO.

---

* Note, for example, the ICO PECR security breach notifications—guidance for service providers, at https://ico.org.uk.
† The data protection regime provides for agreement on codes of conduct with national data protection authorities in relation to specific industry sectors.

TABLE 1.1. Principles

P1	Lawfulness, fairness, and transparency principle
P2	Purpose limitation principle
P3	Data minimization principle
P4	Accuracy principle
P5	Storage limitation principle
P6	Integrity and confidentiality principle
P7	Accountability principle

Principle 1: Lawfulness, fairness, and transparency principle

Personal data (PD) must be processed lawfully, fairly, and in a transparent manner in relation to the data subject.

Principle 2: Purpose limitation principle

PD must be collected for specified, explicit, and legitimate purposes and not further processed in a way incompatible with those purposes.

Principle 3: Data minimization principle

PD must be adequate, relevant, and limited to what is necessary in relation to the purposes for which they are processed.

Principle 4: Accuracy principle

PD must be accurate and, where necessary, kept up to date; every reasonable step must be taken to ensure that inaccurate PD, with regard to the purposes for which they are processed, are erased or rectified without delay.

Principle 5: Storage limitation principle

PD must be kept in a form that permits identification of data subjects for no longer than is necessary for the purposes for which the PD are processed. PD may be stored for longer periods insofar as the data will be processed solely for archiving purposes in the public interest, for scientific or historical research purposes, or for statistical purposes in accordance with Article 89(1), subject to implementation of the appropriate technical and organizational measures required by the regulation in order to safeguard the rights and freedoms of the data subject.

TABLE 1.1. (CONTINUED) Principles

Principle 6: Integrity & confidentiality principle

PD must be processed in a manner that ensures appropriate security of the PD, including protection against unauthorized or unlawful processing and against accidental loss, destruction, or damage, using appropriate technical or organizational measures.

Principle 7: Accountability principle

The controller shall be responsible for, and be able to demonstrate compliance with, Principles 1–6.

So, in addition to the core principles, the DPO must appraise the organization of the accountability principle. In order to be able to demonstrate compliance with the principles, consideration will include the recorded and verified methods of so demonstrating compliance. These records or compliance proofs will need to be kept and made available in the event of the supervisory authority requesting them, which can arise in a variety of scenarios (Table 1.2).

In addition, the DPO might consider the further obligation to maintain records described in Article 30, and its relationship with the accountability principle. Those records referred to in Article 28 will also need to be kept and may be requested by the supervisory authority (Table 1.3).

The records obligation applies to processors in addition to controllers. This will need to be considered by DPOs in the respective organizations (Table 1.4).

The record obligations may not apply to organizations with less than 250 employees. Article 30(5) states that "The obligations referred to in paragraphs 1 and 2 shall not apply to an enterprise or an organization employing fewer than 250 persons unless the processing it carries out is likely to result in a risk to the rights and freedoms of data subjects, the processing is not occasional, or the processing includes special categories of data as referred to in Article 9(1) or personal data relating to criminal convictions and offenses referred to in Article 10."

Therefore, the record obligations apply where

- The organization has 250 or more employees.

- The processing is likely to result in a risk to the rights and freedoms of data subjects (even if less than 250 employees).

- The processing is not occasional (even if less than 250 employees).

- The processing includes special categories of data (per Article 9[1]) or personal data relating to criminal convictions and offenses (per Article 10) (even if less than 250 employees).

DPOs should note that the issue of who counts as an employee is not expressly specified. Therefore, the DPO, being cautious in this regard, may wish to take note of full- and part-time employees as well as (regular or occasional) agency staff, contractors, and consultants. This will particularly be the case when these additional categories of persons engaged are on-site at the main location(s) of the organization. Organizations will wish to avoid the accusation from supervisory authorities that they are seeking to avoid their obligations by engaging non-full-time employees.

It is not immediately clear what the full meaning of "the processing is not occasional" is. However, if it simply means that the organization is carrying out "regular" versus "occasional" processing, this will encompass most organizations. It thus raises the query whether the 250 employees clause is at all effective in practice as a cut off, given that most organizations will be engaging in regular processing that is not occasional. The exception encompasses most—if not all—organizations within the record compliance obligation.

☐ Legitimate Processing

There is a prohibition on the collection and processing of personal data and sensitive personal data, unless

- The processing complies with the *data protection principles.*

- The processing comes with one of a limited number of specified conditions (the *legitimate processing conditions* or *sensitive personal data legitimate processing conditions* [as appropriate]).

- The processing also complies with the security requirements.

☐ Key/Topical Issues, Cases, and Legislation

Some of the key developments and issues that also influence the data protection regime and how it is interpreted include

TABLE 1.2. Accountability: Demonstrating and Recording Compliance

Principle 7: Accountability Principle

The controller shall be responsible for, and be able to demonstrate compliance with, Principles 1–6

P1	P2	P3	P4	P5	P6
Compliance proof 1	Compliance proof 1	Compliance proof 1	Compliance proof 1	Compliance proof 1	Compliance proof 1
Compliance proof 2	Compliance proof 2	Compliance proof 2	Compliance proof 2	Compliance proof 2	Compliance proof 2
Compliance proof 3	Compliance proof 3	Compliance proof 3	Compliance proof 3	Compliance proof 3	Compliance proof 3

TABLE 1.3. Accountability and Records Interface

Principle 6: Accountability Principle

The controller shall be responsible for, and be able to demonstrate, compliance with the principles.

P1	P2	P3	P4	P5	P6
Compliance proof 1	Compliance proof 1	Compliance proof 1	Compliance proof 1	Compliance proof 1	Compliance proof 1
Compliance proof 2	Compliance proof 2	Compliance proof 2	Compliance proof 2	Compliance proof 2	Compliance proof 2
Compliance proof 3	Compliance proof 3	Compliance proof 3	Compliance proof 3	Compliance proof 3	Compliance proof 3

↕ ↕

GDPR Article 30

Each *controller* ... shall maintain a record of processing activities under its responsibility ...

GDPR Article 30

Each ... *representative* ... shall maintain a record of processing activities under its responsibility ...

TABLE 1.4. Record Documentation Types

Records
Records of processing activities
GDPR: Article 30

Controller	Representative	Processor
Controller Records	**Representative Records**	**Processor Records**
The record(s) shall contain all of the following information:	The record(s) shall contain all of the following information:	Processor, and processor representative shall maintain a record of all categories of processing activities carried out on behalf of the controller, containing:
Name and contact details of the controller and, where applicable, the joint controller, the controller's representative and the DPO	Name and contact details of the controller and, where applicable, the joint controller, the controller's representative and the DPO	Name and contact details of processor or processors and each controller on behalf of which the processor is acting and where applicable of the controller's or processor's representative, and the DPO
Purpose of the processing	Purpose of the processing	Categories of processing carried out on behalf of each controller
Description of categories of data subjects and categories of PD	Description of categories of data subjects and categories of PD	
Categories of recipients to whom the PD have been or will be disclosed, including recipients in third countries or international organizations	Categories of recipients to whom the PD have been or will be disclosed, including recipients in third countries or international organizations	

(Continued)

TABLE 1.4. (CONTINUED) Record Documentation Types

Records
Records of processing activities
GDPR: Article 30

Controller	Representative	Processor
Controller Records	**Representative Records**	**Processor Records**
Where applicable, transfers of PD to a third country or an international organization, including the identification of that third country or international organization and, in the case of transfers referred to in Article 49(1) second subparagraph, the documentation of suitable safeguards	Where applicable, transfers of PD to a third country or an international organization, including the identification of that third country or international organization and, in the case of transfers referred to in Article 49(1) second subparagraph, the documentation of suitable safeguards	Where applicable, transfers of PD to a third country or an international organization, including the identification of that third country or international organization and, in the case of transfers referred to in Article 49(1) second subparagraph, the documentation of suitable safeguards
Where possible, the envisaged time limits for erasure of the different categories of data	Where possible, the envisaged time limits for erasure of the different categories of data	
Where possible, a general description of the technical and organization security measures referred to in Article 32(1)	Where possible, a general description of the technical and organization security measures referred to in Article 32(1)	Where possible, a general description of the technical and organizational security measures referred to in Article 32(1)
The records shall be in writing, including in electronic format	The records shall be in writing, including in electronic format	The records shall be in writing, including in electronic format
The controller shall make the records available to the supervisory authority on request	The controller or processor representative shall make the records available to the supervisory authority on request	The processor shall make the records available to the supervisory authority on request

- Data transfers, EU-US Privacy Shield (replacing EU-US Safe Harbor), and other data transfer-legitimizing mechanisms.

- Data breach incidents.

- Insurance for data breach incidents.

- Preparedness and team preparations for incidents that arise.

- Risk assessments.

- Data protection impact assessments.

- Mandated DPOs in organizations.

- Deletion, take down, and the RtbF.

- Security requirements for businesses.

- Children and data protection.

- Deletion issues and children.

- Deletion issues and students.

- Employee monitoring and consent.

- The GDPR RtbF, the DPD95 RtbF, and the *rights* to be forgotten.

- Employee activities at home and off-site.

- Director and officer liability.

- Spam and DM.

- The relationship between the controller and the processor, which needs to be formalized in a contract pursuant to the data protection regime and GDPR. Increasingly, more specifics of the relationship, activities, obligations, and rights need to be detailed.

- Disposal of computer hardware. Particular care is needed when considering the disposal of IT hardware, equipment, and software, which may still contain personal data files. This can continue to be the case even when it appears that files have been wiped or deleted. There are many examples of accessible personal data still being available even after they are believed to have been deleted and the device handed over to a third party, or worse, sold on. The new recipient could be able to access the original personal data and records. This could quite easily be a breach of a number of principles of the data protection regime. It is always advised to take professional legal, IT, and/or forensic advice when considering the disposal of computer devices.

- Websites and social media compliance with the data protection regime.

- Online abuse.

- Offline abuse.

- Vehicles.

- Location.

- Location marketing.

- Profiling.

- Internet of things (IoT) and devices.

- Health and fitness data, new devices, new collections, new uses, and potential transfer disclosees such as insurance companies, banks, and law enforcement.

- Body recognition such as facial recognition on closed-circuit television (CCTV), profiles, and other images; and related issues of transparency, consent, new consent, backward recognition, and present–future recognition (separate issues arise in relation to law enforcement, criminal law, and evidence).

- New sensory data collection, such as when sensors or a device come into contact with a person's head to record, for example, what a person is doing, thinking, or directing without recourse to outward body communications. New forms of personal data can be collected, some without transparency and without consent. Consider a new game headset, glasses, or other head device. These may have a secondary capability to monitor or record new sources of personal data via brain signals. Such mind data collections and mind directions are already occurring under, for example, research into what a person is thinking based on a head-monitoring device to flying a drone solely using brain signals.

- Cloud services and storage.

- Localization storage of cloud data.

- Data protection as an organizational and service selling point.

- DPbD.

- Data transfers and the EU-US Privacy Shield.

- The potential for further cases attacking the EU-US Privacy Shield (and potentially other EU transfer-legitimizing mechanisms).

- EU citizens enforcing their data protection rights, pursuant to the US Judicial Redress Act, which is pursuant in part to and required by the EU-US Privacy Shield in order to extend protection in the United States to EU citizens in relation to their personal data once they are in the United States, effectively permitting EU citizens to sue within the United States.

- Activities that erode the so-called household exemption (from compliance with the data protection regime), such as online selling from home (e.g., eBay) or renting one's home as tourist accommodation (e.g., Airbnb).

- The ongoing ripples from the Snowden disclosures.

Many organizations have altered various data protection–related practices pursuant to the supervisory authority audits, with certain issues ongoing.

☐ Categories of Personal Data

Organizations need to be familiar with two separate categories of personal data in relation to their data protection actions and compliance obligations. This also affects which personal data they may collect in the first instance. The categories of personal data are, namely, *general personal data* and *sensitive personal data*.

The importance of sensitive personal data is that they trigger additional and more onerous obligations of compliance and initial collection conditions. Unless they fall within the definition of sensitive personal data, all personal data fall into the general personal data category.

Why is there a distinction? Certain types of personal data are more important and sensitive to individuals than other categories of personal data. This is recognized in the data protection regime, and additional rules are put in place. First, sensitive personal data are defined differently. Second, in order to collect and process sensitive personal data, an organization must satisfy processing conditions in addition to the *data protection principles* and the general *legitimate processing conditions*, namely, complying with the *sensitive personal data legitimate processing conditions*.

☐ General Personal Data

General personal data generally refers to any data or information relating to a living individual who is (or can be) identified, either from the data or from the data in conjunction with other information that is in, or is likely to come into, the possession of the controller. The definition refers to *"any* information relating to and identified or *identifiable* natural person." The definition of what is encompassed is therefore wide.

☐ Sensitive Personal Data

Sensitive personal data are associated with higher compliance obligations and conditions. Such data can be summarized as personal data relating to

- Racial or ethnic origin

- Political opinions

- Religious or philosophical beliefs

- Trade union membership

- Genetic data

- Biometric data

- Data concerning heath

- Sex life

- Sexual orientation (Article 9(1))

  Note also the restriction regarding personal data relating to

- Criminal convictions, offenses, or related security measures (Article 10)

  Article 8 of the DPD95 refers to the processing of special categories of data. It states that Member States shall prohibit the processing of personal data revealing racial or ethnic origin, political opinions, religious or philosophical beliefs, trade union membership, and the processing of data concerning health or sex life. This provision shall not apply where

- The data subject has given their explicit consent to the processing, except where the laws of the Member State provide that the prohibition* may not be lifted by giving consent.

- Processing is necessary for the obligations of the controller in the field of employment law, if authorized by Member State law with adequate safeguards.

- Processing is necessary to protect the vital interests of the data subject or of another person if they are physically or legally incapable of giving their consent.

- Processing is carried out in the course of its legitimate activities with appropriate guarantees by a foundation, association, or any other nonprofit-seeking body with a political, philosophical, religious, or trade union aim, and on condition that the processing relates solely to the members of the body or to persons who have regular contact with it in connection with its purposes and that the personal data are not disclosed to a third party without the consent of the data subjects.

- The processing relates to personal data that are manifestly made public by the data subject or are necessary for the establishment, exercise, or defense of legal claims.

  There is a carve-out in the DPD95 from the restriction where processing of data is required for the purposes of preventive medicine, medical diagnosis, the provision of care or treatment, or the management of health-care services, and where those data are processed by a health

---

* Referred to in para 1 *ibid.*

professional subject under Member State law or rules established by national competent bodies to the obligation of professional secrecy or by a person subject to an equivalent obligation of secrecy. Subject to the provisions with suitable safeguards, Member States may, for reasons of substantial public interest, provide certain additional exemptions either by national law or by decision of the supervisory authority. Processing of data relating to offenses, criminal convictions, or security measures may be carried out only under the control of official authority or national law safeguards, subject to derogations that may be granted by the Member State under national provisions providing suitable specific safeguards. A complete register of criminal convictions may be kept only under the control of an official authority. Member States may provide that data relating to administrative sanctions or judgments in civil cases shall also be processed under the control of an official authority.*

Article 9 of the GDPR relates to the processing of special categories of personal data. The processing of personal data, revealing racial or ethnic origin, political opinions, religious or philosophical beliefs, or trade union membership, and the processing of genetic data, biometric data for the purpose of uniquely identifying a natural person, data concerning health, or data concerning a natural person's sex life or sexual orientation are prohibited.†

Article 9(2) of the GDPR provides that the Article 9(1) processing prohibitions shall not apply if one of the following applies:

- The data subject has given explicit consent to the processing of those personal data for one or more specified purposes, except where Union or Member State law provides that the prohibition referred to in Article 9(1) may not be lifted by the data subject.

- Processing is necessary for the purposes of carrying out the obligations and exercising specific rights of the controller or of the data subject in the field of employment and social security and social protection law, in so far as it is authorized by Union or Member State law or by a collective agreement pursuant to Member State law providing for appropriate safeguards for the fundamental rights and interests of the data subject.

---

* Member States shall determine the conditions under which a national identification number or any other identifier of general application may be processed; DPD95 Article 8.
† GDPR Article 9(1).

- Processing is necessary to protect the vital interests of the data subject or of another natural person, where the data subject is physically or legally incapable of giving consent.

- Processing is carried out in the course of its legitimate activities with appropriate safeguards by a foundation, association, or any other not-for-profit body with a political, philosophical, religious, or trade union aim, and on condition that the processing relates solely to the members or to former members of the body or to persons who have regular contact with it in connection with its purposes and that the personal data are not disclosed outside that body without the consent of the data subjects.

- The processing relates to personal data that are manifestly made public by the data subject.

- Processing is necessary for the establishment, exercise, or defense of legal claims, or whenever courts are acting in their judicial capacity.

- Processing is necessary for reasons of substantial public interest on the basis of Union or Member State law, which shall be proportionate to the aim pursued, respect the essence of the right to data protection, and provide for suitable measures to safeguard the fundamental rights and interests of the data subject.

- Processing is necessary for the purposes of preventative or occupational medicine; for the assessment of the working capacity of the employee; medical diagnosis; the provision of health, social care, or treatment; the management of health or social care systems and services on the basis of Union or Member State law; or pursuant to contact with a health professional and subject to the conditions and safeguards referred to in Article 9(3).

- Processing is necessary for reasons of public interest in the area of public health, such as protecting against serious crossborder threats to health or ensuring high standards of quality and safety of health-care and medicinal products or medical devices, on the basis of Union or Member State law, which provides for suitable and specific measures to safeguard the rights and freedoms of the data subject, particularly with respect to professional secrecy.

- Processing is necessary for archiving purposes in the public interest, scientific or historical research purposes, or statistical purposes in accordance with Article 89(1) based on Union or Member State law, which shall be proportionate to the aim pursued, respect the essence of the right to data protection, and provide for suitable and specific measures to safeguard the fundamental rights and interests of the data subject.

Personal data referred to in Article 9(1) may be processed for the purposes referred to in Article 9(2)(h) when those data are processed by or under the responsibility of a professional subject to the obligation of professional secrecy under Union or Member State law, or to rules established by national competent bodies, or by another person also subject to an obligation of secrecy under Union or Member State law, or under rules established by national competent bodies.

Member States may maintain or introduce further conditions, including limitations, with regard to the processing of genetic data, biometric data, or data concerning health.

☐ Conclusion

It is important for DPOs and organizations to distinguish, in advance of collecting personal data, whether the proposed data collection relates to general personal data or sensitive personal data. They also need to be able to confirm compliance procedures in advance of collecting and maintaining personal data, particularly sensitive personal data. The organization could be asked to demonstrate, at a future date, that it obtained consent and how it maintains general compliance. If it cannot, it may have to delete the data. It may have committed breaches and offenses, and may potentially face prosecution, fines, and/or being sued by the data subjects. Depending on the circumstances, personal liability can also arise. Now, the new GDPR risk assessments, data protection impact assessments, risk consultations, and DPbD require more nuanced policies, records, and methodologies.

New Profession

☐ Introduction

Chapter IV, Section 4 of the new General Data Protection Regulation (GDPR) creates the new professional role of—and requirement for organizations to designate—a formal data protection officer for the organization. There are rules in relation to

- Organizations' designation of the data protection officer

- Groups of undertakings and the appointment of a single data protection officer

- The appointment of a single data protection officer by public bodies or public authorities

This essentially creates a new profession, perhaps one of a number of new professions and career paths related to data protection issues and the new data protection regime. This emphasizes the new importance attached to personal data.

Chapter IV, Sections 4 and 5 of the new GDPR contains Articles 37–42. Specifically, these relate to the

- Designation of the data protection officer (Article 37)

- Position of the data protection officer (Article 38)

- Tasks of the data protection officer (Article 39)

- Codes of conduct (Article 40)

- Certification (Article 42)

The data protection officer will be chosen on the basis of professional qualities and, in particular, expert knowledge of data protection law and practices and the ability to fulfill the relevant tasks (Article 37[5]).

The data protection officer will have expert knowledge of data protection law and practices, including

- Regulations.

- Technical and organizational measures and procedures.

- Expertise on technical requirements for data protection by design and by default, and for data security.

- Industry and sector-specific knowledge.

- Experience with the size of the controller or processor.

- Awareness of the sensitivity of the data processed.

- Ability to carry out inspections, consultation, documentation, and analysis (including outsourcing or delegating).

- Ability to work with data subjects' and employees' representation organizations.

- The organization must enable the data protection officer to take part in ongoing advanced training measures to maintain specialized knowledge.

☐ Designation of the Data Protection Officer

The organization's new data protection officer should have professional qualities, expertise, and experience, and a particular expert knowledge of data protection law and practice.

- He or she needs to have the ability to understand and fulfill the tasks required under the GDPR and national data protection law.

- The data protection officer may be an employee of the organization or a contractor.

- The contact details for the new data protection officer need to be publicly available.

- These contact details should also be sent to the national data protection supervisory authority.

The designation of a data protection officer is required in any case where

- The processing of data is carried out by a public authority or body (except for courts).

- The core activities consist of processing, which by virtue of nature, scope, and/or purpose, requires "regular and systematic monitoring of data subjects on a large scale."

- The core activities of the controller or processor are on a large scale of special categories of data pursuant to Article 9 and personal data relating to criminal convictions and offenses referred to in Article 10.

☐ Independence

Article 38 (Position of the Data Protection Officer) states that

> The controller and the processor shall ensure that the Data Protection Officer is involved, properly and in a timely manner, in all issues which relate to the protection of personal data.

Also,

> The controller and the processor shall support the Data Protection Officer in performing the tasks ... by providing resources necessary to carry out those tasks and access to personal data and processing operations, and to maintain his or her knowledge.

And importantly,

> The controller or processor shall ensure that the Data Protection Officer does not receive any instructions regarding the exercise of those tasks. He or she shall not be dismissed or penalised by the controller or the processor for performing [the] tasks. The Data Protection Officer shall directly report to the highest management level of the controller or the processor.

It is expressly made clear that the data protection officer "shall ... not receive *any instructions* regarding the *exercise of [the] tasks.*" This means that the organization shall not interfere with or pressure the data protection officer in his or her carrying out and exercising of tasks. The data protection officer is effectively independent in undertaking these tasks.

The data protection officer is also independent in that he or she is free from direction or reporting requirements to other staff, managers, section heads, or particular product or service project managers. This means that the data protection officer cannot be pressured into approving certain activities or projects when certain doubts may exist as regards a new (or existing) data collection or processing activity. Equally, the data protection officer should not be pressured into ignoring a data protection analysis of new (or existing) activities that may raise data protection compliance concerns.

☐ Cannot Be Dismissed or Penalized for Doing Job

Article 38 (Position of the Data Protection Officer) states that

> [The Data Protection Officer] shall not be dismissed or penalised by the controller or the processor for performing [the] tasks.

It is therefore clear that significance, independence, insulation, and protection are being afforded to the new role of the data protection officer.

Once the data protection officer has begun undertaking his or her official role and tasks, the organization cannot victimize, dismiss, or penalize the data protection officer.

It is more of an open issue as to whether sanctions can arise in relation to data protection tasks and or other issues. However, given the possibility of threats, implicit threats, and constructive dismissal, it may well be difficult—if not impossible—to impose sanctions in relation to core data protection tasks, duties, and functions. It may seem easier to impose sanctions for purported errant activity that is outside of or unrelated to the core tasks and activities of the data protection officer. This may be difficult to demonstrate in practice, however, if there is a possibility of this other activity being referred to as a tacit punishment stemming from something occurring or not occurring in the data protection sphere. It may prove, in practice, to be difficult to disassociate data protection from other functions, with subsequent effects. This is in order to assist and ensure the independence of the data protection officer in carrying out his or her tasks, and to ensure that he or she has the confidence to be able to undertake and follow through on tasks without impermissible pressure, third-party interference, or unwarranted direction or intimidation.

However, it should be noted that the data protection officer may be permitted to undertake tasks and duties other than data protection–related tasks. If there are any other such tasks, or duties, they must "not result in a conflict of interests." It might be argued that the insulation and protection afforded to the data protection officer may not extend to disciplinary procedures as regards these non-data protection–related activities. However, it is notable that the provision states that the data protection officer "shall not be dismissed or penalised ... for performing [the] tasks," suggesting the possibility of dismissal for performing other nonpersonal data tasks. The reference to duties and tasks does not necessarily distinguish between the different duties and tasks of the data protection officer (referring only to "[the] tasks" in Article 38[3]). It can quite likely be said that the protection that the data protection officer receives means that he or she may *not* be dismissed, regardless of the data protection and non-data protection tasks and duties undertaken, or at least that an organization may have a most difficult task in seeking to justify a particular sanction or dismissal.

☐ Reporting Line

Article 38 (Position of the Data Protection Officer) states that

The Data Protection Officer shall directly report to the highest management level of the controller or the processor.

It is clear, therefore, that significance is being afforded to the new role of the data protection officer.

Again, this assists and ensures the independence of the data protection officer in carrying out his or her tasks, and ensures that he or she has the confidence to be able to undertake and follow through on tasks without impermissible pressure, third-party interference, or unwarranted direction or intimidation.

☐ Data Protection Officer

There may have existed a traditional view within organizations that the role of the person tasked with dealing with data protection issues was limited to dealing with *outward-facing* data protection queries such as access requests, data protection website queries, and the like. There may have been an understanding that human resources (HR) managers were responsible for dealing with all employee-related queries, including references to and copies of employee documentation and personal data.

This is no longer the case. Now, there must be a designated data protection officer appointed within an organization. Furthermore, the role and tasks of the data protection officer are not limited to outward-facing issues. The data protection officer will also be concerned with inward-facing issues. Employees and similar internal-facing individuals have data protection rights and will be able to address queries to the data protection officer independently of the HR function.

Therefore, organizations must consider data protection officer issues and the GDPR in terms of internal-facing functions. Chapter IV, Section 4 of the new GDPR refers to data protection officers and the obligation for organizations to appoint data protection officers.

The controller and the processor shall designate a data protection officer in any case where

- The processing of data is carried out by a public authority or body

- The core activities involve processing with "regular and systematic monitoring of data subjects on a large scale"

- The core activities involve processing of special categories of data or of criminal convictions or offenses data on a large scale*

---

* GDPR Article 37(1).

A group of undertakings may appoint a single data protection officer.*

Where the controller or the processor is a public authority or body, a single data protection officer may be designated for several such authorities or bodies, taking account of their organizational structure.†

In cases other than those referred to in Article 37(1), the controller, processor, or associations and other bodies representing categories of controllers or processors may designate a data protection officer.‡

The data protection officer shall be designated on the basis of professional qualities and, in particular, expert knowledge of data protection law and practices and the ability to fulfill the tasks referred to in Article 39. In some instances, therefore, the necessary level of expert knowledge may be determined, *inter alia*, according to the data processing carried out and the protection required for the personal data processed by the organization.

The data protection officer may be a staff member of the controller or processor, or may fulfill the tasks on the basis of a service contract.§

The controller or the processor shall publish the contact details of the data protection officer and communicate these to the supervisory authority.¶

The controller or the processor shall ensure that the data protection officer is involved in a proper and timely manner in all issues that relate to the protection of personal data.**

The controller or processor shall ensure that the data protection officer performs the tasks and duties independently and without instructions regarding the exercise of the functions.††

Data subjects may contact the data protection officer on all issues related to the processing of the data subject's personal data and the exercise of his or her rights under the GDPR.‡‡

The controller or processor shall support the data protection officer in performing his or her tasks and shall provide the resources needed to carry out the duties and tasks.§§ This could include, for example, staff, premises, and equipment.

The data protection officer shall have at least the following tasks:

---

* GDPR Article 37(2).
† GDPR Article 37(3).
‡ GDPR Article 37(4).
§ GDPR Article 37(6).
¶ GDPR Article 37(7).
** GDPR Article 38(1).
†† GDPR Article 38(3).
‡‡ GDPR Article 38(4).
§§ GDPR Article 38(2).

- To inform and advise the controller or the processor and the employees who carry out data processing of their obligations pursuant to the regulation and to other Union or Member State data protection provisions

- To monitor compliance with the regulation, with other Union or Member State data protection provisions, and with the policies of the controller or processor in relation to the protection of personal data, including the assignment of responsibilities, awareness-raising, and training of staff involved in processing operations and related audits

- To provide advice where requested regarding data protection impact assessment and monitoring of its performance, pursuant to Article 35

- To cooperate with the supervisory authority

- To act as the contact point for the supervisory authority on issues relating to processing, including the prior consultation referred to in Article 36, and to consult, where appropriate, with regard to any other matter*

Importantly, the data protection officer shall, in the performance of the tasks, have due regard to the risks associated with processing operations, taking into account the nature, scope, context, and purposes of processing.†

☐ Qualifications and Expertise of the Data Protection Officer

The data protection officer shall be designated on the basis of professional qualities and, in particular, expert knowledge of data protection law and practices and the ability to fulfill the tasks referred to in Article 39.‡

The data protection officer may be a staff member of the controller or processor, or may fulfill the tasks on the basis of a service contract.§

---

* GDPR Article 39(1).
† GDPR Article 39(2).
‡ GDPR Article 37(5).
§ GDPR Article 37(6).

Independent in Role and Functions

The controller or processor shall ensure that the data protection officer does not receive any instructions regarding the exercise of these functions. He or she shall not be dismissed by the controller or the processor for performing his or her functions.*

Resources

The controller and processor shall support the data protection officer in performing the necessary tasks and functions. The controller or processor, as appropriate, shall provide resources necessary to carry out the duties and tasks,† which may include, for example, staff, premises, equipment, and any other resources. Therefore, a protection exists against under resourcing, even deliberate under resourcing, of the data protection officer.

Description

Organizations must designate a data protection officer

- To monitor internal compliance with the GDPR regime and rules

- Where the data processing is undertaken in the public sector

- Where the data processing requires regular and systematic monitoring of data subjects

- To ensure governance of the organization's data management

- To draft, review, and update compliant data protection policies

- To implement systems, changes, and functions in terms of being compliant

---

* GDPR Article 38(3).
† GDPR Article 38(2).

The data protection officer should be qualified and have particular expertise in data protection law and practice. There is a need for him or her to be able to fulfill his or her tasks in compliance and conformity with the GDPR. It appears that the data protection officer may be an employee or a contractor.

The data protection officer's details must be made publicly available and the supervisory authority should be notified of the appointment.

The organization must ensure timely involvement of the data protection officer in relation to *all* issues related to the protection of personal data and data subject issues, and proper and adequate resources must be supplied to the data protection officer by the organization to allow him or her to undertake the tasks. There is an obligation to ensure that the data protection officer has independence in his or her role and functions, and that he or she cannot be controlled, micromanaged, or instructed in relation to his or her tasks.

The data protection officer will report to the board or to the highest management level as appropriate. This requirement also emphasizes the increasing importance attached to the understanding of and compliance with data protection.

The data protection officer advises the organization and employees in relation to their data protection obligations under national law and the GDPR. He or she will also monitor compliance with the data protection legal regime as well as with internal policies, and will also be involved in assigning responsibilities, raising awareness, and staff education and training.

Data protection officers should highlight changes and the new GDPR to the organization. Key issues need to be identified to appropriate management. New and ongoing change and compliance issues need appropriate resourcing. The data protection officer should assess which personal data the organization collects and processes, for which purpose, and where it is located and secured. Particular attention to outsourcing issues and contracts with processors is needed. Contracts, including service level agreements in relation to information technology (IT) systems, the cloud, and so on may be assessed. The various IT hardware, software, and systems that employees use need to be considered.

The structure of the organization of groups needs to be considered, as well as jurisdiction and location issues. The life cycles, storage, and disposal of personal data are also important considerations for the new data protection officer.

The relevant processes, policies, and documentation must be maintained by the organization, which places particular obligations on the data protection officer to consider the different documentation sets.

CHAPTER

New Role in Organizations

☐ Introduction

All organizations are now required to have a designated data protection officer to deal with data protection compliance obligations, data subject access requests, and so on. There is also a legal requirement for many organizations and particular types of activities to have a data protection officer. That is not to say that board responsibility for data protection compliance is in any way lessened.

☐ Data Protection Officer

Chapter IV, Section 4 of the new General Data Protection Regulation (GDPR) refers to data protection officers and the obligation for organizations to appoint data protection officers.

All organizations should have a data protection officer when they collect and process personal data.

In particular, the controller and the processor shall designate a data protection officer in any case where

• The data processing is carried out by a public authority or body

- The core activities of the controller or the processor consist of processing that requires regular and systematic monitoring of data subjects

- Large scale data processing of sensitive, criminal, or offense-related personal data is undertaken*

A group of undertakings may appoint a single data protection officer.†

Where the controller or the processor is a public authority or body, a single data protection officer may be designated for several such entities, authorities, or bodies, taking account of their organizational structure.‡

In cases other than those referred to in Article 37(1), the controller, processor, or associations and other bodies representing categories of controllers or processors may designate a data protection officer.§

The data protection officer shall be designated on the basis of professional qualities and, in particular, expert knowledge of data protection law and practices and the ability to fulfill the tasks referred to in Article 39. Arguably, there are objective, subjective, and individualized organizational elements to these requirements.

The data protection officer may be a staff member of the controller or processor, or may fulfill the tasks on the basis of a service contract.¶

The controller or the processor shall publish the contact details of the data protection officer so that they are available to the public, and shall also communicate these details to the supervisory authority.**

☐ Position of the Data Protection Officer

The controller or the processor shall ensure that the data protection officer is involved in a proper and timely manner in all issues related to the protection of personal data.††

The controller or processor shall support the data protection officer in performing his or her tasks by providing the resources necessary to carry out those tasks and duties.‡‡

---

* GDPR Article 37(1).
† GDPR Article 37(2).
‡ GDPR Article 37(3).
§ GDPR Article 37(4).
¶ GDPR Article 37(6).
** GDPR Article 37(7).
†† GDPR Article 38(1).
‡‡ GDPR Article 38(2).

Data subjects may contact the data protection officer about all issues related to the processing of the data subject's data and the exercise of their rights under the GDPR.*

The controller or processor shall ensure that the data protection officer does not receive any instructions regarding the exercise of his or her function.† He or she shall not be dismissed by the controller or the processor for performing his or her tasks.‡ The data protection officer shall report directly to the highest management level of the controller or the processor.§

The data protection officer may fulfill other tasks and duties. The controller or processor shall ensure that any such tasks and duties are compatible with the data protection tasks and duties, and do not result in a conflict of interest.¶

☐ Tasks of the Data Protection Officer

The data protection officer shall have at least the following tasks:

- To inform and advise the controller or the processor and the employees who carry out data processing of their obligations pursuant to this regulation and to other Union or Member State data protection provisions

- To monitor compliance with this regulation, with other Union or Member State data protection provisions, and with the policies of the controller or processor in relation to the protection of personal data, including the assignment of responsibilities, awareness-raising, and training of staff involved in processing operations and related audits

- To provide advice where requested regarding the data protection impact assessment and monitoring of its performance, pursuant to Article 35

- To cooperate with the supervisory authority

---

* GDPR Article 38(4).
† GDPR Article 38(3).
‡ GDPR Article 38(3).
§ GDPR Article 38(3).
¶ GDPR Article 38(6).

- To act as the contact point for the supervisory authority on issues relating to processing, including the prior consultation referred to in Article 36, and to consult, where appropriate, with regard to any other matter*

The data protection officer shall, in the performance of his or her tasks, also have due regard to the risks associated with processing operations, taking into account the nature, scope, context, and purposes of processing.

* GDPR Article 39(1).

SECTION 2

The Regulation

CHAPTER 4

New Data Protection Regime

☐ General Data Protection Regulation Sections

The new General Data Protection Regulation (GDPR) presents a new data protection regime for organizations and data protection officers.

There will be some immediate issues that will require the attention of the data protection officer, once appointed. Other issues will need more detailed consideration by data protection officers, supervisory authorities, lawyers, and ultimately by courts.

However, all data protection officers will need to become familiar with the requirements and content of the new GDPR. This content is referred to more specifically in this chapter. However, some of the new data protection regime issues that will need to be assessed in detail include

- New rights

- New obligations

- Remedies and sanctions

- Fines amounting to a percentage of annual worldwide turnover may be imposed for noncompliance

- Criteria to set out the level of fine will include the degree of technical and organizational security measures and procedures

- Data protection by design and by default (DPbD)

- Security of processing

- Data protection impact assessment

- Data protection compliance review

- Risk assessments

☐ General Data Protection Regulation Chapters

There are 11 chapters in the GDPR. These chapters and their subject matter are

- Chapter I: General provisions

- Chapter II: Principles

- Chapter III: Rights of the data subject

- Chapter IV: Controller and processor

- Chapter V: Transfer of personal data to third countries or international organizations

- Chapter VI: Independent supervisory authorities

- Chapter VII: Cooperation and consistency

- Chapter VIII: Remedies, liability, and penalties

- Chapter IX: Provisions relating to specific data processing situations

- Chapter X: Delegated acts and implementing acts

- Chapter XI: Final provisions

☐ General Provisions

Chapter I general provisions refer to

- Article 1: Subject matter and objectives

- Article 2: Material scope

- Article 3: Territorial scope

- Article 4: Definitions

☐ Principles

Chapter II principles refer to

- Article 5: Principles relating to processing of personal data

- Article 6: Lawfulness of processing

- Article 7: Conditions for consent

- Article 8: Conditions applicable to a child's consent in relation to social services information

- Article 9: Processing of special categories of personal data

- Article 10: Processing of personal data relating to criminal convictions and offenses

- Article 11: Processing which does not require identification

☐ Rights of the Data Subject

Chapter III refers to the rights of data subjects and contains five sections, as follows:

- Section 1: Transparency and modalities

- Section 2: Information and access to data

- Section 3: Rectification and erasure

- Section 4: Right to object and automated individual decision-making

- Section 5: Restrictions

Section 1, referring to transparency and modalities, contains the following:

- Article 12: Transparent information, communication, and modalities for the exercise of the rights of the data subject

Section 2, referring to information and access to personal data, contains the following:

- Article 13: Information to be provided where personal data are collected from the data subject

- Article 14: Information to be provided where personal data have not been obtained from the data subject

- Article 15: Right of access by the data subject

Section 3, referring to rectification and erasure, contains the following:

- Article 16: Right to rectification

- Article 17: Right to erasure (right to be forgotten)

- Article 18: Right to restriction of processing

- Article 19: Notification obligation regarding rectification or erasure of personal data or restriction of processing

- Article 20: Right to data portability

Section 4, referring to right to object and automated individual decision-making, contains the following:

- Article 21: Right to object

- Article 22: Automated individual decision-making, including profiling

    Section 5, referring to restrictions, contains

- Article 23: Restrictions

☐ Controller and Processor

Chapter IV, referring to controllers and processors, contains five sections as follows:

- Section 1: General obligations

- Section 2: Security of personal data

- Section 3: Data protection impact assessment and prior authorization

- Section 4: Data protection officer

- Section 5: Codes of conduct and certification

    Section 1, referring to general obligations, contains the following:

- Article 24: Responsibility of the controller

- Article 25: DPbD

- Article 26: Joint controllers

- Article 27: Representatives of controllers or processors not established in the Union

- Article 28: Processor

- Article 29: Processing under the authority of the controller and processor

- Article 30: Records of processing activities

- Article 31: Cooperation with the supervisory authority

Section 2, referring to the security of personal data, contains the following:

- Article 32: Security of processing

- Article 33: Notification of a personal data breach to the supervisory authority

- Article 34: Communication of a personal data breach to the data subject

Section 3, referring to data protection impact assessment and prior consultation, contains the following:

- Article 35: Data protection impact assessment

- Article 36: Prior consultation

Section 4, referring to data protection officers, contains the following:

- Article 37: Designation of the data protection officer

- Article 38: Position of the data protection officer

- Article 39: Tasks of the data protection officer

Section 5, referring to codes and certification, contains the following:

- Article 40: Codes of conduct

- Article 41: Monitoring of approved codes of conduct

- Article 42: Certification

- Article 43: Certification bodies

☐ Transfer to Third-Party Countries or International Organizations

Chapter V, referring to the transfer of personal data to third-party countries or international organizations, contains the following:

- Article 44: General principle for transfers

- Article 45: Transfers on the basis of an adequacy decision

- Article 46: Transfers subject to appropriate safeguards

- Article 47: Binding corporate rules

- Article 48: Transfers or disclosures not authorized by Union law

- Article 49: Derogations for specific situations

- Article 50: International cooperation for the protection of personal data

☐ Independent Supervisory Authorities

Chapter VI, referring to independent supervisory authorities, contains the following sections:

- Section 1: Independent status

- Section 2: Competence, tasks, and powers

    Section 1, referring to independent status, contains the following:

- Article 51: Supervisory authority

- Article 52: Independence

- Article 53: General conditions for the members of the supervisory authority

- Article 54: Rules on the establishment of the supervisory authority

Section 2, referring to competence, tasks, and powers, contains the following:

- Article 55: Competence

- Article 56: Competence of the lead supervisory authority

- Article 57: Tasks

- Article 58: Powers

- Article 59: Activity reports

☐ Cooperation and Consistency

Chapter VII, referring to cooperation and consistency, contains the following sections:

- Section 1: Cooperation

- Section 2: Consistency

- Section 3: European Data Protection Board

☐ Cooperation

Section 1 refers to cooperation, and contains the following:

- Article 60: Cooperation between the lead supervisory authority and the other supervisory authority

- Article 61: Mutual assistance

- Article 62: Joint operations of supervisory authority

☐ **Consistency**

Section 2, referring to consistency, contains the following:

- Article 63: Consistency mechanism

- Article 64: Opinion of the Board

- Article 65: Dispute resolution by the Board

- Article 66: Urgency procedure

- Article 67: Exchange of information

☐ **European Data Protection Board**

Section 3, referring to the European Data Protection Board, contains the following:

- Article 68: European Data Protection Board

- Article 69: Independence

- Article 70: Tasks of the Board

- Article 71: Reports

- Article 72: Procedure

- Article 73: Chair

- Article 74: Tasks of the Chair

- Article 75: Secretariat

- Article 76: Confidentiality

☐ Remedies, Liability, and Sanctions

Chapter VIII, referring to remedies, liability, and sanctions, contains the following:

- Article 77: Right to lodge a complaint with a supervisory authority

- Article 78: Right to an effective judicial remedy against a supervisory authority

- Article 79: Right to an effective judicial remedy against a controller or processor

- Article 80: Representation of data subjects

- Article 81: Suspension of proceedings

- Article 82: Right to compensation and liability

- Article 83: General conditions for imposing administrative fines

- Article 84: Penalties

☐ Provisions for Specific Data Processing Situations

Chapter IX, referring to provisions relating to specific processing situations, contains the following:

- Article 85: Processing and freedom of expression

- Article 86: Processing and public access to official documents

- Article 87: Processing of the national identification number

- Article 88: Processing in the context of employment

- Article 89: Safeguards and derogations relating to processing for archiving purposes in the public interest, for scientific or historical research purposes, or for statistical purposes

- Article 90: Obligations of secrecy

- Article 91: Existing data protection rules of churches and religious associations

☐ Delegated Acts and Implementing Acts

Chapter X, referring to delegated acts and implementing acts, contains the following:

- Article 92: Exercise of the delegation

- Article 93: Committee procedure

☐ Final Provisions

Chapter XI, referring to final provisions, contains the following:

- Article 94: Repeal of Directive 95/46/EC

- Article 95: Relationship to Directive 2002/58/EC

- Article 96: Relationship with previously concluded Agreements

- Article 97: Commission reports

- Article 98: Review of other Union legal acts on data protection

- Article 99: Entry into force and application

SECTION 3

Role

CHAPTER

5

Role, Obligations, and Position

☐ Introduction

Organizations are now required to have a data protection officer. In addition, the role and task requirements are now more explicit. The data protection officer must also have an appropriate independence in his or her activities and cannot be compromised or dictated to in a manner that undermines the role and duties in relation to personal data. It is now clear that the profession of the independent and expert data protection officer has arrived.

☐ New Role of Data Protection Officer

Chapter IV, Section 4 of the new General Data Protection Regulation (GDPR) refers to the new role and requirement of data protection officers and the obligation for organizations to appoint data protection officers.

While a data protection officer is recommended in all instances, the controller and the processor shall designate a data protection officer in any case where

• The data processing is carried out by a public authority or body, except for courts acting in their judicial capacity.

- The core activities of the controller or the processor consist of data processing operations that, by virtue of their nature, scope, and/or purposes, require regular and systematic monitoring of data subjects on a large scale.

- The core activities of the controller or the processor consist of data processing on a large scale of special categories of data pursuant to Article 9 and personal data relating to criminal convictions and offenses referred to in Article 10*.

☐ Role and Position

The controller or processor needs to involve the data protection officer in a proper and timely manner in all of the various issues that relate to personal data and the protection of personal data.

Sufficient resources and support must be supplied by the controller or processor to ensure that the data protection officer can successfully carry out his or her tasks.

The data protection officer reports directly to the highest management level within the respective organization of the controller or processor.

The data protection officer will be very active in terms of ensuring that the organization approaches data protection issues and compliance seriously. Appropriate policy and procedures must be implemented. These will be tailored and specific to the organization and the data processing activities envisaged.

Appropriate governance structures must be implemented to meet the data protection issues, concerns, risks, documentation record requirement, and general compliance issues. A variety of measures, from audits to assessments, consultations, early warning systems, and so on, must be implemented across the organization proportionate to the issues and risks arising. Sectoral issues will also be an important factor in dictating the appropriate policies required.

☐ Independent in Role and Tasks

The data protection officer must be allowed to act independently and to not be under direction or instruction regarding his or her individual tasks.

---

* GDPR Article 37(1).

The controller or processor shall ensure that the data protection officer does not receive any instructions regarding the exercise of his or her function. He or she shall not (ordinarily or at all) be dismissed by the controller or the processor for performing his or her tasks.*

☐ Resources

The controller or processor shall support the data protection officer in performing the tasks referred to in Article 37 by providing resources necessary to carry out these tasks. The controller or processor, as appropriate, must therefore by implication provide staff, premises, equipment, and any other resources necessary for the data protection officer to carry out the required duties and tasks.

☐ Group Data Protection Officer

A group of undertakings may appoint a single data protection officer.†

Where the controller or the processor is a public authority or body, a single data protection officer may be designated for several of its entities, taking account of their organizational structure.‡

In cases other than those referred to in Article 37(1), the controller, processor, or associations and other bodies representing categories of controllers or processors may, or where required by Union or Member State law shall, designate a data protection officer. The data protection officer may act for such associations and for other bodies representing controllers or processors.§

Of course, organizations should not appoint a single data protection officer when in fact more than one is required, nor seek to only have one data protection officer in order to avoid properly resourcing compliance with data protection and/or downgrading it compared with other issues.

---

* GDPR Article 38(3).
† GDPR Article 37(2).
‡ GDPR Article 37(3).
§ GDPR Article 37(4).

☐ Contact Details

The controller or the processor shall publically publish the contact details of the data protection officer and communicate them to the supervisory authority.*

Data subjects may contact the data protection officer on all issues related to the processing of the data subject's data, the exercise of their rights under the GDPR, and to exercise their rights.†

☐ Reporting

The data protection officer shall report directly to the highest management level of the controller or the processor.‡

---

* GDPR Article 37(7).
† GDPR Article 38(4).
‡ GDPR Article 38(3).

CHAPTER

Independence Needed

☐ Independence

Article 38(3) (Position of the Data Protection Officer) states that

> The controller and processor shall ensure that the Data Protection Officer does not receive any instructions regarding the exercise of those tasks. He or she shall not be dismissed or penalised by the controller or the processor for performing [the] tasks. The Data Protection Officer shall directly report to the highest management level of the controller or the processor.

☐ Instructions Regarding Tasks

Data protection officers, both of controllers and of processors, must be independent and able to act without constraint, direction, or instruction. While this obligation is expressly stated as an obligation that controllers and processors must ensure, it can be said that data protection officers must also be cognizant of this obligation and that there is therefore also an obligation on them to act independently. The data protection officer should be alert and should object to communications that may be interpreted as placing him or her under pressure of being directed, pressured, or otherwise compromised in his or her duties. If there is a risk of such communications to the data protection officer, or some other activity that makes clear that the controller, or processor, is in breach of their explicit obligations (or a risk that this may be the case), the data protection officer cannot ignore this, or worse still, acquiesce to this.

☐ Cannot Be Dismissed or Penalized for Performing Tasks and Functions

This is one of the protections for data protection officers, in part to ensure that the he or she can and will act independently in his or her functions. The data protection officer cannot be dismissed or otherwise penalized for performing his or her tasks.

It might also be implied that this protection includes not being dismissed, or penalized, for refusing or protesting against instructions regarding the exercise of tasks.

While these protections are critically important to the data protection officer and to the organization itself, these new provisions will also need to be fully understood by the human resources department of the organization.

Prudent organizations will also ensure that there is an expressly established route for the data protection officer to object and protest about what are unlawful efforts to direct, instruct, and compromise the data protection officer in his or her tasks and functions. It is implicit that this route will also need to exist at the highest level of the organization. It may of course be appropriate for the data protection officer to raise these issues directly where this problem occurs, but for the provisions to work most efficiently, there should be an established route to go above the person creating the problem. Unfortunately, as this person may be the direct member of senior management to whom the data protection officer already reports to, the established route must involve some person more senior than that person.

☐ Report to Highest Management Level

It is also specified that "The Data Protection Officer shall directly report to the highest management level of the controller or the processor." This is a critical tool in ensuring independence by the data protection officer in his or her functions and tasks. It also ensures that data protection is taken seriously by the organization. By requiring senior management involvement, the provision also ensures that the data protection officer is not compromised by being overruled, ignored, or otherwise compromised by nonsenior management or section heads in various parts of the organization.

It may be important to caution against a non-manager, junior section head, or other junior executive being considered sufficiently senior to be the person to whom the data protection officer reports. The data protection officer should be reporting to someone at senior level, which should be board level management. (It is for this reason that if the senior person is the cause of a problem that compromises independence, for example, of the data protection officer, the alternative contact point to whom the problem should be reported should be a more senior member of the management board—or indeed the managing director.)

This can also be taken to mean that the obligation is directed at the controller, processor, and data protection officer.

Relationship with the Management Board

☐ The Management Board in General

The importance of data protection compliance, new issues and developments, and general updates on data protection issues within the organization will be communicated to the board by the data protection officer.

There is potential for this communication to be either direct or indirect via the board member to whom the data protection officer should ideally report. This may depend on the organization itself, its size, maturity, and so on. It may also be an issue of compliance that evolves over time and as the Commission, European Data Protection Board, and national supervisory authorities deal more with the General Data Protection Regulation (GDPR) and the new data protection regime.

Such reporting to and contact with the management board may also be influenced in part by the urgency of the data protection issue involved.

☐ Reporting to Management Level

Article 36(2) (referring to the position of the Data Protection Officer) requires that "The Data Protection Officer *shall* directly report to the highest management level of the controller or the processor." This signifies the senior or highest management of the organization, and is not to be misunderstood as being any individual who may have a title of "manager," or who may be a junior official or manager. Such misunderstanding would create the potential situation of data protection not being treated properly and seriously as is required, by downgrading the ability of the data protection officer and the organization to perform the required tasks, functions, and compliance obligations. It would also create the possibility for an individual junior manager or section head to refuse to cooperate with the data protection officer or to ignore the advice or directions of the data protection officer in relation to a risky—or even unlawful—processing activity. Section heads responsible for developing new products and services are under a particular pressure to roll out new projects as quickly and as commercially as possible. This sometimes creates tension in terms of appropriate consideration of data protection issues. If the data protection officer has to report to this person, this can create further tension where data protection compliance advice might sometimes be ignored, or the data protection officer encouraged, directed, or instructed to row back on his or her compliance advice. Even where these is no reporting line between the data protection officer and the section head, there is a risk that such a section head may feel superior to and able to ignore or dictate to the data protection officer if the management reporting line is not at a level higher than the section head in question.

The highest level of reporting will, by necessity, require that the data protection officer is reporting to someone at board level. Downgrading the reporting line to below this level may not fully satisfy the requirement and may raise additional problems.

In some instances, and depending on the size, sector, and maturity of the organization, the data protection officer may be reporting to the managing director. However, this may create a potential escalation point issue in terms of maintaining the independence of the data protection officer. Alternative solutions may need to be considered, and are possible, depending on the circumstances.

☐ Promoting Data Protection to the Management Board

Some of the roles and functions will necessitate that the data protection officer is promoting and effectively "selling" data protection, security, prudent use of technology (and new technology), prudent development and launch of new products and services, and pre-problem-solving (e.g., with data protection by design or data protection by default) to the organization and to the management board.

It goes without saying that, given the arrival of the GDPR and the new data protection regime, the data protection officer will be busy updating the management board and the organization in general about the new rights, obligations, and other issues arising.

The required activities of the data protection officer in relation to the management board (and organization in general) may also vary, depending upon whether there is an existing data protection officer within the organization or whether the position is newly appointed as a result of the GDPR.

In the latter instance, the data protection officer will possibly have more work to do in bringing the board up to speed with the importance of data protection and data protection compliance. (To some extent, the issue of the new fines and penalties regime may be of some assistance in focusing minds.)

However, data protection is not limited to a mere compliance issue. There are many advantages, including competitive advantages, to respecting personal data. The data protection officer should be conscious of selling the advantages of data protection best practice to the management board.

Particularly within an organization new to data protection or new to having a data protection officer, having the board "on board" with the message of data protection will assist in promoting data protection throughout all levels of the organization. It will filter down more efficiently once the data protection officer ensures that the board understands and treats data protection properly.

Obviously, in order to "sell" data protection to the management board (and others), the data protection officer will need to fully understand the issues and nuances of the data protection regime, the new GDPR, and sector-specific issues related to the organization itself. (This understanding ties in with the requirements for being a data protection officer and being suitably qualified and experienced.)

The data protection regime, GDPR, new and expanded rights, rules, obligations, and the advantages of data protection will all be relevant to what the data protection officer is promoting to the management board.

It may also be important for the data protection officer to contextualize the new data protection regime. It is not a mere or inconvenient compliance issue. Rather, many issues and developments have occurred since the European Union Data Protection Directive 95/46/EC of 1995 (DPD95), and indeed since the even earlier Council of Europe Convention.

Organizational data collections have increased in size, scale, and detail, and general awareness of data protection has increased. Individuals are more conscious of the issues related to their personal data. The media too regularly concentrates upon the growing myriad of data protection issues. The issues of data breach, data loss, hacking, and even blackmail related to personal data all heighten the importance of data protection and security for personal data.

The existing—and now expanded—data protection regime will also assist organizations considering new potential products, services, and data collections. Location issues and drones, for example, are just some of the new technological developments that might be more difficult to consider and to correctly and ethically roll out in the absence of the guidance and balance of the data protection regime. These new and developing issues demonstrate that there is a need for the expertise and guidance that the data protection officer brings to the organization.

The new and significant levels of fines and penalties in the GDPR bring a new focus for ensuring that the management board (fully) appreciates what is required.

Security threats related to data involve customer personal data, employee personal data, commercial data, and proprietary data and will need to be communicated to the management board, both by the data protection officer and the information technology (IT) personnel. Some of these threats will be internal, while others will come from outside sources. There is increasing emphasis on the need to properly plan, test, and react to security threats and data breaches. The new data protection regime provides a number of provisions in this regard including security, risk assessments, pre-problem-solving, and breach reporting. The data protection officer will need to set out and define these problems and assist in highlighting preventative, minimization, and remedial solutions.

There is a growing appreciation that, when threats or problem issues are highlighted internally, they need to be acted upon. A number of organizations have not only suffered data breaches, but it has also been revealed that the particular problem vulnerabilities were known and warned against internally and nothing was done. This creates problems for the organization, the management board, executives, and other officials who ignored the advice. In some instances, senior executives and other staff have had to leave the organization as a result. Increasingly, the media, investors, shareholders, and adversely affected users and/or customers will focus not just on the breach issue but on its effects, whether the issue was known and preventable, and what (if any) steps were taken or knowingly ignored. Where employee personal data have been breached or disclosed, they will also be interested to know the details of what happened. Furthermore, there are already examples of organizations being sued by users, customers, and employees in relation to data breaches, particularly where remedial actions were not taken despite the risk having previously been highlighted internally.

One can also envisage the new fines and penalties regime being invoked in instances where breach issues occur in relation to problems that were warned against but not acted upon. In addition, one can envisage that deliberate nonaction on foot of internal warnings might become an aggravating factor to be considered by national supervisory authorities when these issues arise, and also by the courts when litigation matters arise.

In ensuring that security, breach, and other issues are treated seriously throughout all departments and sections of the organization, it will assist the data protection officer to have the encouragement and sponsorship of the management board and of a senior management board member. The message from the data protection officer to other sections of the organization is thus stronger.

The organization needs to be updated on the things that can go wrong, and so these issues need to be raised by the data protection officer. These various problem issues are occurring on an ongoing basis. There are many case studies and examples that the data protection officer can refer to in order to make the point, and also to attain the sponsorship and support needed to deal with the issues.

Once the issues are highlighted, appropriate reaction plans and actions can be implemented within the organization.

While a solution that entirely removes every potential problem may not be possible, the risks should at least be significantly reduced or reduced to acceptable levels.

Part of the activities of the data protection officer may also involve asking questions. Policies, collections, uses, and solutions will all be influenced to a greater or lesser extent by the particular issues, potential risks, potential damage, and potential fallout, and by what is deemed an acceptable risk and an acceptable usage. These questions may be more frequent where an organization is addressing data protection and appointing a data protection officer for the first time. More questions may be appropriate for new potential data collections and data uses, as opposed to existing and established uses and processing systems.

Particular types of data, such as sensitive personal data, will raise additional issues.

One issue for the data protection officer to consider is whether there is passive acceptance of breaches existing in organizational (acceptable usage) policies. Ignoring breaches or lack of enforcement of policies can undermine the efficacy of such policies. In certain instances, it may not be possible to actually enforce a policy breach provision against an employee if previous breaches were regularly ignored. This solution gap needs to be regularly highlighted by the data protection officer. Of course, this only concerns inward-facing problems.

The costs of dealing with problem issues and the fallout cost of data breach issues, for example, are increasing. These cost issues should ideally be communicated to the management board for consideration. When these issues are highlighted, it should be increasingly clear that full compliance is more appropriate than the cost of doing nothing or of not incurring preventative costs. The cost of noncompliance has undoubtedly increased significantly under the new data environment and separately under the new data protection regime.

The cost of compliance will also vary from one sector to another, as some sectors, such as banking and health, are involved in particularly sensitive activities. In addition to considering these sector- and organization-specific issues, the data protection officer may wish to promote comparisons (in relation to issues, compliance costs, controls costs, system costs, etc.) with competing or comparative organizations within the sector. If the organization is spending significantly less on security in all circumstances, this may highlight an elevated risk factor.

It is also worth considering that the data protection officer role may be somewhat wider than the IT (security) function. From a technical IT perspective, the risk assessment may relate to assessing the cost or risk of an IT asset being damaged, lost, or made permanently or temporarily inaccessible. It may perhaps include direct costs of replacement and/or direct costs of reprogramming, reinputting, or reconfiguring systems or data. The damage, loss, costs, fines, penalties, reputation, types of data subjects, litigation, and so on that the data protection officer will need to consider are increasingly wider than an asset-only specific analysis.

8

CHAPTER

Relationship with Management Director Responsible for Data Protection

☐ Management Director

Article 38(3) of the General Data Protection Regulation refers to the position of the data protection officer. It requires that "The Data Protection Officer shall directly report to the highest management level of the controller or the processor."

A management board director will therefore be the normal reporting point for the data protection officer.

This requirement also ties in with the increasing importance of data protection compliance being addressed by the organization at management board level. That the data protection officer reports to a management board director helps to satisfy this requirement for management board level involvement.

That the data protection officer is reporting directly to a management board director ensures that data protection is taken seriously at the highest level and is not downgraded and potentially undermined by layers of internal bureaucracy. It also eliminates the potential for individual junior functions seeking to influence, direct, instruct, or ignore the data protection officer.

Having the sponsorship of the management board and a management board member ensures the independence of the data protection officer from adverse downstream influence and strengthens the weight of the data protection message coming from the data protection officer.

In addition to the new legal requirement, it is also important in practical terms that a good working relationship exists between the data protection officer and the management board member.

As highlighted elsewhere, one further issue to consider is the possibility of a less-than-optimum relationship or unlawful attempts by a director or other person to influence, direct, or instruct the data protection officer. It may be beneficial to explicitly provide in advance the channel by which the data protection officer can protest the issue and protect his or her independence. This might involve setting out who the named, more senior management board member or CEO may be that the data protection officer will approach in the event of a conflict arising with the director to whom he or she regularly report.

Relationship with Information Technology

☐ Data Protection Officer and the Information Technology Function

In some sense, the relationship between the data protection officer and the information technology (IT) department or IT function of the organization will benefit in that there will already be some awareness of data risks and of (some of the) data protection issues.

Historically, some IT officers may even have acted in a dual capacity, taking on some of the data protection functions.

To that extent, the phrase "preaching to the converted" will be broadly appropriate.

However, quite apart from the new legal obligations under the General Data Protection Regulation (GDPR), it is now appropriate that the heretofore acceptance of a dual function of IT being designated as responsible for data protection issues be discontinued.

The heightened importance of the issues that can arise with personal data, and the need for data protection, demonstrates that the proper fulfillment of the data protection function within an organization requires a particular degree of independence of role (hence a designated data protection officer) and also an independence in carrying out the data protection functions, role, and duties.

This is also why it is so beneficial, and some would say necessary, that the data protection officer reports directly to and is supported by a management board member.

If there was not an independence in role and function, there would exist grave potential for conflict, resulting in both the organization and data being procedurally compromised. If, for example, the IT function maintained full control of data protection issues, they may feel an inclination to favor their IT instincts over a valid data protection issue that could be raised. The potential for conflict would therefore increase. Another example might be the potentially greater susceptibility of an IT function to fully follow instructions or requests from product development, sales, or marketing to roll out a new, novel, and technically interesting application, without a proper (or any) data protection analysis. A separate and independent data protection officer will be less conflicted. He or she will be more capable of properly and independently assessing the data protection implications.

It will inevitably be the case that some data protection officers will have to caution against certain proposed activities, applications, products, and services (or aspects of the same) as being impermissible and unlawful under the data protection regime. The data protection officer will have to stand in the way of certain proposals of others in the organization.

Of course, it may be that this can be a constructive approach, especially when the data protection officer is engaged and involved at an early stage of the development process. However, there will be examples of certain sections within an organization being arguably overenthusiastic and wishing to proceed, regardless of fully considering what is permitted under the data protection regime or without wishing to consult the data protection officer early (or at all).

The later the temporal consultation with the data protection officer, the more likely the potential in some instances for data protection issues to arise. This also increases the likelihood that, if data protection issues do arise, the late nature of the issues being identified mean the greater the difficulty in incorporating remedial changes. On occasion, the entire proposal may have to be discontinued. In other instances, delays to launch or "go-live" may be incurred as changes need to be made.

Potentially, therefore, there may exist what could be perceived by some as a conflict with what they may be doing or proposing. However, it remains the role and function of the data protection officer to raise data protection issues, regardless of where they arise within the organization.

Some may also perceive that the data protection officer is not entitled to interfere with or even dictate what the IT or other function can or cannot do. They may feel that only they are in charge of what happens in their section.

So while there is a lot in the respective roles of IT and data protection to complement each other, and an existing awareness, there is also potential for conflict; this is partially the reason for the strong emphasis on the independence of the role and functions of the data protection officer, as provided for in the new GDPR.

While, technically, electronic data can now be stored almost permanently, the data protection regime ensures that personal data must not be stored for an unnecessary or extended period beyond the primary purpose. The IT function therefore needs to be kept informed of data protection compliance, and the data protection officer needs to ensure that compliance is carried through in the IT department.

Data protection officers, particularly new ones, will need to obtain details from the IT function as to the type, form, location, and age of personal data held by the organization. Data protection life cycle issues need to be appraised by the data protection officer and promoted within the IT function.

The data protection officer and the IT function will both be concerned with such issues as confidentiality, security, tools, processes, procedures, standards, encryption, access, electronic access control, risk, monitoring, surveillance, policies, employment, data protection and employment rules, commercial activities, commercial third-party arrangements, intellectual property, levels or hierarchies of access, and so on.

Numerous issues and problems can arise. It may not yet be the case that pre-problem-solving, such as privacy by design and by default where compliance and protection are "built in" from the earliest stage of development or installation, are adopted by the IT function.

This needs to be highlighted, promoted, and monitored by the data protection officer. The policy involves being proactive and not reactive, and preventative but not remedial. Data protection must become the default setting and be embedded into the design of all processing activities. This will apply from creation, initiation, and across the full life cycle of the activity.

While the Internet of things (IoT), social media, new devices, offsite activity, and so on, may be compelling to embrace from a technology perspective, the data protection officer needs to ensure that caution and vetting of risks are undertaken initially, and if permitted, during the life cycle of such use.

Both the IT department and the data protection officer should be interested in data collection, data use, context, data classification and storage, security, risk appraisal, and so on, and thus share common interests. Each will also be concerned with data access, data disclosures, data location, data separation, and data ring-fencing and containment, whether permitted and otherwise.

Each will also be particularly concerned with IT events, breaches, risk, monitoring, assessment, response, action planning, event categorization, reactions, minimization, and so on.

The IT function can also assist the data protection officer in conducting audits of personal data held, and also with data protection compliance.

Audits will also engage each department; existing policies; data, additions and changes to data; data collection, storage, and compliance with the data protection regime; identifying problems, risks, and remedial actions; data protection incident handling procedures; logging incidents and remedial steps; data subject access requests; access request handling procedures; logging access requests and replies; data protection risk assessment procedures; training; training needs, policies, and record logs; retention, storage, and destruction policy (including the various retention periods); security, separation, and encryption; documentation, records, and proof that policies and procedures are being followed and adhered to; identifying types and categories of personal, general, and sensitive data; contracts with third-party outsourced data processors (or joint data controllers); how personal data are collected; data subject transparency, consent, and fair obtaining notices; sources of personal data; transfers of personal data; purposes; separate policies for obtaining and using sensitive personal data; closed- circuit television (CCTV); facial recognition; biometric data; health data; when and how data subjects are informed of the purpose(s) of the data collection; disclosures, transfers, recordal of original purposes, and linkage to data collected; maintaining the same; recordal of life cycles and purpose time line and expiry; possible secondary uses; validity of such processing; how and where data are to be stored; on-site and off-site access; IT system and technical access controls; security procedures; organizational physical access controls; password policies; event continuity needs and continuity planning; outsource data processor selection, contracts, and auditing; processor assistance, obligations, and records; overseas transfers; transfers outside of the European Economic Area (EEA); transfers to the United States; the EU-US Privacy Shield; lawfulness, adequacy, and security at the recipient destination; transfer frequency, volume, and need; and corrective updates downstream and across the third-party transfer stream.

The IT function may not be concerned with the frequency of data review, update, and correction, but the data protection officer needs to be concerned with this. Other issues and queries include, for example

- How often data integrity and quality are evaluated

- Whether data are used for marketing purposes

- Compliance with ePrivacy regulations

- That there is a clear purpose for each item of personal data collected

- Whether and how expectations may be set with data subjects regarding data retention

- A formal data retention/destruction policy

- Decommissioning and end of life of hardware and storage media

- Policies differentiating between categories of personal data

- The data destruction methods used

- Third-party processors involved in the data retention/storage processes

- Records and verification of data destruction

- Data subject access request identification, receipt and response procedure, and related recording log

- Who is authorized (and how) to make disclosures of personal data

- Redaction and exemption considerations

- Supervisory authority considerations

- Scheduling reviews

- Procedure for notifying issues to the supervisory authority

- Procedure for notifying the supervisory authority in the event of a breach event

- Procedure for notifying data subjects in the event of a breach event

- Recordal of breach events

- Electronic evidence and securing of workstations

- Securing portable equipment and storage media

- Premises access control and related security

10

CHAPTER

Relationship with Product Development

☐ Product Development

Those who develop new products, services, and so on in an organization will generally be less familiar with the nuances of data protection compared with the information technology (IT) function. Their activities and priorities are somewhat different.

The data protection officer will need to establish an ongoing relationship and communication process with those functions involved in expanding and cross-selling activities using personal data collected for a previous or ongoing purpose. The data protection officer will need to assess what, if any, such additional intended purposes may be undertaken, and also what additional compliance steps may be needed.

In addition, many organizations will have sections that are heavily involved in developing new products and services. Particular examples are companies developing software or software-related products, and companies involving the Internet and social media.

Frequently, newer organizations may be primarily concerned with development and ensuring product/service launch and "go-live" as soon as possible. The predominant focus on the product launch can sometimes ignore the fact that there is also a requirement to consider safety and data protection compliance. The data protection officer needs to be informed of the development issues at the earliest stage possible and to be afforded the time, access, and resources to carry out a data protection assessment.

This brings the potential for certain conflict with product development, sales, and/or marketing, particularly if data protection problems arise and are only highlighted by the data protection officer at a very late stage—most likely because the data protection officer was only made aware of the intended launch.

Such late notification places enormous pressure on the data protection officer, and unfairly so. However, the data protection officer must remain independent and insist on the full time needed to examine the aspects of the proposed product/service. He or she must also be independent in his or her assessment, and rise above the pressure of other functions and their own agendas.

However, over time the data protection officer should be able to establish good working relationships whereby other functions in the organization are sufficiently trained to appreciate data protection issues, there should be regular ongoing feedback traveling in both directions, and the data protection officer should be kept informed at the conceptual stage of potential new products and services.

The data protection officer also needs to promote pre-problem-solving such as data protection by design and by default. This will help to reduce the potential for agitation, conflict, or resentment between development and similar functions and the data protection officer.

Relationship with Human Resources

☐ Human Resources

The human resources (HR) function within an organization deals with a vast amount of employee personal data as well as past and prospective employees, spouses, and so on. This is inward-facing personal data. Depending on the organization, there may also be sensitive personal data in addition to general personal data relating to employees.

It is important, therefore, for there to be a regular and ongoing relationship between the data protection officer and the HR function. Issues may arise, and the HR function must generally be kept updated and educated in relation to personal data compliance issues.

In particular, the HR function needs to be fully updated in general in relation to the new General Data Protection Regulation (GDPR) and the new data protection regime. It also needs to be apprised of particular important issues that are specific to employees in the organization.

Article 88 of the GDPR, for example, refers to the processing of personal data in the employment context. It states:

> Member States may, by law or by collective agreements, provide for more specific rules to ensure the protection of the rights and freedoms in respect of the processing of employees' personal data in the employment context, in particular for the purposes of the recruitment, the performance of the

contract of employment, including discharge of obligations laid down by law or by collective agreements, management, planning and organisation of work, equality and diversity in the workplace, health and safety at work, protection of employer's or customer's property and for the purposes of the exercise and enjoyment, on an individual or collective basis, of rights and benefits related to employment, and for the purpose of the termination of the employment relationship.

The rules shall include suitable and specific measures to safeguard the data subject's human dignity, legitimate interests, and fundamental rights, with particular regard to the transparency of processing, the transfer of personal data within a group of undertakings, or a group of enterprises engaged in a joint economic activity and monitoring systems at the workplace.

Each Member State shall notify the Commission of those provisions of its law that it adopts and, without delay, any subsequent amendment affecting them.* Obviously, data protection officers will therefore need to examine particular national legislative changes as may occur.

In addition, the HR function needs to be informed of the full role, function, and tasks of the data protection officer. One of these functions involves the data protection officer being the point of contact in the organization for queries and access requests related to personal data. This will include being the point of contact for access requests made by employees of the organization.

Heretofore, the HR function might have been expected to be the point of contact for all employee-related queries. This realignment will need to be notified to the HR function.

The data protection regime provides for expanded and new data subject rights. Employees, like other data subjects, are entitled to these rights. A process needs to be implemented for ensuring that employees are aware of their rights, including the access right. This will need to be discussed between the Data Protection Officer and the HR function.

The various policies that refer to data protection and employees will need to be reviewed and updated as appropriate, in light of the changes brought about by the new GDPR. Template employment contracts and employee handbook(s) also need to be reviewed.

Data protection and security can form an important element of the trust and value proposition that the organization provides to, for example, its customers and users. There should be full confidence and assurance on the customer's part in dealing with the organization. Similar assurances and expectations exist in relation to employees and inward-facing issues. Data protection should be a core organizational value.

---

* GDPR Article 88(3).

CHAPTER 12

Obligation to Maintain Records and Documentation

Article 30 of the General Data Protection Regulation (GDPR) relates to the documentation records of processing activities. Article 30(1) provides that each controller and processor and, if any, the controller's representative, shall maintain a record of processing operations under its responsibility.

The documentation records referred to shall contain all of the following information:

a. The name and contact details of the controller and, where applicable, the joint controller, the controller's representative, and the data protection officer

b, The purposes of the processing

c. A description of the categories of data subjects and of the categories of personal data

d. The categories of recipients to whom the personal data have been or will be disclosed, including recipients in third-party countries or international organizations

e. Where applicable, transfers of personal data to a third-party country or an international organization, including the identification of that country or international organization and, in the case of transfers referred to in the second subparagraph of Article 49(1), the documentation of suitable safeguards

f. Where possible, the envisaged time limits for erasure of the different categories of data

g. Where possible, a general description of the technical and organizational security measures referred to in Article 32(1)

Each processor and, where applicable, the processor's representative shall maintain a record of all categories of processing activities carried out on behalf of a controller, containing

- The name and contact details of the processor or processors and of each controller on behalf of which the processor is acting (and, where applicable, of the controller's or the processor's representative) and the data protection officer

- The categories of processing carried out on behalf of each controller

- Where applicable, transfers of personal data to a third-party country or an international organization, including the identification of that country or international organization and, in the case of transfers referred to in the second subparagraph of Article 49(1), the documentation of suitable safeguards

- Where possible, a general description of the technical and organizational security measures referred to in Article 32(1)

The records shall be in writing, including in electronic format.

The controller or the processor and, where applicable, the controller's or the processor's representative, shall make the records available to the supervisory authority on request.

The obligations shall not apply to an enterprise or an organization employing fewer than 250 persons unless the processing it carries out is likely to result in a risk to the rights and freedoms of data subjects, the processing is not occasional, or the processing includes special categories of data as referred to in Article 9(1) or personal data relating to criminal convictions and offenses referred to in Article 10.

Records will relate to such issues as prior information, collections, principles, purposes and purpose limitation, legitimate processing conditions, general and sensitive personal data, locations, security measures, data transfers, processors and third parties, roles, responsibilities, policies, procedures, protocols, contracts, training documentation and programs, awareness building, information assets, electronic device assets, indexation and updating of records, data collections, data deletions and end of data life cycle, maintaining and updating records, retention periods, retention schedules, and disposal of data and devices.

This requirement will also intersect with or compliment the Accountability Principle.

CHAPTER

Staff Training Guides

☐ Staff Training

Article 39(1) is headed "Tasks of the Data Protection Officer." It states

> The Data Protection Officer shall have at least the following tasks:
>
> a. to inform and advise the controller or the processor and the employees who carry out processing of their obligations pursuant to this Regulation and to other Union or Member State data protection provisions;
> b. to monitor compliance with this Regulation, with other Union or Member State data protection provisions and with the policies of the controller or processor in relation to the protection of personal data, including the assignment of responsibilities, awareness-raising and training of staff involved in processing operations, and the related audits.

Training will be a constant and ongoing task for the data protection officer. It also needs to be maintained at a general level across the organization and followed up with more particular and nuanced training and awareness building designed to meet the needs of different units within the organization. The human resources (HR) section will have particular needs in relation to data protection understanding and compliance. The marketing and advertising department will undertake activities that sometimes bring them into potential conflict with the data protection regime. The data protection officer will need to be constantly aware of issues that may arise in terms of marketing, hence the need for ongoing data protection education in relation to marketing, consent, and related issues.

The training media will also vary and may include e-mails, hard-copy documents, policies, updates, introductions to data protection, responsibilities and general compliance, training for specific roles, issue-specific training, e-learning, the intranet, information technology (IT) access issue–related documentation, device issues and training, general awareness, and ongoing changes and updates.

SECTION **4**

Tasks

Tasks

☐ Tasks under the New Regulation

The controller and the processor shall ensure that the data protection officer is involved in all issues that relate to the protection of personal data in a proper and timely manner.*
The data protection officer shall have at least the following tasks:

- To inform and advise the controller or the processor and the employees who carry out data processing of their obligations pursuant to the General Data Protection Regulation (GDPR) and to other Union or Member State data protection provisions

- To monitor compliance with the GDPR, with other Union or Member State data protection provisions, and with the policies of the controller or processor in relation to the protection of personal data, including the assignment of responsibilities, awareness-raising and training of staff involved in processing operations, and related audits

---

* GDPR Article 38(1).

- To provide advice, where requested, regarding the data protection impact assessment and to monitor its performance pursuant to Article 35

- To cooperate with the supervisory authority

- To act as the contact point for the supervisory authority on issues related to data processing, including the prior consultation referred to in Article 36, and to consult, where appropriate, on any other matter*

The data protection officer will therefore inform and advise on the organization's and employees' obligations under the data protection regime.

He or she shall also monitor for compliance with the obligations of the data protection regime, including policies, assignment of responsibilities, awareness-raising, and training of staff.

The data protection officer may fulfill other tasks and duties. The controller or processor shall ensure that any such tasks and duties do not result in a conflict of interest.†

The data protection officer will also supervise, advise, and/or assist in relation to data protection impact assessments, and will monitor their performance and make recommendations.

He or she will also monitor and address any requests from the supervisory authority and be the designated point of contact for the supervisory authority. He or she will also cooperate with the national supervisory authority.

It is important that the data protection officer is aware of the organization-specific risks that may arise in relation to personal data and processing issues (including security issues). Depending on the sector, there may also be code of conduct and/or certification issues for the data protection officer to be concerned with. Data protection seals and certification are meant to help organizations demonstrate compliance.

The data protection officer will also, in the performance of his or her tasks, have due regard for the risks associated with processing operations, taking into account the nature, scope, context, and purposes of processing.

---

* GDPR Article 39(1).
† GDPR art 35(6).

☐ Tasks Required by the New Regulation

The new data protection regime contains *explicit required tasks* and *implicit required tasks* for the data protection officer. The former are explicitly set out in the new GDPR. The latter are required by implication of the GDPR and the role of the data protection officer.

☐ Explicit Required Tasks under the New Regulation

Article 39(1) is headed "Tasks of the Data Protection Officer." It states that

The Data Protection Officer shall have at least the following tasks:

a. to inform and advise the controller or the processor and the employees who carry out processing of their obligations pursuant to this Regulation and to other Union or Member State data protection provisions

b. to monitor compliance with this Regulation, with other Union or Member State data protection provisions and with the policies of the controller or processor in relation to the protection of personal data, including the assignment of responsibilities, awareness-raising and training of staff involved in processing operations, and the related audits;

c. to provide advice where requested as regards the data protection impact assessment and monitor its performance pursuant to Article 35;

d. to cooperate with the supervisory authority;

e. to act as the contact point for the supervisory authority on issues relating to processing, including the prior consultation referred to in Article 36, and to consult, where appropriate, with regard to any other matter

Article 39(2) states that

The Data Protection Officer shall in the performance of his or her tasks have due regard to the risk associated with processing operations, taking into account the nature, scope, context and purposes of processing.

Therefore, the explicit required tasks of the data protection officer are to

• Inform and advise the controller, processor, and employees of their obligations

- Monitor compliance, including responsibilities, awareness-raising, training, and audits

- Advise on data protection impact assessment and monitor its performance

- Cooperate with the supervisory authority

- Be the contact point for the supervisory authority, and consult with it

- Have due regard to the risks associated with processing operations, taking into account the nature, scope, context, and purposes of processing

☐ Implicit Required Tasks under the New Regulation

Article 38(1) (Position of the Data Protection Officer) states that

> The controller or the processor shall ensure that the Data Protection Officer is involved, properly and in a timely manner, in all issues which relate to the protection of personal data.

As such, the data protection officer is concerned with proper and timely involvement in *all* data protection issues.

Article 38(3) (Position of the Data Protection Officer) states that

> The controller and processor shall ensure that the Data Protection Officer does not receive any instructions regarding the exercise of those tasks. He or she shall not be dismissed or penalised by the controller or the processor for performing his tasks. The Data Protection Officer shall directly report to the highest management level of the controller or the processor.

As such, the data protection officer is to be concerned with independence, maintaining independence, ensuring that he or she is not improperly instructed, and reporting as appropriate. The data protection officer is to be concerned with self-assurance, from his or her perspective, that he or she does not receive any instructions regarding the exercise of required tasks. This includes instructions in relation to any disciplinary or similar action that does not relate to his or her tasks. The data protection controller must also ensure that he or she directly reports to the highest management level of the controller/processor.

Article 38(2) (Position of the Data Protection Officer) states that

> The controller and processor shall support the Data Protection Officer in performing the tasks ... by providing resources necessary to carry out those tasks and access to personal data and processing operations, and to maintain his or her expert knowledge.

The data protection officer must therefore be cognizant of whether he or she has sufficient resources. This can include sufficient support and staff resources.

Article 38(2) (Position of the Data Protection Officer) states that

> The controller and processor shall support the Data Protection Officer in ... access to personal data and processing operations.

The data protection officer must therefore ensure that he or she is satisfied that appropriate access to both personal data and to the data processing operations is available to him or her.

Article 37(5) (Designation of Data Protection Officer) states that

> The Data Protection Officer shall be designated on the basis of professional qualities and, in particular, expert knowledge of data protection law and practices and the ability to fulfil the tasks referred to in Article 39.

As such, the data protection officer is to be concerned with qualifications, expertise, and knowledge, and maintaining same by way of continuing professional development and related activities. The data protection officer will also be cognizant of the particular data processing being carried out by the organization and what is necessary to fulfill the tasks relevant to the organization.

The data protection officer shall, in the performance of his or her tasks, have due regard for the risks associated with processing operations, taking into account the nature, scope, context, and purposes of the particular processing.

Article 38(6) (Designation of Data Protection Officer) states that

> The Data Protection Officer may be a staff member of the controller or processor, or fulfil the tasks on the basis of a service contract.

While this refers to the controller and processor, the data protection officer must also ensure and be assured that if there are other duties, such duties do not create a conflict or potential conflict.

Article 38(3) (Designation of Data Protection Officer) states that

> The ... Data Protection Officer ... shall not be dismissed or penalised by the controller or the processor for performing [the] tasks. The Data Protection

Officer shall directly report to the highest management level of the controller or the processor.

As such, the data protection officer is to be concerned with ensuring that his or her contract is compliant; that he or she is not improperly dismissed; and that there is not undue pressure placed upon him or her in the exercise of his or her role and function by mechanisms of renewal of term, nonrenewal, dismissal, and/or related threats. Threats of improper discipline as a means of undue pressure could become an issue of unfair dismissal for the data protection officer to consider.

Article 37(7) (Designation of Data Protection Officer) states that

> The controller or the processor shall publish the contact details of the data protection officer and communicate them to the supervisory authority.

As such, the data protection officer should ensure that his or her contact details are actually published and communicated to the supervisory authority.

Article 38(4) (Position of the Data Protection Officer) states that

> Data subjects may contact the Data Protection Officer with regard to all issues related to processing of their personal data and to exercise their rights under this Regulation.

As such, the data protection officer is to ensure that he or she is the contact point for data subjects on all issues related to the processing of the data subject's data and the exercise of his or her rights.

Therefore, the implicit required tasks of the data protection officer are to

- Ensure proper and timely involvement in all data protection issues.

- Ensure independence, maintenance of independence, and that he or she is not improperly instructed, and to report as appropriate. The data protection officer is to ensure, from his or her perspective, that he or she does not receive any instructions regarding the exercise of his or her tasks. This includes instructions in relation to any disciplinary or similar actions that do not relate to his or her tasks. The data protection controller must also ensure that he or she reports directly to the appropriate management level of the controller/processor.

- Ensure that they have appropriate access to personal data and to the data processing operations.

- Be cognizant of whether he or she has sufficient resources.

- Be concerned with qualifications, expertise, and knowledge, and the maintenance of same by way of continuing professional development and related activities. The data protection officer will also be cognizant of the particular data processing being carried out by the organization and the necessity to fulfill the tasks.

- Have due regard to processing risks, taking into account the nature, scope, context, and purposes of particular processing.

- Ensure and be assured that, if there are other duties, they are compatible and that no conflict exists.

- Ensure that his or her contract is compliant, that he or she is not improperly dismissed, and that there is not undue pressure placed upon him or her in the exercise of the data protection officer role and function by mechanisms of dismissal and or related threats. Threats of improper discipline, as a means of undue pressure, could become an issue of unfair dismissal for the data protection officer to consider.

- Ensure that his or her contact details are actually published and also communicated to the supervisory authority.

- Be the contact point for data subjects on all issues related to the processing of the data subject's data and the exercise of his or her rights.

☐ Further Implicit Required Tasks

There are additional implicit required tasks that the data protection officer must undertake and comply with. These are and include the matters referred to in this section (but should by no means be seen as a final closed list).

The new GDPR sets out provisions and obligations for controllers and processors as well as rights for the individual data subjects. The data protection officer is concerned with these provisions and obligations and must ensure compliance as follows:

CHAPTER I	General provisions		Article 1	Subject matter and objectives
			Article 2	Material scope
			Article 3	Territorial scope
			Article 4	Definitions
CHAPTER II	Principles		Article 5	Principles relating to processing of personal data
			Article 6	Lawfulness of processing
			Article 7	Conditions for consent
			Article 8	Conditions applicable to a child's consent in relation to information from social services
			Article 9	Processing of special categories of personal data
			Article 10	Processing of personal data relating to criminal convictions and offenses
			Article 11	Processing that does not require identification
CHAPTER III	Rights of the data subject	Section 1 Transparency and modalities	Article 12	Transparent information, communication, and modalities for the exercise of the rights of the data subject
		Section 2 Information and access to personal data	Article 13	Information and access to personal data collected from the data subject
			Article 14	Information to be provided where personal data have not been obtained from the data subject
			Article 15	Right of access by the subject

(Continued)

		Article 83	General conditions for imposing administrative fines
		Article 84	Penalties
CHAPTER IX	Provisions relating to specific processing situations	Article 85	[]
		Article 86	[]
		Article 87	[]
		Article 88	Processing in the context of employment
		Article 89	[]
		Article 90	[]
		Article 91	[]
CHAPTER X	[]		
CHAPTER XI		Article 94	Repeal of Directive 95/46/EC

Therefore, some of the issues that need to be dealt with include

- Principles relating to the processing of personal data

- Lawfulness of data processing

- Conditions for consent

- Child's consent and information from social services

- Processing of special categories of personal data

- Processing of personal data and criminal convictions and offenses

- Processing that does not require identification

- Transparent information, communication, and modalities for the exercise of the rights of the data subject

- Information to be provided where personal data are collected from the data subject

- Information to be provided where personal data have not been obtained from the data subject

- Right of access by the data subject

- Right to rectification

- Right to erasure ("right to be forgotten")

- Right to restriction of processing

- Notification obligation regarding rectification or erasure of personal data or restriction of processing

- Right to object

- Measures based on profiling

- Restrictions

- Controller and processor general obligations

- Responsibility of the controller

- Data protection by design and by default

- Joint controllers

- Representatives of controllers not established in the Union

- Processor

- Processing under the authority of the controller and processor

- Documentation

- Cooperation with the supervisory authority

- Data security

- Security of processing

- Notification of a personal data breach to the supervisory authority

- Communication of a personal data breach to the data subject

- Data protection impact assessment

- Prior authorization and prior consultation

- Data protection officer

- Designation of the data protection officer

- Position of the data protection officer

- Tasks of the data protection officer

- Codes of conduct

- Certification

- Transfer of personal data to third-party countries or international organizations

- General principle for transfers

- Transfers with an adequacy decision

- Transfers by way of appropriate safeguards

- Transfers by way of binding corporate rules

- Derogations

- International cooperation for the protection of personal data

- Remedies, liability, and sanctions

- Right to lodge a complaint with a supervisory authority

- Right to a judicial remedy against a supervisory authority

- Right to an effective judicial remedy against a controller or processor

- Common rules for court proceedings

- Right to compensation and liability

- Penalties

- Administrative sanctions

- Provisions relating to specific data processing situations

- Processing of personal data and freedom of expression

- Processing of personal data for health

- Processing in the employment context

- Processing for historical, statistical, and scientific research purposes

- Obligations of secrecy

- Existing data protection rules of churches and religious associations

    Additional and/or more specific tasks will implicitly include

    Training

- Training staff in general about data protection compliance and issues

- Training specific staff who deal with personal data

- Training specific staff or management who deal with specific risks related to personal data processing

    Policies

- Drafting data protection policies

- Implementing data protection policies

- Updating data protection policies

    - Reviewing other policies related to data protection sections and issues

Contracts, Terms, and so on

- Reviewing data protection terms, references, and clauses in the organization's contracts, terms, and so on

Existing Information Technology (IT) Projects and Processing

- Reviewing and engaging in existing IT projects related to the impact on personal data and data processing compliance issues and risks

New IT Projects and Processing

- Reviewing and engaging in new IT projects related to the impact on personal data and data processing compliance issues and risks

Access Requests (additional)

- Being the point of contact for general queries regarding personal data

- Dealing with access requests

- Implementing an access request policy and procedures

- Reviewing and updating existing access request policies in light of the new data protection regime

Queries

- Being the point of contact for data access queries and requests

Point of Contact

- Being the organization's official data protection point of contact for data subjects

- Being the organization's official data protection point of contact for customers

- Being the organization's official data protection point of contact for users

- Being the organization's official data protection point of contact for the supervisory authority

- Being the organization's official data protection point of contact for other supervisory authorities (if relevant)

- Being the organization's official data protection point of contact for other communications or queries

Communications

- Being the point of contact for third-party communications, queries, and requests for information regarding the organization and data protection issues

- Being the point of contact for third-party requests for communications and media commentary (this may also involve the designated press or media contact [if any])

- Being the point of contact for requests to speak at conferences regarding data protection

Audits (internal)

- Audits

Audits (by supervisory authority)

- Audits

Audits (of new proposed products and services)

- Audits

Employment Contract of Data Protection Officer

- Reviewing the new or existing contract of employment of the data protection officer (or the contract of engagement if he or she is an external contractor) to ensure that it does not conflict with the independence, role, and tasks of the data protection officer

Pierre Vernhes,* former data protection officer at the Council of Europe, refers to the tasks and related duties as follows:

- Ensuring, in an independent manner, the application of the data protection regime

- Providing information and raising awareness on data protection

- Ensuring that controllers and data subjects are informed of the rights and obligations

- Providing the organization with recommendations and advice

- Assisting data subjects

- Monitoring compliance

- Keeping a register of processing operations

- Cooperating with the supervisory authority

- Notifying processing operations likely to present specific risks

- Promoting a data protection culture

- Developing an appropriate IT system from the outset

- Keeping oneself informed

- Cooperating with internal and external stakeholders

---

* Vernhes, The Data Protection Officer at Work, Workshop on Data Protection, European Parliament, Brussels, 8 June 2011.

CHAPTER

15

Tasks in Detail

☐ Explicit Required Tasks

The explicit required tasks are described in greater detail in the following sections.

Advising on Obligations

Inform and Advise the Controller of Their Data Protection Obligations

Article 39(1) states that "The Data Protection Officer shall have at least the following tasks: (a) to inform and advise the controller ... of their obligations pursuant to this Regulation and to other Union or Member State data protection provisions."

The importance of the data protection officer to inform and advise the controller organization of their data protection obligations and the requirements of compliance cannot be overestimated. This goes to the core of legal compliance and what the organization can and cannot do in terms of the intended collection, use, processing, storage, and transfer of personal data. The criteria for data collection and processing are now more stringent. The risks now attached to storing personal data are frequently greater than they were previously. Organizations also need to be aware,

119

and the data protection officer will be central to informing and advising on these issues, that the consequences of noncompliance and getting data protection wrong are severe. These can include significant media attention, damaged reputation and goodwill, lost business, lost customers, regulatory attention (including from data protection supervisory authorities), the closing or discontinuing of particular activities, processes or trading while an incident is ongoing, hot desks, replacement of hardware and data, additional staff, redirecting staff, engaging outside experts, disciplining staff, hiring new staff, including executives (indeed, there are growing examples of senior managers, executives, and even managing directors losing their positions after particular data breach incidents at companies such as Target and Sony), and so on. Sales and profits can be significantly adversely affected in particular instances. These issues can all have significant cost implications for the organization. Furthermore, and particularly under the new data protection regime, there can be significant monetary costs associated with official fines and penalties. These penalties are set out under the new General Data Protection Regulation (GDPR) and involve fines of up to millions of euro or a percentage of the global turnover of the organization, which can also amount to millions of euro.

The provision also expressly states that the obligations listed are the minimum, and are hence just some of the issues that the data protection officer is tasked with being responsible for.

Inform and Advise the Processor of Their Data Protection Obligations

Article 39(1) states that "The Data Protection Officer shall have at least the following tasks: (a) to inform and advise the ... processor ... of their obligations pursuant to this Regulation and to other Union or Member State data protection provisions."

The importance of the data protection officer to inform and advise the processor organization of their data protection obligations and the requirements of compliance cannot be overestimated.

This goes to the core of legal compliance and what the organization can and cannot do in terms of the intended collection, use, processing, storage, and transfer of personal data, and as directed by the controller. The criteria for data processing are now more stringent.

The consequences of noncompliance and getting data protection wrong are severe, and can include significant media attention, damaged reputation and goodwill, lost business, lost customers, regulatory attention (including from data protection supervisory authorities), closing or discontinuing particular activities, processes or trading while an incident is ongoing, hot desks, replacement of hardware and data, additional staff, redirecting staff, engaging outside experts, disciplining staff, hiring new staff (including executives; indeed, there are growing examples of senior managers, executives, and even managing directors losing their positions after particular data breach incidents at companies such as Target and Sony), and so on. Sales and profits can be significantly adversely affected in particular instances. These issues can all have significant cost implications for the organization. Furthermore, and particularly under the new data protection regime, there can be significant monetary costs associated with official fines and penalties. These penalties are set out under the new GDPR and involve fines of up to millions of euro or a percentage of the global turnover of the organization, which can also amount to millions of euro.

Inform and Advise Employees of Their Data Protection Obligations

Article 39(1) states that "The Data Protection Officer shall have at least the following tasks: (a) to inform and advise the ... employees who carry out processing of their obligations pursuant to this Regulation and to other Union or Member State data protection provisions."

In practice, the data protection officer will be involved in many employee data protection issues. In addition, he or she will pay particular attention to those employees involved in direct processing of personal data.

All organizations operate by way of their employees. It is therefore most important that the data protection officer is tasked with informing, appraising, and advising all employees (and in this sense, generally including executives) in relation to general data protection and their general (and specific) obligations within the organization. This advice may also include issues of policies and contracts.

It is interesting to also consider the issue of the new and enhanced rights of individual data subjects. While focus may frequently be directed at the *outward-facing* data protection issues of customers, prospective customers, and users, the data protection officer should also consider that employees will, as data subjects, also have data protection rights. While it might traditionally have been assumed that all employee-related issues would be dealt with via the employee's manager and/or human resources (HR) department, data protection officers will also need to consider (a) officially dealing with employees regarding the employees' data protection rights, concerns, and complaints; (b) the relationship of the data protection officer and the HR department as regards employees' data protection rights, concerns, and complaints; and (c) the issue of informing and advising employees of their data protection rights at the same time as "inform[ing] and advis[ing] employees of their data protection obligations." This will, no doubt, be an evolving area.

Organizations need to respect the data protection rights of their employees and even of potential employees. In addition, particular care and attention need to be paid to access requests from employees. Compliance is an ongoing issue as new changes and business practices will always present new internal challenges.

The data protection officer is tasked with a very onerous and wide-ranging responsibility to deal with and monitor compliance across the data controller or processor organization. Indeed, a data protection officer for a controller may be involved in dealing with aspects of ensuring or satisfying the organization that the processor engaged by the controller is acting appropriately and in compliance with the data protection regime. More importantly, he or she must be satisfied that the processor ensures data protection compliance by the controller as regards the personal data and processing activities that the organization delegates to the external processor organization.

The reference to "policies" highlights the need for the data protection officer to monitor, review, amend, or indeed initiate implementation of data protection policies and polices that refer to data protection and personal data issues. This is an initial obligation for new data protection officers, but also an ongoing task for all data protection officers.

The inclusion of the phrase "including assignment" or "assignment of responsibilities" is not entirely clear. It may not detract from the provision or the role and tasks of the data protection officer. In considering its meaning, it could refer to the assignment or transfer of data to processors; transfer of data from controller to controller (e.g., company sale or asset sale); transfer of contracts or policies relating to transfers, or outsourcing by controller organizations to processors; or assignment or transfer of personnel (dealing with processing activities) from controller to processor or from controller to controller. It is notable that during company or asset transfers or assignments in corporate sales transaction, and in intergroup company transfers or assignments, personal data will at least be involved or may even be the core (value) of what is being transferred or assigned.

Consideration of external contractors within the organization and data protection issues, awareness, and training also arises.

In considering policies, procedures, practices, and so on, the data protection officer will, among other things

- Provide guidelines to the organization board and to members of staff

- Provide guidelines to new members of staff

- Provide guidelines to new members (e.g. non-staff/permanent staff)

- Provide guidelines to contractors and external third parties accessing personal data

- Liaise with HR in relation to policies, procedures, and practices, specifically for individuals such as employees, retired employees, interviewees, and employee applicants

- Liaise with the information technology (IT) department in relation to developing policies, procedures, and practices in relation to information security, risk, data handling, outsourcing, monitoring, and data breach planning

- Liaise with sales and marketing functions to ensure compliance with the data protection regime and other applicable regulations for marketing, advertising, and public relations (PR)

Monitor Compliance

Monitor Compliance with Data Protection Rules

Article 39(1) states that "The Data Protection Officer shall have at least the following tasks: ... (b) to monitor compliance with this Regulation."

The data protection officer must monitor compliance by the organization with the data protection regime. This is an important, complex, wide-ranging, and ongoing task. It must at least be implied that the role is not limited to mere monitoring. The data protection officer will, without doubt, be proactive in monitoring, assessing, reviewing, amending, and implementing data protection compliance measures and will have a variety of tools available to him or her for doing so. It is also the case that he or she will not be limited to using specific tools and carrying out certain activities as regards assessing, implementing, and enhancing compliance measures by the organization. The obligation is also more nuanced in that it requires the assessment of individual data protection rules and evaluating compliance with these rules.

Monitor Compliance with Other EU Data Protection Rules

Article 39(1) states that "The Data Protection Officer shall have at least the following tasks: ... (b) to monitor compliance with ... other Union ... data protection provisions."

The data protection officer will also need to consider any other EU data protection rules that may apply to the particular organization. One example is electronic communications and electronic communications services. These areas need to be monitored to ensure that the organization is aware of, and is properly monitoring and complying with, additional applicable rules.

Monitor Compliance with National Data Protection Rules

Article 39(1) states that "The Data Protection Officer shall have at least the following tasks: ... (b) to monitor compliance with ... Member State data protection provisions."

In addition, the data protection officer will need to be aware of and monitor compliance with national data protection rules. These can include rules in the country of establishment as well as in other countries where the organization is offering goods and services, or otherwise operating.

Monitor Compliance of the Policies with Data Protection

Article 39(1) states that "The Data Protection Officer shall have at least the following tasks: ... (b) to monitor compliance ... [of] the policies of the controller or processor in relation to the protection of personal data."

The data protection officer is tasked with a very onerous and wide-ranging responsibility to deal with and monitor compliance across the organization of the data controller or processor organization. Indeed, a data protection officer for a controller may be involved in dealing with aspects of ensuring or satisfying the organization that the processor engaged by the controller is acting appropriately and in compliance with the data protection regime. More importantly, he or she must be satisfied that the processor ensures data protection compliance by the controller as regards the personal data and processing activities that the organization delegates to the external processor organization.

The reference to "policies" highlights the need for the data protection officer to monitor, review, amend, or indeed initiate implementation of data protection policies and polices that refer to data protection and personal data issues. This is an initial obligation for new data protection officers and also an ongoing task for all data protection officers.

Consideration of external contractors within the organization and data protection issues, awareness, and training also arises.

In considering policies, procedures, practices, and so on, the data protection officer will, among other things

- Provide guidelines to the organization board and to members of staff

- Provide guidelines to new members of staff

- Provide guidelines to new members

- Provide guidelines to contractors and external third parties accessing personal data

- Liaise with HR in relation to policies, procedures, and practices, specifically for individuals such as employees, retired employees, interviewees, and employee applicants

- Liaise with the IT department to develop policies, procedures, and practices in relation to information security, risk, data handling, outsourcing, monitoring, and data breach planning

- Liaise with sales and marketing functions to ensure compliance with the data protection regime and other applicable regulations for marketing, advertising, and PR

Monitor Assignment of Responsibilities

Article 39(1) states that "The Data Protection Officer shall have at least the following tasks: ... (b) to monitor compliance ... and ... policies of the controller or processor in relation to ... the assignment of responsibilities ..."

The inclusion of the phrase "assignment of responsibilities" is new, and may not detract from the provision or the role and tasks of the data protection officer. In considering its meaning, it could refer to the assignment or transfer of data to processors; transfer of data from controller to controller (e.g., company or asset sale); transfer of contracts or policies relating to transfers or outsourcing by controller organizations to processors; or assignment or transfer of personnel (dealing with processing activities) from controller to processor or controller to controller. It is notable that, in company or asset transfers or assignments in corporate sale transactions and in intergroup company transfers or assignments, personal data will at least be involved or may even be the core (value) of what is being transferred or assigned.

This can also be viewed as monitoring by the data protection officer of the assignment of responsibilities of the controller/processor/employees. Article 39(1) states that "The data protection officer shall have at least the following tasks: ... (b) to monitor compliance with this Regulation, with other Union or Member State data protection provisions and with the policies of the controller or processor in relation to the protection of personal data, including the assignment of responsibilities, awareness-raising and training of staff involved in processing operations, and the related audits." Therefore, there is potentially a very wide ambit in the levels and instances of assignment of responsibility and delegation regarding processing, data protection, and personal data.

Awareness-Raising of the Controller/Processor

Article 39(1) states that "The Data Protection Officer shall have at least the following tasks: ... (b) to monitor compliance with this Regulation, with other Union or Member State data protection provisions and with the policies of the controller or processor in relation to the protection of personal data, including the assignment of responsibilities, awareness-raising and training of staff involved in processing operations, and the related audits."

The importance of data protection compliance, and the issues and concerns with which it seeks to deal with, are obviously very important and are increasingly being presented to organizations as issues. National supervisory authorities and other official organizations have themselves been highlighting data protection issues for a number of years. International events such as Data Protection Day and Safer Internet Day highlight the growing importance of data protection and related risks. The data protection officer is required to undertake awareness-raising activities within the organization. The specifics of these activities are clearly at the discretion of the data protection officer, to a large extent, but often include educating, training, and updating not just employees but also management personnel. They may involve seminars, conferences, documentation, booklets, policies, e-mail updates, and so on. Activities may also include, for all or for specific staff, the need to attend external conferences and briefings. New issues and developments will need to be constantly communicated to those within the organization. Regular updates and refreshers may be undertaken from time to time. Therefore, raising awareness is general, specific, spanning multiple issues, and executed on an ongoing basis.

Data protection officers are also responsible for staff training. This is separate to raising awareness in the sense that it requires training on data protection, compliance, risks, solutions, tasks, roles, and responsibilities specific to individual employees or categories of employees. It will also involve highlighting the risks to the organization, employees, and customers.

Awareness-Raising of Staff

Article 39(1) states that "The Data Protection Officer shall have at least the following tasks: ... (b) ... awareness-raising ... of staff involved in processing operations."

The data protection officer is therefore concerned with awareness-raising activities focused at the staff and employees of the organization, particularly those involved with processing and personal data.

Training of the Controller/Processor

Article 39(1) states that "The Data Protection Officer shall have at least the following tasks: ... (b) ... training."

The data protection officer is therefore concerned with training issues within the controller and/or processor organization, as the case may be, with respect to processing and personal data.

Training of Controller/Processor Employees Involved in Processing Operations

Article 39(1) states that "The Data Protection Officer shall have at least the following tasks: ... (b) ... training of staff involved in processing operations."

The data protection officer is therefore concerned with ensuring appropriate training, and ongoing training, of employees within the organization—especially those actively involved in processing and personal data activities. This will include those specifically doing these activities and those doing so because the section or activity that they are associated with in the organization may potentially be involved in personal data issues.

Internal Audits

Internal audits raise a number of potential issues and a range of activities for the data protection officer dealing with and considering audit issues. Article 39(1) states that "The Data Protection Officer shall have at least the following tasks: ... (b) to monitor ... audits."

Article 39(1) also states that "The Data Protection Officer shall have at least the following tasks: ... (b) to monitor ... controller or processor ... audits" and "The Data Protection Officer shall have at least the following tasks: ... (b) to monitor compliance ... assignment of responsibilities, awareness-raising and training of staff involved in processing operations, and the related audits."

Finally, article 39(1) states that "The Data Protection Officer shall have at least the following tasks: ... (b) to monitor ... protection of personal data ... and the related audits."

These statements exemplify some of the different audit possibilities that may arise and should be considered.

The data protection officer is also responsible for "related audits."* The provision does not specify the types of audits this relates to, but it is clear that there is a variety of audits that can arise under the new data protection regime. Audits can be internal or external. Internal audits can vary from formal to less formal. A new data protection officer may wish to get a quick overview of the types of personal data held; the locations, access requests, or complaints; the different data collection points and the purpose or purposes of each; the products, services, and divisions of the organization; and so on, and a short audit may assist in accomplishing this task. From time to time, a more detailed and formal data protection audit across the organization is also advisable. Particular or more focused audits may also arise on specific issues or for specific departments, sections, or processes of the organization. Equally, they may be specific to a particular section of the organization.

External audit issues also arise where a third-party organization is engaged to carry out a particular audit for the organization or to advise on particular issues in relation to the audit or an aspect of the audit, such as specific IT technical issues, forensic issues, or legal issues. The supervisory authority may also wish to carry out an audit of the organization. This generally arises when the organization is designated as one of a number of nominee organizations in a particular sector for general audit purposes. Over the last number of years, supervisory authorities have increasingly engaged in these sector-specific general audit activities. These types of official general audits will no doubt continue to increase over the coming years under the new data protection regime. Official supervisory authority audits may also arise for a particular organization on foot of a specific issue being identified to the data protection supervisory authority. Examples include where the supervisory authority becomes aware of a data breach in the organization or is notified of a complaint by, or on behalf of, an individual data subject. Indeed, it is now possible under the new data protection regime for organizations and/or supervisory authorities to receive complaints by representative organizations acting on behalf of groups of data subjects.

The related documentation will also be relevant in assisting the data protection officer in updating the supervisory authority on the documentary compliance obligations.

---

* GDPR Article 37(1)(b).

Advising on Data Protection Impact Assessments

Provide Advice on Data Protection Impact Assessments

Article 39(1) states that "The Data Protection Officer shall have at least the following tasks: ... (c) to provide advice where requested as regards the data protection impact assessment and monitor its performance pursuant to Article 35."

This point raises a number of further points to consider. It is required, and no doubt necessary, for the data protection officer to be deeply involved in the data protection impact assessment from planning to draft finalization, rollout, report, conclusions, and follow on actions. However, the wording "provide advice" may be interpreted as the data protection officer providing advice and input as opposed to initiating or being in control of the data protection impact assessment document, process, inputs, outputs, and follow on. There is, in certain circumstances, the potential for a conflict to arise or for the advice of the data protection officer to be ignored, downgraded, and/or otherwise not taken on board (or not taken on board to the extent necessary for data protection compliance). Of course, this concern may be ameliorated by the fact that a data protection impact assessment, by its nature, will involve input from a variety of personnel and potentially external expertise. Indeed, the replies to a data protection impact assessment will involve a significant number people across the organization assisting and providing replies.

The new issue of prior authorization and prior consultations for particular activities means that the data protection officer will be reviewing the issues in question, advising on the need for prior authorization, liaising with the supervisory authority, and may in certain instances assess whether data protection impact assessments have been performed previously.

Cooperate with the Supervisory Authority

Cooperate with the Supervisory Authority

Article 39(1) states that "The data protection officer shall have at least the following tasks: ... (d) to cooperate with the supervisory authority."

This statement is important for a number of reasons. It means, from an official perspective, that the supervisory authority has a designated officer within the organization that they may contact and deal with immediately, both in a routine sense and also if and when problems arise. This is also important in helping to create a speedier, efficient, and more streamlined line of communication.

This also emphasizes the importance of data protection compliance within organizations; they are required to not just deal with these issues but to formally appoint a designated, professional, and experienced data protection officer, where this officer will be responsible for undertaking important data protection tasks across the organization. Once the organization looks at the tasks, obligations, and requirements of the data protection officer, such as reporting to a designated board member (as well as the separate responsibilities of that board member), it will be further emphasized that data protection compliance is necessary and that the data protection officer's role must be fully facilitated. Indeed, it is suggested that the importance of the data protection officer, and his or her position within the organization, will only increase over time as the dedicated line of communication and contact between the data protection officer for the organization and the supervisory authority.

Contact for the Supervisory Authority

Being the Contact Point for the Supervisory Authority on Personal Data

Article 39(1) states that "The Data Protection Officer shall have at least the following tasks: ... (e) to act as the contact point for the supervisory authority on issues relating to processing."

While there may not be any formal requirement for the general registration or notification (selective or otherwise) by organizations with supervisory authorities under the new data protection regime, and in view of the new emphasis on risk and occasional need for prompt communication with the most effective and responsive officer in a particular organization, there is a recognition that the supervisory authority needs to know who the data protection officer is, or at least be able to locate the contact details for the data protection officer as quickly as possible. This may assist smoother relations and response times in the event of, for example, a security or breach issue.

There is also recognition that there may be a variety of matters on which the supervisory authority may contact the data protection officer, one being in relation to prior consultations. Others may relate to enforcement issues, audit issues, and evidencing documentation of general or specific data protection compliance. The supervisory authority will also continue to contact organizations in the event of receiving complaints from individual data subjects.

The emphasis on the requirement of the data protection officer as a formal contact for supervisory authorities is also a general recognition of the new profession of data protection officers and the importance of data protection officers and their role in organizations.

Furthermore, it should not be forgotten that data protection officers may undoubtedly have reason to contact data protection supervisory authorities from time to time, as and when particular queries arise. This is, after all, intended to be a two-way, amicable, facilitative working relationship. The stronger the contact and relationship between the data protection officer profession and supervisory authorities in general, the more potentially problematic issues can be resolved before they become a real or live issue.

Being the Contact Point for the Supervisory Authority on Prior Consultation

Article 39(1) states that "The Data Protection Officer shall have at least the following tasks: ... (e) to act as the contact point for the supervisory authority on issues relating to ... prior consultation referred to in Article 36."

The data protection officer is therefore concerned with dealing with the supervisory authority on prior consultation issues, both proactively and as a contact point when issue and queries arise.

Consulting with Supervisory Authority on Any Other (Data Protection) Matters

Article 39(1) states that "The Data Protection Officer shall have at least the following tasks: ... (e) ... contact point for the supervisory authority ... and to consult."

The data protection officer is therefore concerned with being the contact point on any and all other data protection issues, as may potentially arise.

Consulting on Any Other (Data Protection) Matters

Article 39(1) states that "The Data Protection Officer shall have at least the following tasks: ... (e) ... to consult ... with regard to any other matter."

The data protection officer is therefore concerned with consulting and querying issues with the supervisory authority. The supervisory authority, after all, may be able to provide advice and guidance on queries or problem issues that may arise. New developments will always need to be considered, and it can be useful to consult and query the supervisory authority as developments with potential relevance to the organization arise.

Due Regard to the Risk Associated with Processing

Article 39(2) states that "The Data Protection Officer shall in the performance of his or her tasks have due regard to the risk associated with processing operations, taking into account the nature, scope, context and purposes of processing."

The Data Protection Officer must, therefore, in the performance of the tasks, have due regard to the risk associated with processing operations.

This means that, in considering all data protection and processing issues, he or she must also consider the actual and potential risk issues. This is an onerous obligation and requires full attention. As just one example of how onerous this can be, the Data Protection officer simply needs to look as far as the developing problem of data loss and data breach in commercial organizations. (That is not to say that public sector organizations are immune from these considerations.)

There will be a number of components when considering risk issues. Included within this range of issues, the article points to certain considerations of risk taking into account the nature, scope, context, and purposes of processing.

☐ Implicit Required Tasks of the New Regulation

The implicit required tasks are referred to in the following sections.

All Data Protection Issues

Maintain Proper and Timely Involvement in All Data Protection Issues

Article 38(1) states that "The controller and the processor shall ensure that the data protection officer is involved, properly and in a timely manner, in *all* issues that relate to the protection of personal data."

As such, the data protection officer is concerned with being involved in all data protection issues in a proper and timely manner. It is not just an obligation for the controller or processor to ensure this involvement; the data protection officer must also be proactive in ensuring it.

Article 38(2) states that "The controller and processor shall support the Data Protection Officer … providing resources necessary to carry out those tasks and access to personal data and processing operations, and to maintain his or her expert knowledge." The data protection officer must therefore have

• Resources adequate and necessary for the tasks

• Access to personal data

• Access to processing

As before, this is an obligation for the data protection officer as well as for the controller or processor.

Champion and Ensure Adequate Resources

Performing Tasks with Resources Necessary to Carry Out These Tasks

Article 38(2) refers to the data protection officer having the "resources necessary to carry out those tasks and access to personal data and processing operations, and to maintain his or her expert knowledge."

As such, the data protection officer should be concerned with having adequate resources proportionate and necessary to the tasks; the resources needed for access to personal data; and the resources to deal with and assess the various processing operations from a data protection perspective. Again, this is not just an obligation for the controller or processor, but also for the data protection officer who must be proactive in ensuring this.

Accessing Personal Data and Processing Operations

Access to Personal Data and Processing Operations

Article 38(2) refers to the data protection officer having "access to personal data and [access to] processing operations."

As such, the data protection officer may be concerned, on occasion, with access to personal data and processing operations. This may not be needed on all occasions or on a continual daily basis. However, risks and problems can begin to arise for the data protection officer if he or she is excluded from assessing or considering the personal data and the operations involved. The importance of the data protection officer could thus potentially be undermined or reduced. It may be that practical issues arise in terms of certain technical issues that may require the involvement of technical expertise, internal or external to the data protection officer's team.

Maintaining Expertise

Maintain Expert Knowledge

Article 38(2) refers to the "expert knowledge" of the data protection officer. Article 38(2) also refers to the "resources necessary" to the data protection officer role.

As such, the data protection officer should be concerned with maintaining his or her expert knowledge. Again, this should not be an obligation just for the controller or processor to ensure; the data protection officer must also be proactive in ensuring the maintenance of knowledge as well as requesting the resources for same.

Contact Point for Data Subjects

Be the Contact Point for Data Subjects on All Issues Related to the Processing of the Data Subject's Data

Article 37(7) states that the contact details of the data protection officer shall be "publish[ed]"—essentially, to the public. Article 38(4) states that "Data subjects may contact the Data Protection Officer with regard to all issues related to processing of their personal data."

As such, the data protection officer should be concerned with being the contact point for data subjects on *all* issues related to the processing of data subjects' data.

Be the Contact Point for Data Subjects on All Issues Related to the Exercise of Their Rights

Article 38(4) states that "Data subjects may contact the Data Protection Officer with regard to all issues related to ... the exercise of their rights under this Regulation."

As such, the data protection officer should be concerned with being the contact point for data subjects on *all* issues related to the exercise of their rights.

Avoiding Instructions on Tasks

Ensure That No Instructions Regarding the Exercise of Tasks Are Received

Article 38(3) states that "The controller and processor shall ensure that the Data Protection Officer does not receive *any* instructions regarding the exercise of [the] tasks."

As such, the data protection officer should be concerned with assuring himself or herself, from his or her perspective, that no instructions regarding the exercise of tasks and functions are received. This includes any issues of dismissal or similar threats, implicit or otherwise, in relation to their tasks and functions. The Data Protection Controller must also ensure that he or she directly reports to the highest management level of the controller/processor, again in order to ensure independence and the avoidance of instruction.

Avoiding Dismissal/Discipline on Tasks

Ensuring That Any Dismissal or Similar Actions Do Not Relate to Data Protection Officer Tasks (Which Are Protected)

Article 38(3) states that "the Data Protection Officer ... shall not be dismissed or penalized ... for performing [their] tasks."

As such, the data protection officer should be concerned with assuring himself or herself, from his or her perspective, that there is full independence in his or her role and the exercise of tasks. This includes, in this instance, avoiding being the subject of any dismissal, penalization, disciplinary, or similar actions relating to their duties, role, activities, and tasks. The Data Protection Officer is protected in relation to such duties, role, activities, and tasks, in terms of independence, intimidation, and/or being similarly compromised.

This provision is a significant safeguard, and a very high standard would need to be shown by an organization seeking to dismiss on this basis, if indeed dismissal is possible at all.

However, a note of concern might relate to, for example, probationary periods being abused in terms of seeking to compromise a new data protection officer during the initial period of employment. Full independence must be maintained. It could be queried whether a probationary period in a fixed two-year period contract would be entirely appropriate.

Report Directly to Highest Management

Ensure Direct Reporting to the Highest Management Level of the Controller/Processor

Article 38(3) states that "The Data Protection Officer shall directly report to the highest management level of the controller or the processor."

As such, the data protection officer should be concerned with ensuring, from his or her perspective, that he or she directly reports to the highest management level of the controller/processor and is not otherwise undermined, diverted, or compromised. This helps to assure sufficient independence to properly perform the tasks and functions.

Risk Issues

Article 39(2) (Tasks of the Data Protection Officer) states that "The Data Protection Officer shall in the performance of his or her tasks have due regard to the risk associated with processing operations, taking into account the nature, scope, context and purposes of processing."

As such, this is an express obligation of the data protection officer.

However, it also raises by implication the wide nature of risks associated with current and proposed data protection issues. This obligation refers to

- Risk associated with processing operations, taking into account the nature of processing

- Risk associated with processing operations, taking into account the scope of processing

- Risk associated with processing operations, taking into account the context of processing

- Risk associated with processing operations, taking into account the purposes of processing

However, there are many other risk issues that a data protection officer may need to consider and that are implicit in their nature in that they are not expressly included in the Article 39(2) clause. For example, the nature of the data, sensitive personal data, volume of data, proportionality and necessity, time required, time required on specific systems (e.g., if no longer immediately needed to a broad extent, data could be relocated to potentially less exposed areas of the organization; wide access could be reduced to more limited access; redaction; or anonymization; etc.), encryption, specific encryption, global encryption, off-site working, devices, and so on. The point is that taking an overly narrow view of particular provisions can cause the organization and the data protection officer to omit to review and consider relevant risk issues, particularly as new risks develop and/or are notified.

Avoid Conflicts

Ensure No Conflict of Interest between Data Protection Tasks and Any Other Tasks and Duties

Article 38(6) states that "The Data Protection Officer may fulfil other tasks and duties. The controller or processor shall ensure that any such tasks and duties do not result in a conflict of interests."

As such, the data protection officer should be concerned with ensuring that no conflict of interest exists between the data protection tasks and any other tasks and duties (if any).

Clearly, the optimum position would appear to be that no additional or other (unrelated) tasks and duties are allocated to the data protection officer. In any event, it is to be expected that the very important, detailed, and complex tasks associated with being a professional and expert data protection officer mean that there is not sufficient unallocated time to take on other tasks and duties, particularly those that are unrelated and noncomplimentary to the data protection role.

Also, the most obvious additional tasks and duties will be related to advancement within the data protection function of a larger organization, such as taking on multiregional responsibility after being concerned with one jurisdiction and, further still, taking on global responsibility.

☐ Further Implicit Required Tasks

The further implicit required tasks are referred to in the following sections.

Compliance with the Data Protection Principles

- Principles relating to personal data processing*

- Lawfulness of processing†

- Conditions for consent‡

- Processing of personal data of a child in relation to information from social services§

- Processing of special categories of personal data¶

- Processing of personal data relating to criminal convictions and offenses**

- Processing that does not require identification††

Compliance with the data protection principles is central to data protection compliance for any organization. In all of the activities of the data protection officer, the organization's compliance with these principles will be a constant feature.

As well as considering these core compliance issues in general, the data protection officer will also be most concerned with considering these issues in terms of compliance in specific, identified processing scenarios. This will be the case for current, ongoing processing operations, but also as and when new proposed collections, uses, and processing operations arise.

---

* GDPR Article 5.
† GDPR Article 6.
‡ GDPR Article 7.
§ GDPR Article 8.
¶ GDPR Article 9.
** GDPR Article 10.
†† GDPR Article 11.

The data protection officer will also consider compliance with the legitimate processing conditions in addition to the data protection principles, again both in terms of current levels of compliance and in relation to new proposed collections, uses, and processing activities.

The application of the data protection principles and legitimate processing conditions and, in particular, lawful compliance with the same, will arise for the data protection officer (and the organization) during instances where official or data subject complaints arise; during data access requests; during data breaches; during engagement with data processors; in the impact of data protection on many corporate commercial activities with third-party organizations; and when new threats, concerns, and problems become specifically or publically known to the organization.

The data protection officer will be concerned with developing processes and procedures to ensure and assist employees and the organization to remain generally data protection compliant in their activities from the outset, and ideally without having to engage the data protection officer in each and every activity of the organization.

Compliance with the Rights of Data Subjects: Transparency and Modalities

Transparent Information and Communication

Increasingly, one of the most common areas of data protection that raises public, media, and supervisory authority attention of an organization's data protection compliance is that of data subjects claiming that their personal data have been misused in some way and that their data protection rights have been breached.

The new GDPR enhances the existing and creates new data protection obligations (e.g., increasing the need for and level of transparency); brings new data protection rights and enhances others; and enhances the detail and modalities of how data subjects are to exercise their rights. These issues will be a direct and regular concern of the data protection officer. Indeed, the creation of the new role and requirement for a data protection officer as the transparent point of contact for individuals is another example of the new data protection regime changing its emphasis and its nuanced mechanics.

The data protection regime provides, or enshrines, a number of rights for individuals in relation to their informational privacy and data protection. These are important because organizations must respect these fundamental rights.* They are also important because the individuals themselves can enforce their rights where, for example, they feel an organization is abusing their rights and obligations. Some of these rights also apply, regardless of any suspicion of a breach by an organization. Additionally, there are increasing instances of groups of data subjects cooperating together against organizations. This possibility is further facilitated under the new GDPR, whereby data subject representative organizations are permitted.

The data protection regime provides, or enshrines, a number of rights to individuals in relation to their informational data, privacy, and protection. These rights are enhanced and expanded under the new GDPR. Transparency and consent are very important aspects of respecting and enabling such fundamental rights to be vindicated, utilized, and enforced by data subjects. Individual data subjects have a right of access to personal data. Certain fees may be charged for accessing copies of these data. There are also time limits to be complied with by the controller in relation to replying to a data subject access request (i.e., a request to access or obtain a copy of personal data that the organization holds).

Individuals also have a right to prevent data processing for direct marketing (DM) purposes.

The individual data subject has a right to prevent processing likely to cause damage or distress.

A further right relates to automated decisions being taken without human oversight or intervention. The traditional example often used is adverse credit decisions being taken automatically, without human intervention.†

There has been a lot of publicity in relation to the deletion and right to be forgotten (RtbF) rights of individuals. Importantly, individual data subjects have specific rights in relation to rectification, blocking, erasure, and destruction, and what is becoming known as the RtbF. This has added significance and attention, given the Court of Justice decision in the RtbF takedown case of Google Spain.‡

---

* See Article 8(1) Charter of Fundamental Rights of the EU and Article 16(1) of the Treaty.
† However, it can equally encompass such adverse decisions and activities as so-called neutral algorithmic processing and arranging of information and result outputs. Examples could include search rankings and priorities, search suggestions, search prompts, autosuggest, autocomplete, etc. Other examples could arise in relation to profiling- and advertising-related activities.
‡ Google Spain SL, Google Inc v. Agencia Española de Protección de Datos (AEPD), Mario Costeja González, Court of Justice (Grand Chamber), Case C-131/12, 13 May 2014. This relates to outdated search engine result listings.

Individual data subjects are also entitled to compensation, as well as being entitled to complain to the supervisory authority and to the courts to obtain judicial remedies.

Recital 10 of the Data Protection Directive (DPD) also refers to rights, and states that the objective of national laws on the processing of personal data is to protect fundamental rights and freedoms, notably the right to privacy, which is recognized both in Article 8 of the European Convention* and in the general principles of EU law. The approximation of those laws must not result in any lessening of the protection they afford but must, on the contrary, seek to ensure a high level of protection in the EU.

The new GDPR Recitals refer to data subject rights, principles of fair and transparent processing, prior information requirements, right of access, right of rectification and RtbF, right to complain to single supervisory authority, and automated processing.

Some of the rights are also exercisable regardless of any wrongdoing or breach by the controller.

Data Subject Rights

The main rights of data subjects under the GDPR can be summarized as including the following:

- **The right to transparency (Articles 5 and 12)**
- **The right to prior information (Articles 13 and 14)**
- **The right of confirmation and right of access (Article 15)**
- **The right to rectification (Article 16)**
- **The RtbF and right to erasure (Article 17)**
- **The right to data portability (Article 20)**
- **The right to object (Article 21)**
- **Rights related to automated decisions and profiling (Article 22)**
- **Data protection by design and by default (DPbD) (Article 25)**
- **Security rights (Article 32)**
- **Notification of data breach (Article 34)**
- **Data protection impact assessments, prior authorization, and prior consultation**
- **Data protection officer**
- **Remedies, liability, and sanctions (Chapter VIII)**

---

*European Convention for the Protection of Human Rights and Fundamental Freedoms.

Compliance with Rights of Data Subjects: Information and Access to Data

Information to the Data Subject

These obligations are set out in Articles 13 and 14 of the GDPR.

Right of Access for the Data Subject

One of the rights that individual data subjects has is a *right of access* to personal data. This applies to data subjects; it is an individual data subject's right. Certain fees may be charged for obtaining (additional) copies of personal data held by an organization. These are minimal, however, where and if applicable. There are also time limits to be complied with by controllers in relation to replying to a data subject access request. It is also important to note that certain rights, including the access right, can be invoked by individuals at any time and for any reason. They do not have to wait for an apparent breach by an organization.

The access right is also referred to in Article 15 of the GDPR. It refers to the right of access for individual data subjects. Article 15(1) provides that the data subject shall have the right to obtain confirmation from the controller on whether or not personal data concerning him or her are being processed and, where that is the case, access to the data *and* the following information:

- The purposes of the processing

- The categories of personal data concerned

- The recipients or categories of recipients to whom the personal data have been or will be disclosed, particularly recipients in third countries or international organizations

- Where possible, the envisaged period for which the personal data will be stored or, if not possible, the criteria used to determine that period

- The existence of the right to request rectification or erasure of personal data from the controller, restriction of processing of personal data concerning the data subject, or to object to such processing

- The right to lodge a complaint to the supervisory authority

- Where the personal data are not collected from the data subject, any available information as to their source

- The existence of automated decision-making including profiling, referred to in Article 22(1) and (4) and, at least in those cases, meaningful information about the logic involved in, as well as the significance and the envisaged consequences of, such processing for the data subject.*

Article 15(2) provides that, where personal data are transferred to a third-party country or an international organization, the data subject shall have the right to be informed of the appropriate safeguards relating to the transfer pursuant to Article 46.

The controller shall provide a copy of the personal data undergoing processing. For any further copies requested by the data subject, the controller may charge a reasonable fee based on administrative costs. Where the data subject makes the request by electronic means, and unless otherwise requested by the data subject, the information shall be provided in a commonly used electronic form.

The right to obtain a copy shall not adversely affect the rights and freedoms of others.

The data protection officer should consider implementing a data subject access request log or other recording mechanism. Trends in issues, complaints, and requests should be monitored over time. Redaction and rights of third-party issues need to be considered in detail, as well as any exemption issues.

Customer, Prospective Customer, and User Access Rights

These issues will frequently engage the time resources of the data protection officer. They will concern actual customers, prospective customers, and those who may otherwise engage with the organization (such as users of the organization's website who may not be customers or prospective customers), when their personal data may be utilized, and where this is permitted.

---

* The original Commission proposal for the GDPR referred to the purposes of the processing; the categories of personal data concerned; the recipients or categories of recipients to whom the personal data are to be or have been disclosed, in particular to recipients in third-party countries; the period for which the personal data will be stored; the existence of the right to request rectification or erasure of personal data concerning the data subject from the controller or to object to the processing of such personal data; the right to lodge a complaint to the supervisory authority and the contact details of the supervisory authority; communication of the personal data undergoing processing and of any available information as to their source; and the significance and envisaged consequences of such processing, at least in the case of measures referred to in Article 20.

Employee Access Right

Organizations and data protection officers now need to appreciate that it is not just customers and outward-facing individuals who have data protection rights. It will be important for the data protection officer to apprise the organization of this issue.

It is also necessary to appreciate that inward-facing issues might extend beyond current full-time employees to others such as previous employees, family members, short-term employees, agency staff, consultants, processor's staff, and so on.

The data protection rights generally apply in relation to any individuals whose personal data are being processed. Specifically, these individuals can include

- Employees

- Other workers such as contractors, temps, and casual staff

- Agency staff

- Ex-employees and retired employees

- Job applicants, including unsuccessful applicants

- Volunteers

- Apprentices and trainees

- Customers and clients

- Prospective customers and clients

- Suppliers

    It can also include

- Family members related to these individuals

    The list is also expanding.

Article 15 of the GDPR relates to the right of access for the data subject, which includes employees. Employees and the other categories of person referred to in this section are covered by the data access right.

Article 15(1) provides that the data subject shall have the right to obtain confirmation from the controller as to whether or not personal data concerning him or her are being processed, and where that is the case,

- Access to the personal data and the following information:

- Processing purposes

- Personal data categories

- Data recipients

- Data storage period

- Details of rectification and erasure rights

- Details of supervisory authority complaint mechanism

- Data source of nondirectly collected personal data

- Existence of automated decision-making and profiling

There are other specific provisions regarding employees for organizations to be aware of. Article 88 refers to processing in the employment context. Article 88(1) states that "Member States may, by law or by collective agreements, provide for more specific rules to ensure the protection of the rights and freedoms in respect of the processing of employees' personal data in the employment context, in particular for the purposes of the recruitment, the performance of the contract of employment, including discharge of obligations laid down by law or by collective agreements, management, planning and organization of work, equality and diversity in the workplace, health and safety at work, protection of employer's or customer's property and for the purposes of the exercise and enjoyment, on an individual or collective basis, of rights and benefits related to employment, and for the purpose of the termination of the employment relationship." Those rules shall include suitable and specific measures to safeguard the data subject's human dignity; legitimate interests and fundamental rights, with particular regard to the transparency of processing, the transfer of personal data within a group of undertakings, or a group of enterprises engaged in a joint economic activity; and monitoring systems at the workplace. Each Member State shall notify to the Commission those provisions of its law that it adopts and any subsequent amendment affecting such provisions. Obviously, data protection officers will therefore need to examine particular national law changes as may occur.

Compliance with Rights of Data Subjects: Rectification and Erasure

Right to Rectification

Data subjects have a right to rectification. Chapter III, Section 3 of the GDPR refers to rectification, erasure, and RtbF. Article 16 refers to the right to rectification. It provides that the data subject shall have the right to obtain, without undue delay, the rectification of inaccurate personal data concerning him or her from the controller. Taking into account the purposes of the processing, the data subject shall have the right to have incomplete personal data completed, including by means of providing a supplementary statement.*

Right to Erasure (Right to Be Forgotten)

Article 17(1) of the GDPR provides for the enhanced right to erasure or RtbF. This is known as the right to be forgotten. It provides that the data subject shall have the right to obtain from the controller the erasure of personal data concerning him or her without undue delay, and that the controller shall have the obligation to erase personal data without undue delay where one of the following grounds applies[†]:

- The personal data are no longer necessary in relation to the purposes for which they were collected or otherwise processed.

---

* The original Commission proposal stated "the data subject shall have the right to obtain from the controller the rectification of personal data relating to them that are inaccurate. The data subject shall have the right to obtain completion of incomplete personal data, including by way of supplementing a corrective statement." We see, therefore, that this has been enhanced in the final version by adding the stipulation "without undue delay."

† The original Commission proposal indicated that the "data subject shall have the right to obtain from the controller the erasure of personal data relating to them and the abstention from further dissemination of such data, especially in relation to personal data that are made available by the data subject while they were a child, where one of the following grounds applies …"

- The data subject withdraws the consent on which the processing is based according to Article 6(1)(a) or Article 9(2)(a), and where there are no other legal grounds for the processing.

- The data subject objects to the processing pursuant to Article 21(1) and there are no overriding legitimate grounds for the processing, or the data subject objects to the processing pursuant to Article 21(2).

- The personal data have been unlawfully processed.

- The personal data must be erased for compliance with a legal obligation in Union or Member State law to which the controller is subject.

- The personal data have been collected in relation to the offer of information by social services as referred to in Article 8(1).

Article 17(2) provides that, where the controller has made the personal data public and is obliged pursuant to paragraph 1 to erase the personal data, the controller, taking account of available technology and the cost of implementation, shall take reasonable steps, including technical measures, to inform controllers processing the personal data that the data subject has requested the erasure by such controllers of any links to, or copy or replication of, those personal data.

Article 17(3) provides that paragraphs 1 and 2 shall not apply to the extent that processing is necessary

- For exercising the right of freedom of expression and information

- For compliance with a legal obligation that requires processing by Union or Member State law to which the controller is subject or for the performance of a task carried out in the public interest or in the exercise of official authority vested in the controller

- For reasons of public interest in the area of public health in accordance with Article 9(2)(h) and (i) as well as Article 9(3)

- For archiving purposes in the public interest, scientific or historical research purposes, or statistical purposes in accordance with Article 89(1) in so far as the right referred to in paragraph 1 is likely to render impossible or seriously impair the achievement of the objectives of that processing

- For the establishment, exercise, or defense of legal claims

The controller may implement mechanisms to ensure that the time limits established for the erasure of personal data and/or for a periodic review of the need for the storage of the data are observed.

Where the erasure is carried out, the controller shall not otherwise process such personal data.

There have obviously been various amendments to these requirements and it must be agreed that the RtbF is, or has been portrayed as, contentious, which would have been an issue during the process of finalizing the GDPR.

Article 12 also provides that the "controller shall take appropriate measures to provide any information referred to in Articles 13 and 14 and any communication under Articles 15 to 22 and 34 relating to processing to the data subject in a concise, transparent, intelligible and easily accessible form, using clear and plain language, in particular for any information addressed specifically to a child. The information shall be provided in writing, or by other means, including, where appropriate, by electronic means. When requested by the data subject, the information may be provided orally, provided that the identity of the data subject is proven by other means." In addition, the "controller shall facilitate the exercise of data subject rights under Articles 15 to 22." Also, the "controller shall provide information on action taken on a request under Articles 15 to 22 to the data subject without undue delay and in any event within one month of receipt of the request. That period may be extended by two further months where necessary, taking into account the complexity and number of the requests. The controller shall inform the data subject of any such extension within one month of receipt of the request, together with the reasons for the delay. Where the data subject makes the request by electronic form means, the information shall be provided by electronic means where possible, unless otherwise requested by the data subject."

Synodinou* refers to the "right to oblivion" and notes, in relation to her research, that media interests are not immune to the RtbF. Examples are given where cases have been successful in preventing particular media stories dragging up past events long after they had occurred, including court cases.† Indeed, many countries, such as Germany, Austria, Greece, Finland, Belgium, Hungary, the Netherlands, Poland,

---

* Synodinou, "The media coverage of court proceedings in Europe: striking a balance between freedom of expression and fair process," *Computer Law & Security Review* (2012)(28) 208 at 217. Note also further examples such as Bernal, *Internet Privacy Rights: Rights to Protect Autonomy* (CUP, 2014); Sebastio, "The online right to be forgotten in the European justice evolution," *International Journal of Management* (2015) (4:1) 59; Gilbert, "The right of erasure or right to be forgotten: what the recent laws, cases, and guidelines mean for global companies," *Journal of Internet Law* (2015) (18:8) 1.
† Ibid at 218.

and Portugal, already anonymize party names from decisions and judgments.* The RtbF has also been recognized in France and Belgium.† It is also important to bear in mind that the GDPR introduces enhanced rights as regards deletion and being forgotten and does not introduce such provisions *de novo.*

Data subjects have a right to object to processing in accordance with Article 19.

Right to Data Portability

Article 20 refers to the right to data portability. The data subject shall have the right to receive the personal data concerning him or her, which he or she has provided to a controller, in a structured, commonly used, and machine-readable format, and have the right to transmit those data to another controller without hindrance from the controller to which the personal data have been provided, where

- The processing is based on consent pursuant to Article 6(1)(a) or Article 9(2)(a) or on a contract pursuant to Article 6(1)(b).

- The processing is carried out by automated means.

The data subject has the right to have the personal data transmitted directly from one controller to another, where technically feasible.

Compliance with Rights of Data Subjects: Right to Object and Profiling

Right to Object

Chapter III, Section 4 of the GDPR refers to the right to object and automated individual decision-making. Article 21 refers to the right to object. Article 21(1) provides that the data subject shall have the right to object at any time, on grounds relating to his or her particular situation, to the processing of personal data concerning him or her based on Article 6(1) (e) or (f), including profiling based on those provisions. The controller shall no longer process the personal data unless it demonstrates compelling legitimate grounds for the processing that override the interests,

---

* Ibid at 218 and footnote 106.
† Ibid at 217.

rights, and freedoms of the data subject or for the establishment, exercise, or defense of legal claims.

Where personal data are processed for DM purposes, the data subject shall have the right to object at any time to the processing of personal data concerning him or her for such marketing, including profiling to the extent that it is related to such DM.

Where the data subject objects to processing for DM purposes, the personal data shall no longer be processed for such purposes.

By latest at the time of the first communication with the data subject, the right referred to in paragraphs 1 and 2 shall be explicitly brought to the attention of the data subject and shall be presented clearly and separately from any other information.

In the context of the use of information from social services, and notwithstanding Directive 2002/58/EC, the data subject may exercise his or her right to object by automated means using technical specifications.

Where personal data are processed for scientific or historical research purposes or statistical purposes pursuant to Article 89(1), the data subject, on grounds relating to his or her particular situation, shall have the right to object to processing of personal data concerning him or her, unless the processing is necessary for the performance of a task carried out for reasons of public interest.

Measures Based on Automated Decisions and Profiling

Article 22 of the GDPR refers to automated individual decision-making, including profiling. Article 22(1) provides that the data subject shall have the right not to be subject to a decision based solely on automated processing, including profiling, which produces legal effects concerning him or her or similarly significantly affects him or her.

Paragraph 1 shall not apply if the decision

- Is necessary for entering into, or performance of, a contract between the data subject and a data controller

- Is authorized by Union or Member State law to which the controller is subject and which also lays down suitable measures to safeguard the data subject's rights and freedoms and legitimate interests

- Is based on the data subject's explicit consent

In the case of decisions necessary for entering into, or performance of, a contract between the data subject and a data controller and decisions based on the data subject's explicit consent, the data controller shall implement suitable measures to safeguard the data subject's rights and freedoms and legitimate interests, or at least the right to obtain human intervention on the part of the controller, to express his or her point of view, and to contest the decision.

Decisions referred to in paragraph 2 shall not be based on the special categories of personal data referred to in Article 9(1), unless Article 9(2)(a) or (g) applies and suitable measures to safeguard the data subject's rights and freedoms and legitimate interests are in place.

Data subjects have a right to not be subjected to automated decision-taking processes. This refers to computer-based and automated decisions taken in relation to and affecting individuals and that occur without human intervention. An example would be a financial institution making a credit application decision by automated computer without oversight by personnel of the institution. This is not the only such instance of automated decisions, however. Indeed, such instances may be increasing.

Compliance with Rights of Data Subjects: Restrictions

Restrictions

The data protection officer should consult Article 21 of the new GDPR.

Compliance with Controller and Processor: General Obligations

Responsibility of the Controller

The data protection officer and the organization need to be familiar with the entire GDPR, in particular

- Chapter I: General provisions

- Article 1: Subject matter and objectives

- Article 2: Material scope

- Article 3: Territorial scope

- Article 4: Definitions

- Chapter II: Principles

- Article 5: Principles relating to processing of personal data

- Article 6: Lawfulness of processing

- Article 7: Conditions for consent

- Article 8: Conditions applicable to a child's consent in relation to information society services

- Article 9: Processing of special categories of personal data

- Article 10: Processing of personal data relating to criminal convictions and offenses

- Article 11: Processing that does not require identification

- Chapter III: Rights of the data subject

- Section 1: Transparency and modalities

- Article 12: Transparent information, communication, and modalities for the exercise of the rights of the data subject

- Section 2: Information and access to personal data

- Article 13: Information to be provided where personal data are collected from the data subject

- Article 14: Information to be provided where personal data have not been obtained from the data subject

- Article 15: Right of access by the data subject

- Section 3: Rectification and erasure

- Article 16: Right to rectification

- Article 17: Right to erasure (RtbF)

- Article 18: Right to restriction of processing

- Article 19: Notification obligation regarding rectification or erasure of personal data or restriction of processing

- Article 20: Right to data portability

- Section 4: Right to object and automated individual decision-making

- Article 21: Right to object

- Article 22: Automated individual decision-making, including profiling

- Section 5: Restrictions

- Article 23: Restrictions

- Chapter IV: Controller and processor

- Section 1: General obligations

- Article 24: Responsibility of the controller

- Article 25: DPbD

- Article 26: Joint controllers

- Article 27: Representatives of controllers or processors not established in the Union

- Article 28: Processor

- Article 29: Processing under the authority of the controller or processor

- Article 30: Records of processing activities

- Article 31: Cooperation with the supervisory authority

- Section 2: Security of personal data

- Article 32: Security of processing

- Article 33: Notification of a personal data breach to the supervisory authority

- Article 34: Communication of a personal data breach to the data subject

- Section 3: Data protection impact assessment and prior authorization

- Article 35: Data protection impact assessment

- Article 36: Prior consultation

- Section 4: Data protection officer

- Article 37: Designation of the data protection officer

- Article 38: Position of the data protection officer

- Article 39: Tasks of the data protection officer

- Section 5: Codes of conduct and certification

- Article 40: Codes of conduct

- Article 41: Monitoring of approved codes of conduct

- Article 42: Certification

- Article 43: Certification bodies

- Chapter V: Transfer of personal data to third-party countries or international Organizations

- Article 44: General principle for transfers

- Article 45: Transfers on the basis of an adequacy decision

- Article 46: Transfers subject to appropriate safeguards

- Article 47: Binding corporate rules

- Article 48: Transfers or disclosures not authorized by Union law

- Article 49: Derogations for specific situations

- Article 50: International cooperation for the protection of personal data

- Chapter VI: Independent supervisory authorities

- Section 1: Independent status

- Article 51: Supervisory authority

- Article 52: Independence

- Article 53: General conditions for the members of the supervisory authority

- Article 54: Rules on the establishment of the supervisory authority

- Section 2: Competence, tasks, and powers

- Article 55: Competence

- Article 56: Competence of the lead supervisory authority

- Article 57: Tasks

- Article 58: Powers

- Article 59: Activity reports

- Chapter VII: Cooperation and consistency

- Section 1: Cooperation

- Article 60: Cooperation between the lead supervisory authority and the other supervisory authorities concerned

- Article 61: Mutual assistance

- Article 62: Joint operations of supervisory authorities

- Section 2: Consistency

- Article 63: Consistency mechanism

- Article 64: Opinion by the Board

- Article 65: Dispute resolution by the Board

- Article 66: Urgency procedure

- Article 67: Exchange of information

- Section 3: European Data Protection Board

- Article 68: European Data Protection Board

- Article 69: Independence

- Article 70: Tasks of the Board

- Article 71: Reports

- Article 72: Procedure

- Article 73: Chair

- Article 74: Tasks of the chair

- Article 75: Secretariat

- Article 76: Confidentiality

- Chapter VIII: Remedies, liability, and sanctions

- Article 77: Right to lodge a complaint with a supervisory authority

- Article 78: Right to effective judicial remedy against a supervisory authority

- Article 79: Right to an effective judicial remedy against a controller or processor

- Article 80: Representation of data subjects

- Article 81: Suspension of proceedings

- Article 82: Right to compensation and liability

- Article 83: General conditions for imposing administrative fines

- Article 84: Penalties

- Chapter IX: Provisions relating to specific processing situations

- Article 85: Processing and freedom of expression

- Article 86: Processing and public access to official documents

- Article 87: Processing of the national identity number

- Article 88: Processing in the context of employment

- Article 89: Safeguards and derogations relating to processing for archiving purposes in the public interest, scientific or historical research purposes or statistical purposes

- Article 90: Obligations of secrecy

- Article 91: Existing data protection rules of churches and religious associations

- Chapter X: Delegated Acts and implementing Acts

- Article 92: Exercise of the delegation

- Article 93: Committee procedure

- Chapter XI: Final Provisions

- Article 94: Repeal of Directive 95/46/EC

- Article 95: Relationship to Directive 2002/58/EC

- Article 96: Relationship with previously concluded agreements

- Article 97: Commission reports

Data Protection Principles

The original data protection principles require that personal data are

1. Fairly and lawfully processed

2. Processed for limited purposes

3. Adequate, relevant, and not excessive

4. Accurate and up to date

5. Not kept for longer than is necessary

6. Processed in line with an individual's rights

7. Secure

8. Not transferred to other countries without adequate protection

The new GDPR expresses the principles as the requirement that personal data are

- Processed lawfully, fairly, and in a transparent manner in relation to the data subject ("lawfulness, fairness, and transparency")

- Collected for specified, explicit, and legitimate purposes and not further processed in a manner that is incompatible with those purposes; further processing for archiving purposes in the public interest, for scientific or historical research purposes, or for statistical purposes shall, in accordance with Article 89(1), not be considered to be incompatible with the initial purposes ("purpose limitation")

- Adequate, relevant, and limited to what is necessary in relation to the purposes for which they are processed ("data minimization")

- Accurate and, where necessary, kept up to date; every reasonable step must be taken to ensure that personal data that are inaccurate, with regard to the purposes for which they are processed, are erased or rectified without delay ("accuracy")

- Kept in a form that permits identification of data subjects for no longer than is necessary for the purposes for which the personal data are processed; personal data may be stored for longer periods insofar as the personal data will be processed solely for archiving purposes in the public interest, for scientific or historical research purposes, or for statistical purposes in accordance with Article 89(1), subject to implementation of the appropriate technical and organizational measures required by this regulation in order to safeguard the rights and freedoms of the data subject ("storage limitation")

- Processed in a manner that ensures appropriate security of the personal data, including protection against unauthorized or unlawful processing and against accidental loss, destruction or damage, using appropriate technical or organizational measures ("integrity and confidentiality")

The controller is responsible for, and must be able to demonstrate compliance with, these data protection principles ("accountability").

Organizations, in dealing with individuals and in considering the rights of data subjects, must be fully aware that the data protection principles must also be complied with as regards the data subject.

Controllers must also give a copy of personal data to any individual on request (i.e., an access request).

These rights are very important for organizations to recognize and protect. They need to be incorporated into the organization from day one, as it may not be possible to retrospectively become compliant if the initial collection and processing were illegitimate. This is increasingly significant as data protection authorities become more proactive and as the levels of fines and penalties increase. The rights are expanding and becoming more explicit, and more nuanced, in the GDPR. It is important that organizations keep abreast of the expanding rights and obligations.

Data Protection by Design and by Default

From a headline perspective, privacy by design (PbD) and DPbD may be considered as at least similar, if not identical. However, there is also a real point that DPbD is more formal and legally based in the EU context. Data protection is perhaps a more fundamental right in some respects and may be easier to understand from an obligations and rights perspective than a more nebulous "privacy" perspective. Data protection is a recognized, stand-alone fundamental right in the EU.

It may also be interesting to consider this from a PbD, date protection by design, and data protection by default perspective, which may point toward a slightly different emphasis.

It has been suggested that "law should play a more active role in establishing best practices for emerging online trends."* DPbD is a prime example. One of the most important and developing practical areas of data protection is the concept of DPbD as referred to in the GDPR. Originally developed as a follow on from the data protection legal regime, it is now being recognized more widely and is also being explicitly referred to and recognized in primary legislation itself.

DPbD is important for organizations in terms of being a legal obligation, but also commercially in terms of being a competitive advantage.†

Previously DPbD has been referred to as PbD. The concept of DPbD is complementary to data protection law and regulation. The

---

* McGeveran, "Disclosure, endorsement, and identity in social marketing," *Illinois Law Review* (2009)(4) 1105 at 1105. Note also Zuiderveen Borgesius, *Improving Privacy Protection in the Area of Behavioural Targeting* (Kluwer, 2015).

† See, for example, Mantelero, "Competitive value of data protection: the impact of data protection regulation on online behaviour," *International Data Privacy Law* (2013)(3:4) 229.

idea is acknowledged to have originated with Dr. Ann Cavoukian, the Information and Privacy Commissioner for Ontario, Canada. She states that

"the increasing complexity and interconnectedness of information technologies [requires] building privacy right into system design ... the concept of privacy by design (PbD),... describe[s] the philosophy of embedding privacy proactively into technology itself—making it the default."*

The Information and Privacy Commissioner for Ontario refers to seven principles of PbD.† These are set out below:

1. Proactive, not Reactive; Preventative, not Remedial: The PbD approach is characterized by proactive rather than reactive measures. It anticipates and prevents privacy invasive events before they happen. PbD does not wait for privacy risks to materialize, nor does it offer remedies for resolving privacy infractions once they have occurred—it aims to prevent them from occurring. In short, PbD comes before the fact, not after.

2. Privacy as the Default Setting: We can all be certain of one thing—the default rules of PbD seek to deliver the maximum degree of privacy by ensuring that personal data are automatically protected in any given IT system or business practice. If an individual does nothing, his or her privacy still remains intact. No action is required on the part of the individual to protect his or her privacy—it is built into the system, by default.

3. Privacy Embedded into Design: PbD is embedded into the design and architecture of IT systems and business practices. It is not bolted on as an add-on, after the fact. The result is that privacy becomes an essential component of the core functionality being delivered. Privacy is integral to the system, without diminishing functionality.

4. Full Functionality—Positive Sum, not Zero Sum: PbD seeks to accommodate all legitimate interests and objectives in a positive-sum "win-win" manner, not through a dated, zero-sum approach where unnecessary trade-offs are made. PbD avoids the pretense of false dichotomies such as privacy versus security, demonstrating that it is possible to have both.

---

* At http://privacybydesign.ca/about/.
† At http://www.privacybydesign.ca/content/uploads/2009/08/7foundational principles.pdf.

5. End-to-End Security—Full Life cycle Protection:

PbD, having been embedded into the system prior to the first element of information being collected, extends securely throughout the entire life cycle of the data involved—strong security measures are essential to privacy, from start to finish. This ensures that all data are securely retained and then securely destroyed at the end of the process, in a timely fashion. Thus, PbD ensures "cradle-to-grave," secure life cycle management of information, end to end.

6. Visibility and Transparency—Keep it Open: PbD seeks to assure all stakeholders that, whatever the business practice or technology involved, it is in fact operating according to the stated promises and objectives, subject to independent verification. Its component parts and operations remain visible and transparent to users and providers alike. Remember, trust but verify.

7. Respect for User Privacy—Keep it User-Centric: Above all, PbD requires architects and operators to keep the interests of the individual uppermost by offering such measures as strong privacy defaults, appropriate notice, and empowering user-friendly options. Keep it user-centric.*

DPD95 Recital 46 states that the protection of the rights and freedoms of data subjects with regard to the processing of personal data requires that appropriate technical and organizational measures be taken, both at the time of the design of the processing system and at the time of the processing itself, particularly in order to maintain security and thereby to prevent any unauthorized processing. It is incumbent on the Member States to ensure that controllers comply with these measures, which must ensure an appropriate level of security, taking into account the state of the art and the costs of their implementation in relation to the risks inherent in the processing and the nature of the data to be protected.

DPD95 Recital 53 states, however, that certain processing operations are likely to pose specific risks to the rights and freedoms of data subjects by virtue of their nature, scope, or purposes, such as that of excluding individuals from a right, benefit, or contract, or by virtue of the *specific use of new technologies*. It is for Member States, if they so wish, to specify such risks in their legislation.

---

* At http://www.privacybydesign.ca/content/uploads/2009/08/7foundational principles.pdf.

DPD95 Recital 54 states that, with regard to all the processing undertaken in society, the amount posing such specific risks should be very limited. Member States must ensure that the supervisory authority or the data protection official in cooperation with the authority checks such processing prior to it being carried out. Following this prior check, the supervisory authority may, according to its national law, give an opinion or an authorization regarding the processing. Such checking may equally take place in the course of the preparation, either of a measure of the national parliament or of a measure based on such a legislative measure, which defines the nature of the processing and lays down appropriate safeguards.

The Commission proposed an enhanced data protection regime, including DPbD.* Article 25 of the GDPR refers to DPbD, an increasingly important area in data protection.

Article 25 of the new GDPR refers to DPbD. Note also the related concept of PbD. In some ways, PbD is the impetus for the current DPbD rules.

Taking into account the state of the art, the cost of implementation, and the nature, scope, context, and purposes of processing as well as the risks of varying likelihood and severity for rights and freedoms of natural persons posed by the processing, the controller shall, both at the time of the determination of the means for processing and at the time of the processing itself, implement appropriate technical and organizational measures. These include pseudonymization, which is designed to implement data protection principles such as data minimization in an effective manner and to integrate the necessary safeguards into the processing in order to meet the requirements of this regulation and protect the rights of data subjects.[†]

The controller shall implement appropriate technical and organizational measures for ensuring that, by default, only personal data necessary for each specific purpose of the processing are processed. That obligation applies to the amount of personal data collected, the extent of their processing, the period of their storage, and their accessibility. In particular, such measures shall ensure that, by default, personal data are

---

* See DPR, Spiekermann, "The challenges of privacy by design," *Communications of the ACM* (2012)(55) 38; Spiekermann and Cranor, "Engineering privacy," *IEEE Transactions on Software Engineering* (2009)(35) 67; Tielemans and Hildebrandt, "Data protection by design and technology neutral law," *Computer Law and Security Review* (2013)(29:5) 509; Finneran Dennedy, Fox and Finneran, *The Privacy Engineer's Manifests: Getting from Policy to Code to QA to Value* (Apress Open, 2014); Kroener and Wright, *A Strategy for Operationalizing Privacy by Design* (Routledge, 2014).
† GDPR Article 25(1).

not made accessible to an indefinite number of natural persons without the individual's intervention.*

Many multinationals and other organizations are embracing PbD and DPbD. Microsoft, for example, has endorsed PbD for a number of years. In March 2012, Google rolled out a major privacy policy change regarding users' personal data. It decided to combine the policies of over 60 separate and discrete products and services of Google (and other companies and brand names).

The data protection authorities of the EU, as well as elsewhere around the world (including various officials in the United States), requested that Google not go ahead with this policy change or, in the case of the EU, delay it until officials could consider it further.

The EU data protection authorities, under WP29 and the French data protection authority (CNIL), carried out an investigation of the new privacy policy and its implications. In *WP29 and Data Protection Authorities/Google*,[†] the new Google policy change was found to be in breach of data protection law. Various changes were required. However, one of these included that Google incorporate the policy of DPbD into its products and services.

Organizations must be proactive and not reactive. Data protection considerations need to be assessed and built in from the earliest stage in processes that potentially impact data protection. They must be transparent and visible. Problem issues are addressed and solutions incorporated into the process design and process cycle so that pre-problem-solving is achieved for personal data. DPbD needs to be built in, not merely added or considered once a problem arises at the end or after go-live. However, PbD and DPbD involve incorporating these considerations into the whole life cycle and not just at the beginning and/or the end. They are also incorporated into engineering processes and not just system considerations and data categories. PbD and DPbD are now key concepts and requirements under the new GDPR. There is increasing emphasis on privacy and data protection engineering as a part of the mechanisms needed to achieve DPbD.

In general, DPbD is one of the more important innovations in data protection. This is reflected in the GDPR. All organizations will need to apprise themselves of the concept and the regulatory compliance issues. The Google requirement to implement DPbD is also timely and reflects the importance of enterprises, both large and small, engaging in the benefits as well as the requirements of DPbD.

---

* GDPR Article 25(2).

† See WP29 Letter to Google: http://www.cnil.fr/fileadmin/documents/en/20121016-letter_google-article_29-FINAL.pdf;   Appendix: http://www.cnil.fr/fileadmin/documents/en/GOOGLE_PRIVACY_POLICY-_RECOMMENDATIONS-FINAL-EN.pdf; French DP regulator (CNIL) statement: http://www.cnil.fr/english/news-and-events/news/article/googles-new-privacy-policy-incomplete-information-and-un-controlled-combination-of-data-across-ser/.

Data protection impact assessments* are also referred to in the GDPR and may be relevant in the context of DPbD. DPbD and data protection impact assessments are also relevant in the context of developing cloud services.† Cloud services also raise important data protection and security considerations and should be carefully considered by customers as well as providers.‡ The WP29 has also commented in relation to cloud issues,§ big data issues,¶ Internet of things (IoT),** drones,†† apps on smart devices,‡‡ cookies,§§ device fingerprinting,¶¶ anonymization techniques,*** purpose limitation,††† smart devices,‡‡‡ and so on.

---

* Wright, "The state of the art in privacy impact assessments," *Computer Law & Security Review* (2012)(28) 54; Wright, Wadhwa, Lagazio, Raab and Charikane, "Integrating privacy impact assessment in risk management," *International Data Privacy Law* (2014)(4:2).

† Cloud and data protection reliability and compliance issues are referred to Clarke "How reliable is cloudsourcing? A review of articles in the technical media 2005–11," *Computer Law & Security Review* (2012)(28) 90. Kind and Rajy also research the area of the protection of sensitive personal data and cloud computing; see King and Raja "Protecting the privacy and security of sensitive customer data in the cloud," *Computer Law & Security Review* (2012)(28) 308; Peng, "A new model of data protection on cloud storage," *Journal of Networks* (03/2014)(9:3) 666.

‡ See, for example, the Information Commissioners' Office (ICO) *Guidance on the Use of Cloud Computing*, at http://www.ico.gov.uk/for_organisations/data_protection/topic_guides/online/cloud_computing.aspx; WP29, *Opinion 05/2012 on Cloud Computing*, WP 196, 1 July 2012; Lanois, "Caught in the clouds: the web 2.0, cloud computing, and privacy?" *Northwestern Journal of Technology and Intellectual Property* (2010)(9) 29; Pinguelo and Muller "Avoid the rainy day: survey of US cloud computing caselaw," *Boston College Intellectual Property & Technology Forum* (2011) 1; Kattan, "Cloudy privacy protections: why the stored communications act fails to protect the privacy of communications stored in the cloud," *Vandenburg Journal of Entertainment and Technology Law* (2010–2011)(13) 617.

§ WP29, Opinion 02/2015 on C-SIG Code of Conduct on Cloud Computing; and Opinion 05/2012 on Cloud Computing.

¶ WP29, Statement on Statement of the WP29 on the impact of the development of big data on the protection of individuals with regard to the processing of their personal data in the EU, 2014. The ICO also issued guidance on big data and data protection issues prior to the new GDPD in 2014.

** WP29, Opinion 8/2014 on the Recent Developments on the Internet of Things.

†† WP29, Opinion 01/2015 on Privacy and Data Protection Issues relating to the Utilisation of Drones.

‡‡ WP29, Opinion 02/2013 on apps on smart devices.

§§ WP29, Cookie sweep combined analysis 2015; Opinion 04/2012 on Cookie Consent Exemption.

¶¶ WP29, Opinion 9/2014 on the application of Directive 2002/58/EC to device fingerprinting.

*** WP29, Opinion 05/2014 on Anonymization Techniques. The ICO has previously issued guidance on anonymization techniques prior to the GDPD in an anonymization code of practice (2012).

††† WP29, Opinion 03/2013 on purpose limitation.

‡‡‡ WP29, Opinion 02/2013 on apps on smart devices.

Joint Controllers

Article 26 of the new GDPR needs to be considered by the data protection officer. Particular compliance intricacies exist with joint data controllers. Particular consideration of consent, transparency, purpose limitation, and so on is needed. It must be clear that data are jointly owned and/ or may be transferred between organizations. However, as there may be different activities, controls need to be maintained around the data so that each organization is aware of the purpose limitation. Consideration is also needed of the location of the controllers as this may raise particular issues. The provision provides that "Where two or more controllers jointly determine the purposes and means of processing, they shall be joint controllers. They shall in a transparent manner determine their respective responsibilities for compliance with the obligations under this Regulation, in particular as regards the exercising of the rights of the data subject and their respective duties to provide the information referred to in Articles 13 and 14, by means of an arrangement between them unless, and in so far as, the respective responsibilities of the controllers are determined by Union or Member State law to which the controllers are subject. The arrangement may designate a contact point for data subjects."

The arrangement must also be made available to the data subject.*

Representatives of Controllers or Processors Not Established in the Union

Article 27 of the new GDPR needs to be considered by the data protection officer and refers to representatives when the controller or processor is not established in the Union.

Processor

Article 28 of the new GDPR needs to be considered by the data protection officer. Appropriate contract and contract related terms are required to be in place when engaging outsourced processors. These obligations are now enhanced. The obligations on the processor are also enhanced and more particularized. The provision provides that "Where processing is to be carried out on behalf of a controller, the controller shall use only processors providing sufficient guarantees to implement appropriate technical and organisational measures in such a manner that processing will meet the requirements of this Regulation and ensure the protection of the rights of the data subject."

---

* GDPR Article 26(2).

The processor must not engage another processor without prior specific or general written authorization from the controller. In the case of general written authorization, the processor must inform the controller of any intended changes concerning the addition or replacement of other processors, thus giving the controller the opportunity to object to such changes.

Processing by a processor must be governed by a contract or other legal act under Union or Member State law that is binding on the processor with regard to the controller and that sets out the subject matter and duration of the processing, the nature and purpose of the processing, the type of personal data and categories of data subjects, and the obligations and rights of the controller.

The contract or other legal act shall stipulate, in particular, that the processor

- Processes the personal data only on documented instruction from the controller, including processing with regard to transfers of personal data to a third-party country or an international organization, unless required to do so by Union or Member State law to which the processor is subject; in such a case, the processor shall inform the controller of that legal requirement before processing, unless that law prohibits such information on important grounds of public interest.

- Ensures that persons authorized to process the personal data have committed themselves to confidentiality or are under an appropriate statutory obligation of confidentiality.

- Takes all measures required, pursuant to Article 32.

- Respects the conditions referred to in paragraphs 2 and 4 for engaging another processor.

- Taking into account the nature of the processing, assists the controller by appropriate technical and organizational measures, insofar as this is possible, for the fulfillment of the controller's obligation to respond to requests for exercising the data subject's rights as laid down in Chapter III.

- Assists the controller in ensuring compliance with the obligations pursuant to Articles 32 to 36, taking into account the nature of processing and the information available to the processor.

- At the choice of the controller, deletes or returns all personal data to the controller after the end of the provision of services relating to processing, and deletes existing copies unless Union or Member State law requires storage of the personal data.

- Makes available to the controller all information necessary to demonstrate compliance with the obligations laid down in this article, and allows for (and contributes to) audits, including inspections, conducted by the controller or another auditor mandated by the controller. (It appears that, with regard to this point (h), the processor shall immediately inform the controller if, in its opinion, an instruction infringes this regulation or other Union or Member State data protection provisions).

Where a processor engages another processor to carry out specific processing activities on behalf of the controller, the same data protection obligations (as set out in the contract or other legal act between the controller and the processor as referred to in paragraph 3) shall be imposed on that other processor by way of a contract or other legal act under Union or Member State law. In particular, sufficient guarantees must be provided to implement appropriate technical and organizational measures in such a manner that the processing will meet the requirements of the regulation. Where that other processor fails to fulfill its data protection obligations, the initial processor shall remain fully liable to the controller for the performance of that other processor's obligations.

Adherence of a processor to an approved code of conduct, as referred to in Article 40, or an approved certification mechanism, as referred to in Article 42, may be used as an element by which to demonstrate sufficient guarantees, as referred to in paragraphs 1 and 4 of this article.

Without prejudice to an individual contract between the controller and the processor, the contract or the other legal act referred to in paragraphs 3 and 4 of this article may be based, in whole or in part, on the standard contractual clauses referred to in paragraphs 7 and 8 of this article, including when they are part of a certification granted to the controller or processor pursuant to Articles 42 and 43.

Processing under the Authority of the Controller and Processor

Article 29 of the new GDPR needs to be considered by the data protection officer. This also needs particular consideration from the Data Protection Office, and may require enhanced analysis as it is considered over time.

Records

Article 30 of the new GDPR needs to be considered by the data protection officer. There is now an express obligation on the organization to maintain records and documentation of processing and data protection compliance. The documentation and records must be maintained and available to the supervisory authority when it makes an enquiry or carries out an audit.

The documentation and records will relate to such issues as prior information, collections, principles, purposes and purpose limitation, legitimate processing conditions, general and sensitive personal data, locations, security measures, data transfers, processors and third parties, roles, responsibilities, policies, procedures, protocols, contracts, training documentation and programs, awareness building, information assets, electronic device assets, indexation and updating of records, data collections, data deletions and end of data life cycle, marinating records, updating records, retention periods, retention schedules, disposal of data and devices, and so on.

There is also an obligation to maintain documentation under the accountability aspects of the data protection principles. The controller shall be responsible for and be able to "demonstrate ... compliance" with the principles (Article 5[2]). The data protection officer will be aware that

- Organizations must have, and maintain, appropriate policies and procedures, including those relating to data retention, life cycle, destruction, and data management of the process.

- Policies and procedures must be reviewed on a regular basis.

- Reporting on the activities of the organization, including a summary of policies, processes, and procedures, must take place.

    The documentation should *at least* also contain

- The name and contact details of the controller and, where applicable, the joint controller, the controller's representative, and the data protection officer

- The purposes of the processing

- A description of the categories of data subjects and personal data

- The categories of recipients to whom the personal data have been or will be disclosed, including recipients in third-party countries or international organizations

- Where applicable, transfers of personal data to a third-party country or an international organization, including the identification of that country or organization and, in the case of transfers referred to in the second subparagraph of Article 49(1), the documentation of suitable safeguards

- Where possible, the envisaged time limits for erasure of the different categories of data

- Where possible, a general description of the technical and organizational security measures referred to in Article 32(1)

The records shall be in writing, including in electronic form.

Each processor and, where applicable, the processor's representative shall maintain a record of all categories of processing activities carried out on behalf of a controller, containing

- The name and contact details of the processor (or processors), each controller on behalf of which the processor is acting, the controller's or the processor's representative (where applicable), and the data protection officer

- The categories of processing carried out on behalf of each controller

- Where applicable, transfers of personal data to a third-party country or an international organization, including the identification of that country or organization and, in the case of transfers referred to in the second subparagraph of Article 49(1), the documentation of suitable safeguards

- Where possible, a general description of the technical and organizational security measures referred to in Article 32(1)

The records shall be in writing, including in electronic form.

The documentation may also have to be produced to the supervisory authority.

There is a carve-out, however, for smaller enterprises that employ fewer than 250 employees: "unless the processing it carries out is likely to result in a risk to the rights and freedoms of data subjects, the processing is not occasional, or the processing includes special categories of data as referred to in Article 9(1) or personal data relating to criminal convictions and offenses referred to in Article 10." It will need to be considered what, if anything, is actually excluded, particularly under the "risk" catch-all. Given that the organization will, in any event, have to demonstrate compliance and that the normal way of demonstrating compliance involves documentation and documented processes, procedures, policies, and so on, it is not altogether clear how wide this carve-out will actually be.

Cooperation with the Supervisory Authority

Article 31 of the new GDPR needs to be considered by the data protection officer. Both the controller and the processor must comply with the supervisory authority as and when requested by the supervisory authority. The ambit of these particular obligations will likely expand, as practical compliance with the new General Data Protection Regulation beds in.

Compliance with the Controller and Processor: Data Security

Security of Processing

The new GDPR defines "personal data breach" as a "breach of security leading to the accidental or unlawful destruction, loss, alteration, unauthorized disclosure of, or access to, personal data transmitted, stored or otherwise processed." The importance attached to dealing with data breaches and data breach incidents is highlighted in the GDPR. Now, data breaches must be notified to the supervisory authority and the data subjects. (Bear in mind that employees can also be data subjects.) Data subjects can suffer loss and damage if there has been a data breach, and particularly so if they are unaware of it and are not notified when the organization becomes aware so that, for example, remedial measures can be undertaken by the data subject. For example, they may wish to change passwords or cancel credit cards, depending on the nature of the breach. Indeed, in some instances, organizations may need to recommend remedial or safety measures to data subjects after a data breach.

Issues range from the particular data in question, purposes, locations, data life cycle, the overall policy, the organization, the sector that the organization is in, general risks, specific risks, past risks and incidents, past breach notifications, past official relations, audits, investigations, enforcement, fines (if any), organization training, organization awareness, asset identification, asset management, access control, access protocols and procedures, physical security, operational security, electronic security, communications security, and so on.

The organization and the data protection officer also need to consider third-party relationships, such as those with suppliers and outsourcing.

It is increasingly apparent that properly considered incident management procedures are required. This is obviously a data protection compliance issue. However, it is also a business critical issue, for example, in terms of business continuity.

The Data Security Directive also needs to be considered by data protection officers.

The issue and frequency of data breaches and data breach incidents are frequently highlighted. In addition, it is clear that national supervisory authorities take data breaches very seriously. Significant fines are now regularly leveled at organizations, including large organizations and public organizations, in relation to data breaches. Similarly, even smaller organizations have been fined.

The supervisory authority can carry out audits and inspections of organizations, which can include security and data breach preparedness or can arise from a recent data breach incident. In fact, many data breaches result in media publicity for the organization, in which case the supervisory authority is likely to contact the organization.

Employee involvement is critical in dealing with—and preparing for—data breach incidents. Various teams of employees will be involved. However, as employee personal data can also be the subject of a data breach incident, employees may also need to be specifically considered in this context. For example, they may need to be separately informed that there is a breach relating to their personal data and what actions and safeguards are being followed by the organization to deal with the issue. If the employees need to take specific actions, they may also need to be apprised of this possibility. Potentially liability issues may also arise. For example, employees affected by the massive Sony data breach incidents may have considered suing Sony for breaches relating to their data.

Full details are set out in Article 32.

Notification of a Personal Data Breach to the Supervisory Authority

There must be a notification of a data breach to the supervisory authority. In the case of a personal data breach, the new GDPR requires that the controller shall, without undue delay and, where feasible, not later than 72 hours after having become aware of it, notify the personal data breach to the supervisory authority in accordance with Article 55, unless the personal data breach is unlikely to result in a risk to the rights and freedoms of natural persons. Where the notification to the supervisory authority is not made within 72 hours, it shall be accompanied by reasons for the delay.*

The processor shall notify the controller without undue delay after becoming aware of a personal data breach.†

The notification must at least

- Describe the nature of the personal data breach including, where possible, the categories and approximate number of data subjects concerned and the categories and approximate number of personal data records concerned

- Communicate the name and contact details of the Data Protection Officer or other contact point from where more information can be obtained

- Describe the likely consequences of the personal data breach

- Describe the measures taken or proposed to be taken by the controller to address the personal data breach including, where appropriate, measures to mitigate its possible adverse effects‡

Where, and in so far as, it is not possible to provide the information at the same time, the information may be provided in phases without undue further delay.

The controller shall document any personal data breaches including the facts relating to the personal data breach, its effects, and the remedial action taken. That documentation shall enable the supervisory authority to verify compliance with this article.§

Communication of a Personal Data Breach to the Data Subject

Data breaches must be communicated to the data subjects as specified. Where the personal data breach is likely to result in a high risk to the

---

* GDPR Article 33(1).
† GDPR Article 33(2).
‡ GDPR Article 33(3).
§ GDPR Article 33(5).

rights and freedoms of natural persons, the controller shall communicate the personal data breach to the data subject without undue delay.*

The communication to the data subject, as referred to in paragraph 1 of this article, shall describe the nature of the personal data breach in clear and plain language and contain at least the information and measures referred to in Article 33(3)(b), (c), and (d).†

The communication to the data subject shall not be required if any of the following conditions are met:

- The controller has implemented appropriate technical and organizational protection measures and those measures were applied to the personal data affected by the personal data breach, in particular those that render the personal data unintelligible to any person who is not authorized to access it, such as encryption.

- The controller has taken subsequent measures to ensure that the high risk to the rights and freedoms of data subjects referred to in paragraph 1 is no longer likely to materialize.

- It would involve disproportionate effort. In such a case, there shall instead be a public communication or similar measure whereby the data subjects are informed in an equally effective manner.‡

If the controller has not already communicated the personal data breach to the data subject, the supervisory authority, having considered the likelihood of the personal data breach resulting in a high risk, may require it to do so or may decide that any of the conditions referred to in paragraph 3 are met.§

Employee Data Breaches

Employee involvement is critical in dealing with—and preparing for—data breach incidents. Various teams of employees will be involved.

---

* GDPR Article 34(1). Note, for example, Wainman, "Data protection breaches: today and tomorrow," SCL *Computers and Law*, (30 June 2012). Also see Dekker, Christoffer Karsberg and Daskala, *Cyber Incident Reporting in the EU* (2012); Romanosky, Hoffman and Acquisti, "Empirical analysis of data breach litigation," *Journal of Empirical Legal Studies* (2014)(11:1) 74; Holm and Mackenzie, "The significance of mandatory data breach warnings to identity crime," *International Journal of Cyber-Security and Digital Forensics* (2015)(3:3) 141.
† GDPR Article 34(2).
‡ GDPR Article 34(3).
§ GDPR Article 34(4).

However, as employee personal data can also be the subject of a data breach incident, employees may need to be specifically considered in this context. For example, they may need to be separately informed that there is a breach relating to their personal data, and what actions and safeguards are being followed by the organization to deal with the issue. If the employees need to take specific actions, they may also need to be apprised of this possibility. Potential liability issues may also arise. For example, employees affected by the massive Sony data breach incidents may have considered suing Sony for breaches relating to their data.

Compliance with Controller and Processor: Data Protection Impact Assessment and Prior Authorization

Data Protection Impact Assessments

The requirement for data protection impact assessments (and prior consultations) is an important new requirement of the new data protection regime. Chapter IV, Section 3 of the GDPR refers to data protection impact assessments and prior consultations. As a result of the new GDPR regime, there is now a mandatory impact assessment regime. These assessments must be undertaken when data processing activities involve specific data protection and data protection risks. Particularly when new products and services or changes to existing products and services arise, the organization should ensure that these activities are the subject of a data protection impact assessment.

These data protection impact assessments will help organizations to identify and understand current and new risks in their processing activities, or indeed to their processing activities. Considerations include

- Identifying when a project involves the collection of new information about individuals

- Identifying whether information about individuals will be disclosed to organizations or people who have not previously had routine access to the information

- Identifying whether the project involves use of new technology that may raise privacy and data protection issues, such as overreach or privacy intrusion

- Identifying whether the personal data raise issues or concerns or are in some way objectionable

Where a type of processing, particularly one using new technologies and taking into account the nature, scope, context, and purposes of the processing, is likely to result in a high risk for the rights and freedoms of individuals, the controller shall, prior to the processing, carry out a data protection assessment of the impact of the envisaged processing operations on the protection of personal data. A single data protection impact assessment may address a set of similar processing operations that present similar high risks.*

The data protection officer will consider such issues as the general data protection policy of the organization, particular roles and responsibilities, data collections, processing procedures, purposes and uses, organizational measures, security measures, consultation with stakeholders, replies and reporting issues, an overall project plan, risk issues, risk identification, documenting risks and a possible resister of risks, the assessment, and the ultimate audit and review of the final audit. The final review is relevant both in the present circumstances and also for future purposes.

Article 35(1) provides that "Where a type of processing in particular using new technologies, and taking into account the nature, scope, context and purposes of the processing, is likely to result in a high risk to the rights and freedoms of natural persons, the controller shall, prior to the processing, carry out an assessment of the impact of the envisaged processing operations on the protection of personal data. A single assessment may address a set of similar processing operations that present similar high risks."

The controller shall seek the advice of the data protection officer, where designated, when carrying out a data protection impact assessment.†

A data protection impact assessment, as referred to in Article 33(1), shall particularly be required in the following instances:

- A systematic and extensive evaluation of personal aspects relating to natural persons that is based on automated processing, including profiling, and on which decisions are based that produce legal effects concerning the natural person or similarly significantly affect the natural person

- Processing of special categories of data referred to in Article 9(1) on a large scale, or of personal data relating to criminal convictions and offenses referred to in Article 10

- Systematic monitoring of a publicly accessible area on a large scale‡

---

* GDPR Article 33(1).
† GDPR Article 35(2).
‡ GDPR Article 35(3).

The supervisory authority shall establish and make public a list of the kind of processing operations that are subject to the requirement for a data protection impact assessment, pursuant to paragraph 1. The supervisory authority shall communicate those lists to the Board, as referred to in Article 68.

The supervisory authority may also establish and make public a list of the kind of processing operations for which no data protection impact assessment is required. The supervisory authority shall communicate those lists to the European Data Protection Board (EDPB).

The data protection impact assessment shall contain at least

- A systematic description of the envisaged processing operations and the purposes of the processing including, where applicable, the legitimate interest pursued by the controller

- An assessment of the necessity and proportionality of the processing operations in relation to the purposes

- An assessment of the risks to the rights and freedoms of data subjects referred to in paragraph 1

- The measures envisaged to address the risks, including safeguards, security measures, and mechanisms to ensure the protection of personal data and to demonstrate compliance with the regulation, taking into account the rights and legitimate interests of data subjects and other persons concerned

Compliance with the approved codes of conduct referred to in Article 40 by controllers or processors shall be taken into due account in assessing the impact of the processing operations performed by such controllers or processors, in particular for the purposes of a data protection impact assessment.

Where appropriate, the controller shall seek the views of data subjects or their representatives on the intended processing, without prejudice to the protection of commercial or public interests or the security of processing operations.*

In certain circumstances, previous or prior impact assessments may be considered.†

Where necessary, the controller shall carry out a review to assess if processing is performed in accordance with the data protection impact

---

* GDPR Article 35(9).
† GDPR Article 35(10).

assessment, at least when there is a change of the risk represented by processing operations.*

Vodafone refers to the following reasons for data protection impact assessments:

- Accountability: to demonstrate that the data protection impact assessment process was performed appropriately and in accordance with the program of assessments agreed with the board sponsor for data protection

- Provides a basis for postimplementation review: to ensure any data protection risks identified are allocated a business owner and a timetable for delivery of mitigation actions, therefore providing the data protection officer with a mechanism for ensuring that the agreed actions are delivered according to agreed time scales

- Provides a basis for audit: Vodafone distinguishes between a review that is undertaken by the data protection officer, who is responsible for ensuring that it is implemented and the controls required are delivered; and the audit, which is an objective and neutral assessment undertaken by the group or local audit function or any other suitably qualified audit function that is not part of delivering the overall data protection risk management system

- Provides corporate memory: to ensure that the information gained is available to those completing new assessments if original staff have left, or use a part of a subsequent assessment of the same business or commercial unit or activity

- To enable the experience gained during the project to be shared with the future data protection impact assessment teams and others outside the organization[†]

Nokia also gives reasons for undertaking data protection impact assessments:

- "To measure the implementation of [data protection] requirements, to get an understanding of the current status (risk, controls, root causes, etc.)"[‡].

---

* GDPR Article 35(11).
[†] Deadman and Chandler, "Vodafone's approach to privacy impact assessments," in Wright and de Hert, eds, *Privacy Impact Assessment* (Springer, 2012) 298.
[‡] Brautigam, "PIA: cornerstone of privacy compliance in Nokia," in Wright and de Hert, eds, *Privacy Impact Assessment* (Springer, 2012) 260–261.

- The data protection impact assessment is part of the technical and organizational measures. It assists in finding out if new projects follow the [data protection] requirements, project management, communicating fulfillment of requirements, and generating status reports for management teams, and is an effective tool for assigning responsibility and fixing problems.

- The data protection impact assessment serves as "a repository for information requests from authorities and consumers. Consumers might ask Nokia where and for how long their data is stored. A data protection authority might, for example, ask how consumers are informed about [data protection] practices or who the controller of the data is. [Data protection impact assessment] might also be used to prepare notifications for data protection authorities."*

- "A means to improve general awareness. The [data protection impact assessment] process ... builds up competencies and [data protection] awareness, as it offers an extensive set of questions that might be relevant for [data protection] compliance."†

Some key elements of a data protection impact assessment report are as follows:

- The scope of the data protection impact assessment undertaken

- A summary of the consultative process undertaken

- The project background paper(s) provided to those consulted (appendices)

- An analysis of the data protection issues and risks arising from the data protection impact assessment

- The business case justifying data protection intrusion and implications, where treatment or mitigating actions together with time lines for implementation are included

- References to relevant laws, codes, and guidelines, including internal Vodafone local group policies‡

---

* Ibid.
† Ibid.
‡ Deadman and Chandler, above, 299.

Common characteristics of data protection impact assessments include

- Statement of problem: Is government intervention both necessary and desirable?

- Definition of alternative remedies: These include different approaches such as the use of economic incentives or voluntary approaches.

- Determination of physical effects of each alternative, including potential unintended consequences: The net should be cast wide. Generally speaking, regulations or investments in many areas of public policy can have social, environmental, and other implications that must be kept in mind.

- Estimation of benefits and costs of each alternative: Benefits should be quantified and, where possible, monetized. Costs should be true opportunity costs and not simply expenditures.

- Assessment of other economic impacts, including effects on competition, effects on small firms, and international trade implications.

- Identification of winners and losers, those in the community who stand to gain and lose from each alternative and, if possible, the extent of their gains and losses.

- Communication with the interested public, including the following activities: notification of intent to regulate, requests for compliance costs and other data, public disclosure of regulatory proposals and supporting analysis, and consideration of and response to public comments.

- A clear choice of the preferred alternative, plus a statement defending that choice.

- Provision of a plan for ex-post analysis of regulatory outcomes: It is important to establish a benchmark against which to measure performance. Planning is needed to ensure that procedures are in place for the collection of data to permit such benchmarking.*

---

* OECD, "Regulatory Performance: Ex Post Evaluation of Regulatory Tools and Institutions," Working Party on Regulatory Management and Reform, Draft Report by the Secretariat, OECD, Paris (2004), 7; referred to in Parker, "(Regulatory) Impact Assessment and Better Regulation," in Wright and de Hert, eds, *Privacy Impact Assessment* (Springer, 2012) 80.

Some data protection impact assessment characteristics distinguishing it from other data protection related processes include that

- An assessment focuses on a particular initiative or project

- An assessment is performed at depth, throughout the project life cycle, and involves engagement with stakeholders

- An assessment assesses a project against the needs, expectations, and concerns of all stakeholders, including but not limited to legal requirements

- An assessment assesses all aspects of data protection

- An assessment adopts a multiperspective approach, taking into account the costs and benefits as perceived by all stakeholders

- An assessment adopts a multiperspective approach, taking into account the risks as perceived by all stakeholders

- An assessment is a process used to establish the undertakings an organization needs to give

- An assessment is the process that identifies problems and solutions to them

- An assessment is conducted before and in parallel with a project and ensures that harmful and expensive problems that an audit would later expose are identified, and that unavoidable negative impacts on data protection are minimized and harm mitigated*

The key steps and methodologies in a data protection impact assessment include

- Identifying all of the personal data related to a program or service and looking at how it will be used

- Mapping where personal data are sent after collection

- Identifying data protection risks and the level of the risks

---

* Clarke, "PIAs in Australia: A Work-In-Progress Report," in Wright and de Hert, eds, *Privacy Impact Assessment* (Springer, 2012) 121.

- Finding methods to eliminate or reduce the risks*
  Organizations might consider issues such as the following:

- Preparation

- Undertaking the data protection impact assessment

- The timing of the data protection impact assessment

- Cost and resourcing of the data protection impact assessment

- Who the report is for

- Issues and problems raised

- Independence of those undertaking the data protection impact assessment

- Any constraints

- Legal professional privilege and confidentiality

- After undertaking the data protection impact assessment, draft data protection impact assessment report/comments/final report

- Whether the data protection impact assessment is an individual or ongoing assessment in a (rolling) series

Carrying out a data protection impact assessment, and the like, helps to not only identify privacy and data protection problems and the cases in which these can be addressed, but also helps to identify these problems at the earliest stage possible. Therefore, the least expensive and problematic time to make remedial changes is engaged. Carrying out such data protection impact assessments is not a requirement under the new GDPR regime. This is especially so for high-risk activities and when sensitive personal data may be involved. These data protection impact assessments ensure that organizations understand the data they hold, and the likely problem issues that can arise. Ultimately, the organization, its processes, and the customer relationship will all be improved.

---

* Office of the Privacy Commissioner of Canada, Fact Sheet on Privacy Impact Assessment. Also note OIPC of Alberta, "Commissioner Accepts Privacy Impact assessment for the Alberta Security Screening Directive," press release, 16 January 2003.

Data protection impact assessments are ultimately one of the mechanisms under the new GDPR for assessing, and thus minimizing, risk in the personal data environment.

Organizations must now be proactive and assess when processing activities are likely to raise risks in relation to personal data and processing. The data protection officer and other relevant parties/teams must be involved. Data protection impact assessments must be more systematic. Risk identification and evaluation are now key considerations. Measures to mitigate and address risks must be considered and documented, including risk assessments and data protection impact assessments. In situations where there are substantial risk issues, it may be necessary to consult with the supervisory authority.

Prior Consultation

The controller shall consult the supervisory authority, prior to processing, where a data protection impact assessment under Article 35 indicates that the processing would result in a high risk in the absence of measures taken by the controller to mitigate the risk.*

Where the supervisory authority is of the opinion that the intended processing would infringe the regulation, particularly where the controller has insufficiently identified or mitigated the risk, the supervisory authority shall, within a period of up to 8 weeks of receipt of the request for consultation, provide written advice to the controller and, where applicable, use any of its powers as referred to in Article 58. That period may be extended by 6 weeks, taking into account the complexity of the intended processing. The supervisory authority shall inform the controller and, where applicable, the processor of any such extension within 1 month of receipt of the request for consultation, together with the reasons for the delay. Those periods may be suspended until the supervisory authority has obtained the information it has requested for the purposes of the consultation.

When consulting the supervisory authority, pursuant to paragraph 1, the controller shall provide the supervisory authority with

- Where applicable, the respective responsibilities of the controller, joint controllers, and processors involved in processing, in particular for processing within a group of undertakings

- The purposes and means of the intended processing

---

* GDPR Article 36(1).

- The measures and safeguards provided to protect the rights and freedoms of data subjects pursuant to this regulation

- Where applicable, the contact details of the Data Protection Officer

- The data protection impact assessment as described in Article 35

- Any other information requested by the supervisory authority*

National law may make additional provisions, which will also need to be considered.

Compliance with the Controller and Processor: Data Protection Officer

Designation of the data protection officer[†]

Position of the data protection officer[‡]

Tasks of the data protection officer[§]

See the previous sections.

Compliance with the Controller and Processor: Codes of Conduct and Certification

Codes of conduct[¶]

*Certification***

Article 40 relates to codes of conduct. Member States, the supervisory authorities, the EDPB, and the Commission shall encourage the

---

* GDPR Article 36(3).
† GDPR Article 37.
‡ GDPR Article 38.
§ GDPR Article 39.
¶ GDPR Article 40.
** GDPR Article 42.

drawing up of codes of conduct intended to contribute to the proper application of the regulation, taking account of the specific features of the various processing sectors and the specific needs of micro, small, and medium-sized enterprises.

Associations and other bodies representing categories of controllers or processors may prepare codes of conduct, or amend or extend such codes, for the purpose of specifying the application of the regulation, such as with regard to

- Fair and transparent processing

- The legitimate interests pursued by controllers in specific contexts

- The collection of personal data

- The pseudonymization of personal data

- The information provided to the public and to data subjects

- The exercise of the rights of data subjects

- The information provided to, and the protection of, children, and the manner in which consent from the holders of parental responsibility over children is to be obtained

- The measures and procedures referred to in Articles 24 and 25 and the measures to ensure the security of processing referred to in Article 32

- The notification of personal data breaches to the supervisory authorities and the communication of such personal data breaches to data subjects

- The transfer of personal data to third-party countries or international organizations

- Out-of-court proceedings and other dispute resolution procedures for resolving disputes between controllers and data subjects with regard to processing, and without prejudice to the rights of data subjects pursuant to Articles 77 and 79

Data controllers and processors not subject to the GDPR may also wish to consider complying with codes of conduct.*

---

* GDPR Article 40 (3).

It is necessary for data protection officers to monitor developments in relation to developments from the Commission and supervisory authorities in this regard.

Compliance with Transfer of Personal Data to Third-Party Countries or International Organizations

*General principle for transfers**

Transfers with an adequacy decision[†]

Transfers by way of appropriate safeguards[‡]

Binding corporate rules[§]

Transfers or disclosures not authorized by Union law[¶]

Derogations for specific situations[**]

International cooperation for the protection of personal data[††]

The transfer of personal data, particularly outside of the EU, has been one of the most prominent data protection issues in the compliance, legal, and media commentary over the last couple of years. The striking down of the EU-US Safe Harbor transfer regime by the Court of Justice in the *Schrems v. Commissioner* case raised worldwide headlines as well as particular headaches for thousands of businesses and political policy-makers on both sides of the Atlantic. Recently, the replacement regime was agreed, entitled the EU-US Privacy Shield. Organizations that need to transfer data to the United States now need to quickly find a new legal mechanism for transfers other than the now invalid Safe Harbor regime.

The area of data transfers is also referred to in particular provisions in the new GDPR.

---

[*] GDPR Article 44.
[†] GDPR Article 45.
[‡] GDPR Article 46.
[§] GDPR Article 47.
[¶] GDPR Article 48.
[**] GDPR Article 49.
[††] GDPR Article 50.

The supervisory authority should consider issues such as ownership and who the controller or processor is in relation to transfer and data sharing. Specific policies, procedures, protocols, and agreements should cater for these issues, such as data transfer logs, data sharing and transfer agreements, partnership agreements, outsource agreements, and similar agreements. Particular training and awareness-raising should be considered. Data protection impact assessments may well refer to these issues in review.

Overall, the area of compliance in relation to data transfers requires a high level of attention by organizations and data protection officers, and this will remain the case for some time given the level of attention and indeed contention focused on it.

Compliance with Remedies, Liability, and Sanctions

*Right to lodge a complaint with a supervisory authority**

Right to an effective judicial remedy against a supervisory authority†

Right to an effective judicial remedy against a controller or processor‡

Representation of data subjects§

Suspension of court proceedings¶

*Right to compensation and liability***

General conditions for imposing administrative fines††

Penalties‡‡

All organizations will need to be particularly aware of the penalty issues that may arise as these are now very significant under the new

---

* GDPR Article 77.
† GDPR Article 78.
‡ GDPR Article 79.
§ GDPR Article 80.
¶ GDPR Article 81.
** GDPR Article 82.
†† GDPR Article 83.
‡‡ GDPR Article 84.

data protection regime. This will be an added factor in the organization's enthusiasm to get data protection compliance right.

In addition, the new, more emphasized rights of individual data subjects (and organizations of data subjects), particularly in relation to the right to damages and compensation—and related rights such as injunctions—are a further lightening rod for organizations to get data protection processes and compliance correct.

The Data Protection Officer will be heavily involved in and leading on these compliance issues.

Compliance with Provisions Relating to Specific Data Processing Situations

Processing and freedom of expression and information*

Processing and public access to official documents†

Processing of the national identity number‡

Processing in the employment context§

- *Safeguards and derogations relating to processing for archiving purposes in the public interest, for scientific or historical research purposes, or for statistical purposes¶*

- *Obligations of secrecy***

- *Existing data protection rules for churches and religious associations††*

As always, different or rather more particular additional data protection issues will apply to specific organizations. The new GDPR sets out some specific sector- or issue-related provisions in addition to the general provisions. Data protection officers will need to be aware of these

---

* GDPR Article 85.
† GDPR Article 86.
‡ GDPR Article 87.
§ GDPR Article 88.
¶ GDPR Article 89.
** GDPR Article 90.
†† GDPR Article 91.

particular issues when they apply, and be familiar with how they will be applied to their organization when applicable.

☐ Additional and/or More Specific Tasks

In the following sections, some other references and additional task related issues are set out.

Training

General staff training in relation to data protection compliance and issues

Training specific staff that deal with personal data

Training specific staff or manager that deal with specific risks as regards personal data processing

Some training needs to be general in focus while other training needs to be more direct and nuanced. There will be a need for headline training in relation to the current and new data protection regime and the legal obligations for organizations to comply. Separate to this type of training, particular sections such as HR, marketing, and so on may require more specific and tailored training. Managers or teams that develop new technical products, services, and solutions that impact personal data may require separate training again. Appraising and educating the key people in relation to the advantages, need, and obligations for DPbD is needed.

In considering the training responsibilities, the data protection officer will, *inter alia*,

- Provide facilities for training and raising awareness among existing employees, new employees, officers, management, and the board

- Advise and coordinate inward-facing or in-house training, which will occur by departments, by groups, by heads, and by issues

- Produce regular updates, reviews, and information on new legislation, cases, codes, official findings/decisions, and guidelines

- Raise awareness of new issues and developments as they occur

Policies

Drafting Data Protecting Policies

Policies are both inward facing, in terms of employees (e.g., policy of data protection, intent usage, etc.), and outward facing for customers and others (e.g., Internet policy, terms referring to personal data. These policies are important in terms of referring to transparency, consent, data usage, purpose(s), data transfers, and so on. Policies also need to be reviewed and amended as needed. It is important to keep policies as user friendly as possible. A policy must be understood by those at whom it is directed.

Implementing Data Protection Policies

After a policy is amended or indeed finalized for the first time, the data protection officer will assist in rolling that policy out. The method of implementation will need to ensure that it is implemented in the appropriate places on time, and that the target recipients are properly apprised or made aware of the policy.

Updating Data Protection Policies

As mentioned under the "Drafting Data Protecting Policies" section, no policy is fixed in time. Organizations are dynamic and so are their activities, processes, and including data processing activities. It is necessary, therefore, for the data protection officer to review the policies and also the nature of the surrounding activities as well as external change issues, any of which may require that particular policies or sections of those policies be updated. This of course will be an ongoing task for the data protection officer. In conjunction, the data protection officer will also apprise senior management and others of the instant need for certain updates as they arise.

Reviewing Other Policies in Relation to Data Protection Sections and Issues

Most organizations will also have a variety of other policies and guidelines in addition to the data protection policy, online privacy statement, employee contract, and related employee data protection policy. Some of these will relate to communications usage, social media, company laptops, phones, and other electronic devices, off-site work-related activities (where permitted), company vehicles, monitoring, and location issues. Security-related issues and policies will also be of interest to the data protection officer. Depending on the organization, there may be other documentation and policies to review. For example, a financial organization will have suites of various customer documents, contracts, notices, and so on, all of which may impact personal data and data protection compliance.

Contracts, Terms, and So On

Organizations have a large variety of different contracts, differing in scale, value, importance, parties, terms, and so on. While not all of these will be relevant from a personal data perspective, many will be. The organization and the data protection officer should therefore fully consider the data protection compliance issues. Sometimes the Data Protection Officer may discover that not all of the relevant contracts incurring data protection issues have been properly vetted from a compliance perspective.

Reviewed Data Protection Terms, References and Clauses in the Organization's Contracts, Terms, and So On

Similar to the requirements for contracts and terms, the data protection officer needs to understand the nature and scope of the contract relations, contract types, and the interface with data protection issues in order to plan to ensure that contracts, terms, and so on are assessed for compliance. There will also be additional types of documentation that may not directly be policies or contracts but are directly peripheral to these documents and relations with employees, third parties, and customers. These should not mislead the recipient about what the organization is doing, particularly regarding which personal data may be collected, processed, transferred, and so on. The same applies in relation to security, where data may be stored, where it will not be stored, and so on.

Existing IT Projects and Processing

Reviewing and Engaging in Existing IT Projects as Regards the Impact on Personal Data and Data Processing Compliance Issues and Risks

While the issue of new IT projects and processing activities (see the section "New IT Projects and Processing") will be a particular focus for data protection officers as regards potential problem issues and data protection compliance, the issue of existing IT projects and processing should not be overlooked.

Many projects may already be in existence by the time a data protection officer is appointed or a new data protection officer is installed. These may have important issues to be considered and reviewed from a personal data and data protection perspective. The data protection officer, as well as considering an initial audit of data collections, processing activities, and purposes, may also make specific enquiries about existing IT projects and processing, particularly those involving significant amounts of personal data, risks, and/or past problems.

It can also be the case that those involved in existing projects and processing may not appreciate that a new use for existing personal data may not be permitted in the circumstances. Therefore, these tweaks, extensions, or expansions of processing involving personal data will raise the need for a data protection compliance assessment—even before the change goes live. Therefore, the data protection officer cannot ignore particular projects and processing just because they are up and running.

New IT Projects and Processing

Reviewing and Engaging in New IT Projects as Regards the Impact on Personal Data and Data Processing Compliance Issues and Risks

New IT projects and new processing activities that involve personal data increasingly have the potential to raise compliance issues. In particular sectors, some of these new projects or processing activities raise issues of lawfulness, consent, transparency, and so on, more frequently than other sectors. New technology-related activities will frequently raise data protection issues. The data protection officer, as well as being apprised of these projects, should also be proactive in looking out for signals of new projects or new processing activities in case he or she has not been notified. The earlier that the data protection officer is aware of a potential problem project or issue, the better it may be resolved or dealt with.

Access Requests (Additional)

Being the point of contact for general queries regarding personal data

Dealing with access requests

Implementing access request policy and procedures

Reviewing existing access request policies and updating these in light of the new data protection regime

One of the most significant roles of the data protection officer is to receive and deal with data confirmation and data access requests. There is also an important function of proactively putting advance procedures and templates in place for dealing with such requests. These will need to be monitored and updated from time to time as new issues and/or legislative changes arise.

Some of the particular responsibilities in relation to dealing with data subject access requests include

* Preparing for, managing, and administering data subject access requests

* Being the initial point of contact for customers, users, and others in relation to data subject access requests

* Being the initial point of contact for employees in relation to data subject access requests

* Raising awareness among employees of data subject access requests and the importance of a timely response and time limits

* Ensuring that responses to data subject access requests are compliant with the data protection regime and are provided within the appropriate time frames

* Providing the organization's board and employees with policies, procedures, and practices in relation to compliance with data subject access requests

Queries

Being the Point of Contact for Data Access Queries and Requests

The data protection officer will receive and deal with data confirmation and data access requests. There is also an important aspect of this function in being designated as the official contact point, which ensures that the request or query gets to the appropriate officer in the organization as quickly as possible. This can be important, given that there can be specific timeframes for responding. It can also be important that the organization has, and is able to demonstrate, proper and efficient systems for dealing with data protection issues.

Point of Contact

Being the organization's official data protection point of contact for data subjects

Being the organization's official data protection point of contact for customers

Being the organization's official data protection point of contact for users

Being the organization's official data protection point of contact for the supervisory authority

Being the organization's official data protection point of contact for other supervisory authorities (if relevant)

Being the organization's official data protection point of contact for other communications or queries

The data protection officer is now the official point of contact for outward-facing issues, including contact with the supervisory authority, and also for inward-facing queries and issues. The range of issues will vary between specific issues, ongoing issues, and data protection and compliance in general. It is possible to envisage that the issues and range of contact for the Data Protection Officer will increase in the future, particularly as the importance of the new data protection regime reaches a wider organizational (and public) audience.

Communications

Being the point of contact for third-party communications, queries, and requests for information regarding the organization and data protection issues

Being the point of contact for third-party requests for communications and media comment (this may also involve the designated press or media contact [if any])

Being the point of contact for requests to speak at conferences regarding data protection

In addition to being the point of contact for many people and organizations in relation to the company/organization, the communications role of the data protection officer is also increasing. It will encompass both specific and general data protection issues. In high pressure situations, such a large data breach, the data protection officer will also liaise with the organization's press officer. The data protection officer will also deal with many other officials and teams within the organization. The general position of the data protection officer is becoming more widely known, as outward-facing communications issue arise for data protection officers and data protection officers speak at more and more conferences and seminars. Data protection officers will also publish articles and give interviews on the general importance of data protection compliance and respect for personal data, both for trade publications and the wider media.

Audits (Internal)

Audits

When the data protection officer is initially engaged, he or she will carry out an initial audit to apprise him or herself of the data processing activities and the types of personal data held by the organization. Over time, more detailed general audits will also be carried out. In addition, such audits will help to guide the data protection officer, whether new or established, in targeting their resources, attention, and assistance. Repeated audits over time also assist the data protection officer in monitoring improvements in data protection compliance. They can also assist in identifying new or developing issues that may require specific attention. Some of the advantages of undertaking regular ongoing audits and specific targeted audits are to ensure lawful processing activities, efficient compliance, and cost-effective compliance by ensuring that issues are addressed in advance and without the need for escalation in urgent and costly scenarios, thus reducing (if not eliminating) the need for formal investigations, complaints, audits, enforcement, and so on with the supervisory authority.

Duties and responsibilities in relation to audit obligations may include, for example

- Regular audits for compliance with applicable legislation and regulations

- Advising the company of any changes to policies, procedures, and practices as a result of any annual audit

- Implementation of any authorized changes to policies, procedures, and practices resulting from an audit

- Considering, where necessary, the use of specialist advisors in relation to audits and compliance

Audits (by Supervisory Authorities)

Audits

There are many instances in which the supervisory authority may decide to carry out a large or specifically targeted audit of the organization and its data protection compliance. Specific processing activities and processes may be the subject of a general audit across a specific industry sector. Examples might include cookies, website privacy policies, childrens' personal data collection, heath data, and so on. On occasion, the supervisory authority may also decide to investigate a specific complaint and, as a result of that process, decide to undertake a more general audit of the processing activities within the organization. This audit may be specific to particular issues or wider, covering many processing activities. Even where a complaint has not arisen, the supervisory authority is entitled to randomly audit organizations. This happens quite often across many sectors and across large and small organizations. It is also the case, unfortunately, that security or data breach issues come to the attention of the public. In these instances, a supervisory authority may decide to carry out an investigation and audit of the organization. Indeed, even under the new data protection regime, organizations have increased reporting requirements (both to supervisory authorities and to individual data subjects) in the event of a data breach occurring. The data protection officer will assist the supervisory authority in all of these examples.

Audits (of New Proposed Products and Services)

Audits

Frequently, new products, services, or processing activities commence without proper (or any) regard for the data protection consequences. This means that problems can arise after the new activity has commenced. In other instances, the consideration of data protection issues may only be raised at the very last moment, just before the new activity is meant to go live. At this very late stage, a data protection analysis may delay matters. Redesign of the proposed activities can also be necessary, but this may not always be possible. It may also, depending on the activities in question, mean drawing attention to impermissible or unlawful processing activities, in which case the activity needs to be cancelled.

In order to avoid this problem, the data protection officer needs to be involved in inputting and considering new processing activities, particularly where a new product or service is involved. As part of this ongoing process, the data protection officer will need to liaise and build relationships with development and related teams throughout the organization. Those involved in, and particularly those leading, teams that develop new processing activities, products, and services need to be educated about the need to involve and update the data protection officer as necessary. Senior management and the data protection officer must emphasize that this is a requirement and not a mere box-ticking issue or something that the team can decide on a purely discretionary basis. In addition, the independence and seniority (reporting to senior management and not to a section or team lead) are important factors in these issues.

As part of the role of educating teams and undertaking audits and assessments of new products, services, and processing activities, the data protection officer will refer to the benefits of DPbD and the pre-problem solutions it offers.

Employment Contract of the Data Protection Officer

Reviewing the new or existing contract of employment of the data protection officer, or the contract of engagement of an external contractor, to ensure that it does not conflict with the independence, role, and tasks of the data protection officer

The data protection officer is responsible for a number of important functions within the organization. Significant importance is attached to independence, noninterference, and his or her position being, to a large extent, ring-fenced and protected. There are also important protections in relation to the senior management to whom the data protection officer will report. New data protection officers will need to carefully review their proposed contract of employment to ensure that nothing in the contract conflicts with or would jeopardize this.

Recitals on the GDPR

Recital 13 includes the statement that "In order to ensure a consistent level of protection for natural persons throughout the Union and to prevent divergences hampering the free movement of personal data within the internal market, a Regulation is necessary to provide legal certainty and transparency for economic operators, including micro, small and medium-sized enterprises, and to provide natural persons in all Member States with the same level of legally enforceable rights and obligations and responsibilities for controllers and processors, to ensure consistent monitoring of the processing of personal data, and equivalent sanctions in all Member States as well as effective cooperation between the supervisory authorities of different Member States. The proper functioning of the internal market requires that the free movement of personal data within the Union is not restricted or prohibited for reasons connected with the protection of natural persons with regard to the processing of personal data. To take account of the specific situation of micro, small and medium-sized enterprises, this Regulation includes a derogation for organizations with fewer than 250 employees with regard to record-keeping. In addition, the Union institutions and bodies, and Member States and their supervisory authorities, are encouraged to take account of the specific needs of micro, small and medium-sized enterprises in the application of this Regulation. The notion of micro, small and medium-sized enterprises should draw from Article 2 of the Annex to Commission Recommendation 2003/361/EC."

Recital 98 states that "Associations or other bodies representing categories of controllers or processors should be encouraged to draw up codes of conduct, within the limits of this Regulation, so as to facilitate the effective application of this Regulation, taking account of the specific characteristics of the processing carried out in certain sectors and the specific needs of micro, small and medium enterprises. In particular, such codes of conduct could calibrate the obligations of controllers and processors, taking into account the risk likely to result from the processing for the rights and freedoms of natural persons."

Recital 132 states that "Awareness-raising activities by supervisory authorities addressed to the public should include specific measures directed at controllers and processors, including micro, small and medium-sized enterprises, as well as natural persons in particular in the educational context."

Main Articles of the GDPR

Article 40(1), which relates to certification, states that "The Member States, the supervisory authorities, the Board and the Commission shall encourage the drawing up of codes of conduct intended to contribute to the proper application of this Regulation, taking account of the specific features of the various processing sectors and the specific needs of micro, small and medium-sized enterprises."

Klug also refers to tasks and duties. He states that

"In fulfilling his duties, the [data protection officer] closely interacts with the various business units/departments and, if necessary, with the head of the controller. A detailed up to date register of all relevant data processing operations should be the basis for his work."* He refers to the tasks as

- Supervision and compliance
- Lawful processing
- Corporate data protection provisions
- Transparency and data subject rights
- Employee information and training†

Klug also states that

The [data protection officer]'s main task is to carry out an independent inspection of the processing operations involving personal data such as customer and employee data. As a compliance institution, he is supposed to ensure that personal data is handled in accordance with all relevant data protection provisions covering on and offline processing operations.‡

Referring to employees, Klug states that "People employed in data processing may not collect, process or use personal data without authorization and one of the [data protection officer]'s tasks is to ensure all relevant employees are committed to maintaining confidentiality. The [data protection officer] also has to take steps to familiarize staff with data protection provisions and with particular data protection requirements relevant to each case, including information about administrative or criminal offenses."§

European Data Protection Supervisor

The European Data Protection Supervisor, in relation to the approximate equivalent obligation in EU institutions for a data protection officer albeit

---

* Klug, "Improving Self-Regulation Through (Law-based) Corporate Data Protection Official," at https://www.gdd.de/international/english/DPO_Report_by_Christoph_Klug.pdf. Revised version of article in *Privacy Laws and Business International Newsletter*.
† Ibid.
‡ Ibid.
§ Ibid.

under a separate legal measure, refers to the role and tasks of the data protection officer:*

Adequate Staff and Resources

The European Data Protection Supervisor, in relation to the approximate equivalent obligation in EU institutions for a data protection officer "albeit under a separate legal measure", refers to the role and tasks of the data protection officer.[†] This includes obligations in relation to adequate staff and resources:

> The issue of sufficient resources whether they be IT resources, HR resources or financial resources has also been an important element to enable the [data protection officer] to carry out his/her duties in practice.[‡]

Information and Awareness-Raising Function

Referring to the information and awareness-raising function, the European Data Protection Supervisor states that

> This implies, on the one hand informing staff members of their rights and, on the other hand, informing controllers and the institution/body of their obligations and responsibilities. Raising awareness can take the form of staff information notes, training sessions, setting up of a website, privacy statements.[§]

Advisory Function

Referring to the advisory function, the European Data Protection Supervisor states that

> [data protection officer] must ensure that the Regulation is respected and advise controllers on fulfilling their obligations. The [data protection

---

* European Data Protection Supervisor, "Position paper on the role of Data Protection Officers in ensuring effective compliance with Regulation (EC) 45/2001," at https://secure.edps.europa.eu/EDPSWEB/webdav/site/mySite/shared/DPO_Corner/Getting%20started/05-11-28_DPO_paper_EN.pdf.
† Ibid.
‡ Ibid.
§ Ibid.

officer] may make recommendations for the practical improvement of data protection to the institution/body and advise it, or the controller concerned, on matters concerning the application of data protection provisions. The [data protection officer] may also be consulted by the institution/body, by the controller, by the Staff Committee and by any individual on any matter concerning the interpretation or application of the Regulation.*

Organizational Function

Referring to the organizational function, the European Data Protection Supervisor states that

> [D]ata processing operations must be notified to the [data protection officer]. This requires the drafting of a notification form to be filled in by controllers containing at least information as mentioned in Article 25. The [data protection officer] must organize a register of processing operations. The register must be made accessible to any person. The EDPS believes that it would be most appropriate to have an on-line access to this register, but non electronic access cannot be refused to a person who asks for it. Once the [data protection officer] has received the notification she/he must identify cases falling within the scope of Article 27 and notify the EDPS for prior checking taking into account the two-month delay within which the EDPS must render his opinion. The EDPS has developed a notification form to this effect to be filled in by the controller and/or [data protection officer]. In case of doubt as to the need for prior checking, the [data protection officer] may consult the EDPS.†

Cooperative Function

Referring to the cooperation function, the European Data Protection Supervisor refers states that

> The [data protection officer] has the task of responding to requests from the EDPS and, within the sphere of his competence, cooperate with the EDPS at the latter's request or on his/her own initiative. This task emphasizes the fact that the DPO facilitates cooperation between the EDPS and the institution notably in the frame of investigations, complaint handling or prior checks. The [data protection officer] not only has inside knowledge of the institution, but is also likely to know who the best person to contact within the institution is. The [data protection officer] may also be aware, and duly

---

* Ibid.
† Ibid.

inform the EDPS, of recent developments likely to impact the protection of personal data. The cooperation and possible synergies between the [data protection officer] and the EDPS will be examined in this document.*

Monitoring of Compliance

Referring to the compliance monitoring function, the European Data Protection Supervisor states that

> [T]he [data protection officer] is to ensure the application of the Regulation within the institution. The [data protection officer] may, on his own initiative or at the request of the institution or body, the controller, the staff committee or any individual investigate matters and occurrences directly relating to his/her tasks and report back to the person who commissioned the investigation or to the controller. This function is supported by the fact that the [data protection officer] shall have access at all times to the data forming the subject-matter of processing operations and to all offices, data-processing installations and data carriers.†

Handling Queries and Complaints

Referring to the queries and complaints function, the European Data Protection Supervisor states that

> Although not explicitly mentioned in the Regulation, this function can be deduced from the fact that the [data protection officer] is granted with investigation functions: "Furthermore he or she may, on his own initiative or at the request of the Community institution or body which appointed him or her, the controller, the Staff Committee concerned or any individual, investigate matters and occurrences directly relating to his tasks and which come to his or her notice, and report back to the person who commissioned the investigation or to the controller" (Annex §1). Furthermore the Regulation provides that "No one shall suffer prejudice on account of a matter brought to attention of the competent Data Protection Officer" (Annex §3). The EDPS, as the principal complaint handling instance in the field of data protection, encourages the investigation and handling of complaints by [data protection officers] (see point IV. 3). The fact that the [data protection officer] acts from within the institution and is close to the data subject places him/her in an ideal situation to receive and handle

---

* Ibid.
† Ibid.

queries or complaints at a local level. This does not however prevent the data subject from addressing him/herself directly to the EDPS.*

Guaranteeing Independence

Referring to the independence function, the European Data Protection Supervisor states that

> The [data protection officer] is placed in a difficult position: he/she is a part of the institution and yet must remain independent from this institution in the performance of his/her duties. As already mentioned, the fact of being a part of the institution (idea of proximity) puts him/her in an ideal situation to ensure compliance from the inside and to advise or to intervene at an early stage thereby avoiding possible intervention from the supervisory body. A number of guarantees have been provided for in the Regulation which aim at ensuring that the [data protection officer] fulfils his duties in an independent manner.†

No Conflict of Interest between Duties

Ensuring the full application of the provisions of the regulation should not be jeopardized by an overlap in the data protection officer's functions, thus resulting in conflicting interests. For example, a part-time "[data protection officer] should not act as data controller in his initial activity ... So as to avoid conflicts of interests and to guarantee independence, if the [data protection officer] has several duties, these duties must be evaluated separately. Evaluation of a DPO in the performance of his/her duties as [data protection officer] must not be related in any way to the performance of other tasks ... the [data protection officer] should not be prevented from exercising his duties due to lack of time as a result of other official duties. As mentioned above, in practice, the percentage of time granted to the [data protection officer] in order to perform his/her duty as [data protection officer] has been problematic in many institutions.... Moreover, a new post of [data protection officer] requires a lot of investment at the start in order to raise the awareness of staff and to ensure compliance in the field of notifications. If the post is not new, the function is also time-consuming for a newly appointed [data protection officer] who has to get to grips with the subject. The EDPS therefore recommends the appointment of a full-time [data protection officer] at least at the start of the function."‡

---

* Ibid.
† Ibid.
‡ Ibid.

Staff and Resources to Carry Out Duties

Referring to staff and resources, the European Data Protection Supervisor states that

> ... implies that the [data protection officer] is provided with sufficient financial resources to carry out his/her duties. It could also imply that the [data protection officer] receives adequate support if needed from other services (the legal service, for example) and access to training facilities.*

No Receipt of Instructions Regarding the Performance of Duties

Referring to the nondirection or conflict function, the European Data Protection Supervisor states that

> This article is paramount in ensuring independence of [data protection officer]s. It refers not only to direct instructions from a superior, but also implies that a [data protection officer] must not be in a position to be inclined to accept certain compromises when dealing with controllers in high positions. This could be an issue for "contractual" [data protection officer]s including temporary agents, who feel that their position in a certain context could influence the extension or renewal of their contract. There is also a risk that junior [data protection officer]s are confronted with "authority" problems vis-à-vis high ranking controllers. Furthermore, [data protection officer]s should not suffer prejudice in their career development from the mere fact of having been a [data protection officer]. Finally, the [data protection officer] should only report to his/her appointing authority and not to a direct superior.†

Access to Information and to Offices and Data-Processing Installations

Referring to access issues, the European Data Protection Supervisor states that

> This provision gives the [data protection officer] investigative powers in the performance of his/her duties. This is supported by the fact that the same provision provides that the controller shall be required to assist the

---

* Ibid.
† Ibid.

[data protection officer] in the performance of his/her duties and to give information in reply to questions.*

Ensuring Compliance

Referring to the ensuring compliance function, the European Data Protection Supervisor states that

> [data protection officer]s play an important role in developing knowledge on data protection issues inside the institution/body. The EDPS welcomes this and its consequence in terms of stimulating an efficient preventive approach rather than repressive data protection supervision.... The [data protection officer] also provides advice to the institution/body on practical recommendations for improvement of data protection within the institution/body or concerning the interpretation or application of the Regulation (Annex §1 and 2). This advisory function is shared with the EDPS who shall advise all Community institutions/bodies on matters concerning the processing of personal data (Article 46 sub d)). In this field the EDPS has often been called upon to advise [data protection officer]s on specific issues related to data protection (case by case approach). The EDPS also intends to produce position papers on certain themes so as to afford guidance to the institutions/bodies on certain more general topics.†

Keeping Controllers and Data Subjects Informed of Rights and Obligations

The European Data Protection Supervisor separately refers to the role and tasks of the data protection officer.‡ These include ensuring that controllers and data subjects are informed of their rights and obligations:

> The [data protection officer] shall raise awareness on data protection issues and encourage a culture of protection of personal data within his/her institution/body. Controllers shall be informed of their obligations (see

---

* Ibid.

† Ibid.

‡ Data Protection Supervisor, "Implementing rules concerning the tasks, duties and powers of the Data Protection Officer (Article 24.8)," at https://secure.edps.europa.eu/EDPSWEB/webdav/site/mySite/shared/DPO_Corner/Getting%20started/IR/10-07-29_Guidelines_DPO_tasks_EN.pdf.

below point 6) and data subjects shall be made aware of their rights (see below point 7). This can take different forms:

- Training of staff members and controllers
- Making the register accessible also in electronic form as a tool to ensure transparency as regards the processing operations in place in the institution/body (see below)
- Assistance given by the [data protection officer] to the controllers in notifying processing operations, which may also be formalized in the rules (see below)
- Contribution of the [data protection officer] to the Annual Activity Report of the institution/body, as this is a good tool to raise awareness on data protection issues internally but also externally.

Access to Data

The data protection officer shall have access at all times to the data forming the subject matter of processing operations and to all offices, data-processing installations, and data carriers.

Although not explicitly mentioned in the Regulation, the EDPS encourages the handling of queries or complaints by the [data protection officer], where appropriate. Indeed, the handling of queries and complaints at a local level can help in most cases to solve problems .... It is good practice to elaborate on the investigation powers of the DPO. The procedural aspects should be defined: delay for the [data protection officer] to respond to the person who commissioned the investigations (written reply), obligation and deadline for the controller in charge of the processing operation at stake to respond to the [data protection officer] (written reply), obligation of confidentiality, obligation to conduct the enquiry in full independence, and so on.

Prior Notice of Processing

One requirement is to give prior notice of processing operations:

Controllers should give prior notice to the [data protection officer] of any processing operation.

Information to be given is detailed in Article 25.2. Processing operations should be notified sufficiently well in advance to allow for prior checking by the EDPS (at least two months) because the operation cannot be implemented before the EDPS's opinion is issued;

Any change in the processing implying personal data should be notified promptly to the DPO;

Controllers should cooperate with the [data protection officer] to establish the inventory of processing operations referred to in Article 4(2) hereof;

Where appropriate, controllers should consult the [data protection officer] on the conformity of processing operations, in particular in the event of doubt as to conformity;

Controllers should prepare notifications to the [data protection officer] for all existing processing operations that have not yet been notified;

In case the controller outsources part(s) of the processing operations to a processor, this should be done in compliance with Article 23. Ideally, relevant parts of the article should be quoted.

Tools of the Data Protection Officer

CHAPTER

Tools of the Data Protection Officer

☐ Introduction

The data protection officer has a number of tools, processes, and advantages at his or disposal when dealing with individuals within the organization, assisting the organization, ensuring data protection compliance, and performing his or her tasks and obligations.

☐ Advantages of Data Protection Officers

Some of the advantages that data protection officers bring to the organization include, but are not limited to

- Meeting and satisfying the new legal obligation to have a data protection officer

- Fulfilling the legal obligations relating to data protection compliance

- Data protection controls, processes, and procedures can be implemented where none previously existed

- Data protection controls, processes, and procedures can be optimally improved where they existed heretofore

- The data protection officer will be familiar with company structures and processing operations and be in the best position to deal with issues as and when they arise*

- Reviewing, advising, and implementing of appropriate data protection policies, clauses, rules, and related documentation

- Better understanding and ensuring of global data protection management[†]

- Ensuring that data protection is now a competitive advantage for organizations[‡]

- Organized internal training for all in the organization in relation to data protection compliance

- On hand advice for teams and functions within the organization when data protection queries arise

- On hand advice for teams within the organization when considering new products and services and their data protection implications

- Expertise on hand in relation to ongoing risk identification and pre-problem-solving, such as audits, data protection by design and by default, and so on

- Important expertise in relation to data breach issues and events

- Regular audits and appraisals to reduce the likelihood of problem issues arising

- He or she is an immediately identifiable contact point and liaison for the supervisory authorities

- The supervisory authority is unburdened and facilitated in better directing its resources[§]

---

* Klug, "Improving Self-Regulation Through (Law-based) Corporate Data Protection Official," at https://www.gdd.de/international/english/DPO_Report_by_Christoph_Klug.pdf. Revised version of article in *Privacy Laws and Business International Newsletter*.
† Ibid.
‡ Ibid.
§ Ibid.

☐ Significant Cost of Getting Data Protection Wrong

The data protection officer will have to apprise the organization about the very significant consequences of the organization getting data protection compliance wrong. Errors can involve large costs, financial and otherwise.

If the organization does not collect personal data correctly, it is not lawfully entitled to retain or process such data.

This raises the consequence of official audit, penalty, prosecution, or investigation by the supervisory authority. In addition, enforcement orders can be issued by the supervisory authority. In certain circumstances, depending of the scale of the unlawfulness, there may be more than one supervisory authority involved.

If the personal data are unlawfully collected, it may not be possible to remedy the situation, in which case the data may have to be deleted. In addition, the situation may arise where these difficult issues must be notified to the supervisory authority. Considering the importance of personal data to certain new start-up companies and technology-related companies, their databases may be considered significant (sometimes even the most valuable) company assets. To have to delete the database would have adverse consequences for the company—and indeed its business or transactional model.

Individual data subjects may also be upset with what the organization has done, and may seek to enforce their respective data protection rights. Indeed, these rights are now enhanced and expanded under the new data protection regime.

Data subjects are also entitled to sue the organization, and this can include injunctive-type remedies. On occasion, individuals may also seek to sue for compensation and damages, particularly where financial loss issues or concerns arise.

Furthermore, organizations and data protection officers will now face the prospect of having to deal with an increasing number of queries, if not litigation, from data subject representative organizations on behalf of groups of data subjects.

In all of the instances where an organization gets its data protection compliance wrong, there is a real possibility of media attention for the wrong reasons. Such media attention and commentary can be quite critical of the organization.

Increasingly, where media attention arises as a result of the organization getting its data protection compliance strategy wrong, the organization will also be the focus of significant social media attention.

This can involve individual data subjects, customers, potential customers, and users. The comments of such criticism can be less circumspect than more restrained mainstream media comments.

Brand, risk, and tarnishment considerations must be considered significant issues for organizations in relation to their data protection compliance regime. Getting data protection compliance wrong can have significant and long-term consequences to the brand and to the bottom line. Customer, trade, turnover, and profits can be hit in many breach and unlawful data processing situations. It can be a lengthy and costly exercise to restore the brand and the reputation of the organization. On certain occasions, this might not be possible if the breach is so significant as to make the entire brand toxic.

Sometimes, the time and resources necessary to deal with unlawful data processing and/or data breach require that the organization ceases, or is directed to cease, processing activities. Not every organization will have the resources to sustain an extended period of no remunerated commercial activity while correct and lawful processes are being restored. Indeed, there may well be significant efforts required to relaunch the brand and the commercial activities of the organization. Sometimes, the brand can be rehabilitated, sometimes not.

An organization may also be required to expend significant time and financial resources engaging a variety of external third-party expertise, depending on the particular nature of the unlawfulness or breach at hand.

Depending on the nature of the unlawful activity, and particularly where this is not the first instance of unlawfulness, the supervisory authority may decide to prosecute the organization. This will have costs and consequences, regardless of the outcome of such a prosecution. Organizations and data protection officers will no doubt be aware of the increasing trend for such supervisory prosecutions over the last number of years. Such prosecutions may be predicted to increase under the new data protection regime, with the increased emphasis on modern personal data, data protection compliance, risk issues, risk identification, and pre-problem-solving.

The cost of getting data protection compliance wrong can now result in very significant fines and penalties for the organization in breach. These are detailed in the "Fines and Penalties" section of this chapter but, suffice to say, fines and penalties of up to 200 million euros (and potentially more in some instances, based on worldwide turnover) should be a lightning bolt to focus the attention of any organization.

In addition, individual officers and directors of an organization can be the subject of fines, penalties, and sanctions. There is also the potential for named officers to be included in litigation by data subjects or representative organizations for data subjects.

Organizations also need to be aware, and the data protection officer will be central to informing and advising on these issues, that the consequences of noncompliance and getting data protection wrong are severe. These can include significant media attention; damaged reputation and goodwill; lost business; lost customers; regulatory attention (including from the data protection supervisory authorities); closing or discontinuing particular activities, processes, or trading while an incident is ongoing; hot desks; replacement of hardware and data; additional staff; redirecting staff; engaging outside experts; disciplining staff; hiring new staff; including executives (indeed there are growing examples of senior managers; executives; and even managing directors losing their position after particular data breach incidents such as those at Target and Sony), and so on. Sales and profits can be significantly adversely affected in particular instances. These issues can all raise significant cost issues for the organization. Furthermore, and particularly under the new data protection regime, there can be significant monetary costs involved in official fines and penalties. These costs are set out under the new General Data Protection Regulation (GDPR) and involve fines of up to millions of euros or a percentage of the global turnover of the organization, which can also amount to millions of euros.

☐ Fines and Penalties

As highlighted in the previous section, the organization can be the recipient of very significant fines and penalties, running into millions of euros. Article 83 of the new GDPR refers to the general provisions for supervisory authorities imposing administrative fines.

The administrative fines are to be effective, proportionate, and dissuasive. The fine will be fixed with regard, *inter alia*, to the nature, gravity, and duration of the breach; the intentional or negligent character of the infringement; the degree of responsibility of the natural or legal person and of previous breaches by this person; the technical and organizational measures and procedures implemented; and the degree of cooperation with the supervisory authority to remedy the breach.

Administrative fines shall, depending on the circumstances of each individual case, be imposed in addition to, or instead of, the measures referred to in points (a) to (h) and (j) of Article 58(2). When deciding whether to impose an administrative fine and deciding on the amount of the fine in each individual case, due regard shall be given to the following:

- The nature, gravity, and duration of the infringement, taking into account the nature, scope, or purpose of the processing concerned as well as the number of data subjects affected and the level of damage suffered by them

- The intentional or negligent character of the infringement

- Any action taken by the controller or processor to mitigate the damage suffered by data subjects

- The degree of responsibility of the controller or processor, taking into account the technical and organizational measures implemented by the controller pursuant to Articles 25 and 32

- Any relevant previous infringements by the controller or processor

- The degree of cooperation with the supervisory authority to remedy the infringement and mitigate the possible adverse effects of the infringement

- The categories of personal data affected by the infringement

- The manner in which the infringement became known to the supervisory authority, in particular whether (and if so, to what extent) the controller or processor notified the infringement

- Measures referred to in Article 58(2) that have previously been ordered against the controller or processor with regard to the same subject matter, and compliance with those measures

- Adherence to approved codes of conduct pursuant to Article 40 or approved certification mechanisms pursuant to Article 42

- Any other aggravating or mitigating factor applicable to the circumstances of the case such as financial benefits gained or losses avoided, directly or indirectly, from the infringement

If a controller or processor intentionally or negligently, for the same or for linked processing operations, infringes several provisions of this regulation, the total amount of the administrative fine shall not exceed the amount specified for the gravest infringement.

Infringements of the following provisions shall, in accordance with paragraph 2, be subject to administrative fines of up to 10 million euros, or in the case of an undertaking, up to 2% of the total worldwide annual turnover of the preceding financial year, whichever is higher. This is in accordance with

- The obligations of the controller and the processor, pursuant to Articles 8, 11, 25–39, 42, and 43

- The obligations of the certification body, pursuant to Articles 42 and 43

- The obligations of the monitoring body, pursuant to Article 41(4)

Infringements of certain provisions shall, in accordance with paragraph 2, be subject to administrative fines of up to 20 million euros or, in the case of an undertaking, up to 4% of the total worldwide annual turnover of the preceding financial year, whichever is higher, This is in accordance with

- The basic principles for processing, including the conditions for consent, pursuant to Articles 5, 6, 7, and 9

- The data subjects' rights, pursuant to Articles 12–22

- The transfers of personal data to a recipient in a third-party country or an international organization, pursuant to Articles 44–49

- Any obligations pursuant to Member State law adopted under Chapter IX

- Noncompliance with an order or a temporary or definitive limitation on processing or the suspension of data flow by the supervisory authority, pursuant to Article 58(2), or the failure to provide access in violation of Article 58(1)

Noncompliance with an order by the supervisory authority as referred to in Article 58(2) shall, in accordance with paragraph 2 of this article, be subject to administrative fines of up to 20 million euros, or in the case of an undertaking, up to 4% of the total worldwide annual turnover of the preceding financial year, whichever is higher.

A Member State may lay down the rules on whether and to what extent administrative fines may be imposed on public authorities and bodies established in that Member State.

Where the legal system of the Member State does not provide for administrative fines, this article may be applied in such a manner that the fine is initiated by the competent supervisory authority and imposed by competent national courts while ensuring that those legal remedies are effective and have an equivalent effect to the administrative fines imposed by supervisory authorities. In any event, the fines imposed shall be effective, proportionate, and dissuasive.

☐ Director and Officer Responsibility

Directors and officers of the organization now need to be cognizant of the fact that they can individually, in addition to the corporate organization, be named as the subject of official actions. Indeed, there are already examples in a number of Member States of directors being the subject of official fines and penalties. There are also examples of directors having being prosecuted. Directors have also been restricted in terms of enforcement and prosecution actions.

☐ Data Subject Actions

Individuals are also entitled to enforce their data protection rights and to seek court remedies in relation to damage and loss suffered as a result of the misuse of their personal data. They are not confined to simply making complaints to the supervisory authority. It is important to note that certain remedies that an individual may seek are not available from or through the supervisory authority.

Data subjects are entitled to sue an organization in relation to data protection noncompliance. Article 79, headed "Right to an effective judicial remedy against a controller or processor," states:

> Without prejudice to any available administrative or non-judicial remedy, including the right to lodge a complaint with a supervisory authority pursuant to Article 77, each data subject shall have the right to an effective judicial remedy where he or she considers that his or her rights under this Regulation have been infringed as a result of the processing of his or her personal data in non-compliance with this Regulation.

Article 79(2) states that "Proceedings against a controller or a processor shall be brought before the courts of the Member State where the controller or processor has an establishment. Alternatively, such proceedings may be brought before the courts of the Member State where the data subject has his or her habitual residence, unless the controller or processor is a public authority of a Member State acting in the exercise of its public powers."

So, the organization can be sued by data subjects when it breaches the data protection regime.

This recognition of judicial, as well as official, routes to remedies is also contained in the GDPR's Recitals. Every data subject should have the right to lodge a complaint with a single supervisory authority in any Member State and have the right to a judicial remedy if he or she considers that his or her rights under this regulation are infringed, or where the supervisory authority does not react on a complaint or does not act where such action is necessary to protect the rights of the data subject.*

For proceedings against a controller or processor, the plaintiff should have the choice to bring the action before the courts of the Member States where the controller or processor has an establishment or where the data subject resides, unless the controller is a public authority of a Member State acting in the exercise of its public powers.†

The controller or processor should compensate any damage that a person may suffer as a result of processing that infringes the regulation. The controller or processor should be exempt from liability if it proves that it is not in any way responsible for the damage. The concept of damage should be broadly interpreted in light of the case law of the Court of Justice and in a manner that fully reflects the objectives of the regulation. This is without prejudice to any claims for damage deriving from the violation of other rules in Union or Member State law. Processing that infringes this regulation also includes processing that infringes delegated and implemented acts adopted in accordance with the regulation—and Member State law—specifying rules of the regulation. Data subjects should receive full and effective compensation for the damage they have suffered. Where controllers or processors are involved in the same processing, each controller or processor should be held liable for the entire damage. However, where they are joined under the same judicial proceedings, in accordance with Member State law, compensation may be apportioned according to the responsibility of each controller or processor for the damage caused by the processing, provided that full and effective compensation of the data subject who suffered the damage is ensured. Any controller or processor that has paid full compensation

---

* GDPR Recital 141.
† GDPR Recital 145.

may subsequently institute recourse proceedings against other controllers or processors involved in the same processing.*

Article 22 of the DPD95 provides that "Member States shall provide for the right of every person to a judicial remedy for any breach of the rights guaranteed [them] by the national law applicable to the processing in question." Article 23 of the European Union Data Protection Directive 95/46/EC of 1995 (DPD95) states that "Member States shall provide that any person who has suffered damage as a result of an unlawful processing operation or of any act incompatible with the national provisions adopted pursuant to [the] Directive is entitled to receive compensation from the controller for the damage suffered." Article 82 of the GDPR states that any person who has suffered material or nonmaterial damage as a result of an infringement of the regulation shall have the right to receive compensation from the controller or processor for the damage suffered.† Any controller involved in processing shall be liable for the damage caused by processing that infringes the regulation. A processor shall be liable for the damage caused by processing only where it has not complied with the obligations of the regulation specifically directed at processors or where it has acted outside or contrary to the lawful instructions of the controller.‡ A controller or processor may be exempt from liability under paragraph 2 if it proves that it is not in any way responsible for the event giving rise to the damage.§

Where more than one controller or processor, or both a controller and a processor, are involved in the same processing and where they are, under paragraphs 2 and 3, responsible for any damage caused by processing, each controller or processor shall be held liable for the entire damage in order to ensure effective compensation of the data subject.

Where a controller or processor has, in accordance with paragraph 4, paid full compensation for the damage suffered, that controller or processor shall be entitled to claim back from the other controllers or processors involved in the same processing that part of the compensation corresponding to their part of responsibility for the damage, in accordance with the conditions set out in paragraph 2.

Court and civil or tortious remedies are available to data subjects; in addition to enforcing compliance with the prior information requirements, *data protection principles, legitimate processing conditions,* and security requirements, the data protection regime contains a number of further important rights for individuals in respect to their personal data. The data

---

* GDPR Recital 118.
† GDPR Article 82(1).
‡ GDPR art 82(2).
§ GDPR art 82(3).

protection rights enshrined in the data protection regime for individuals are set out in the *data protection principles*. They include the following:

- Individuals have the right to be informed by an organization about their identity and details when the organization is collecting and processing the individual's personal data.

- The organization must disclose to the individual the purpose for which it is collecting and processing his or her personal data.

- If the organization is forwarding or transferring the personal data to third-party recipients, it must disclose this to the individual as well as identify the third-party recipients.

- If it is permitted to transfer the personal data outside of the county, the organization must identity the third-party country that will be receiving the personal data.

Possibly the most important right relates to the right of data subjects to access or obtain a copy of their personal data as held by organizations. Organizations must answer and reply to requests from individuals in relation to their data protection rights. This includes requests for access to a copy of the personal data held in relation to the individual. This is known as a *personal data access request*. Every individual for whom a controller keeps personal information has a number of other rights under the data protection regime, in addition to the right of access. These include the right to have any inaccurate information rectified or erased and to have personal data taken off a direct marketing or direct mailing list.

The individual data subject has a right to prevent processing likely to cause damage or distress. A further right relates to automated decision-taking. Importantly, individual data subjects have specific rights in relation to rectification, blocking, erasure, and destruction. This is being further calibrated in the GDPR as encompassing the right to oblivion or the right to be forgotten.

Individual data subjects are entitled to compensation as well as being entitled to complain to the supervisory authority and to file actions in the courts to obtain judicial remedies. The DPD95 notes that data protection laws must not result in any lessening of the protection but must, on the contrary, seek to ensure a high level of protection in the EU.*

---

* DPD95 Recital (10).

☐ Organizational Data Subject Groups

Recital 142 of the GDPR states that where a data subject considers that his or her rights under the regulation are infringed, he or she should have the right to mandate a not-for-profit body, organization, or association that is constituted in accordance with the law of a Member State, has statutory objectives that are in the public interest, and is active in the field of the protection of personal data to lodge a complaint on his or her behalf with a supervisory authority, exercise the right to a judicial remedy on behalf of data subjects or, if provided for in Member State law, exercise the right to receive compensation on behalf of data subjects. A Member State may provide for such a body, organization, or association to have the right to lodge a complaint in that Member State, independently of a data subject's mandate, and the right to an effective judicial remedy where it has reasons to consider that the rights of a data subject have been infringed as a result of the processing of personal data that infringes the regulation. That body, organization, or association may not be allowed to claim compensation on a data subject's behalf independently of the data subject's mandate. Indeed, there are an increasing number of data protection and privacy groups, both nationally and supranationally. Indeed, the Court of Justice case that struck down the Data Retention Directive was taken by one such group.*

---

* Cases C-293/12 and C-594/12, Digital Rights Ireland and Seitlinger and Others, Court of Justice, 8 April 2014. Directive 2006/24/EC and amending Directive 2002/58/EC.

Accessing the Data Sources

☐ Sources and Locations of Personal Data

It is necessary for the data protection officer (DPO) to understand what data the organization has and the purpose of those data. The following is an example of an audit tool from the European Data Protection Supervisor (EDPS). It is aimed mostly at inward-facing personal data collection.

☐ Sample Audit Inventory Queries

One data protection supervisory authority provides the following illustrative questions in relation to data audits (Ireland). The sample audit questions refer to the fair obtaining and processing of personal data. Obviously, the emphasis may differ depending on whether customers or employees merit a particular focus. The sample questions are provided in the next section. These are given from the perspective of an external official audit into an organization as opposed to an internal audit. However, the questions are useful for DPOs to bear in mind in their own considerations.

☐ Customers/Clients

- How do you obtain personal data?

- What types of personal data do you obtain?

- Do you record the personal public service number (PPSN)?

- Is verification documentation sought? If so, what happens to the verification documentation? Is a copy made and retained for your records?

- What procedures are in place to ensure that a person's data are being recorded accurately?

- Do you record incoming or outgoing telephone calls? If so, how do you inform the customer that this is being done?

- Can we view the physical filing area and look at a random sample of files?

☐ Employees

- How do you obtain personal data?

- What types of personal data do you obtain?

- Is verification documentation sought? If so, what happens to the verification documentation?

- What do you do with approved and rejected application forms?

- Are all details received inputted into a computer system?

- What procedures are in place to ensure that a person's data are being recorded accurately?

- For how long are personal data retained, both in computer and manual form?

- Do you record incoming or outgoing telephone calls? If so, how do you inform staff that this is being done?

- How long are personnel files held (computer and manual) after a staff member has left employment?

- Can we view the physical filing area and look at a random sample of files?

☐ Sensitive Personal Data

- Do you process any sensitive personal data such as medical data or data regarding nationality/ethnic origin?

- Under what circumstances do you obtain sensitive data?

- Who has access to sensitive data?

- What constitutes a business need to access medical data?

- Who controls which staff may gain access to the data?

- Is sensitive personal data transmitted internally/externally?

- How are the data transmitted? Encrypted e-mail? Secure fax?

- Is the data subject aware that his or her sensitive personal data are being processed in this way?

- For how long are sensitive personal data retained in both computer and manual form?

☐ Service Application Forms

(May or may not be relevant, depending on the type of organization.)

- Do you conduct reviews of service application forms to ensure that the information sought is not excessive?

- Do you clearly explain, on all service application forms, why certain information is being sought?

- Do you ever use the information gathered on service application forms for other uses besides the original purpose for which the information is sought? Is the consent of the data subject sought to do so?

☐ Third-Party Requests for Disclosure

- Do you receive requests from third parties seeking data regarding your customers/employees?

- Is there a legislative basis cited by any of these third parties when seeking information?

- Are there procedural guidelines to deal with requests for personal data from third parties?

- Do you document all requests handled and responded to?

- How do you handle law enforcement requests for disclosure of information?

☐ Staff Training and Awareness

- Are there set down procedures/reference documents for staff for dealing with day-to-day data protection issues?

- Is there a data protection committee or working group within the organization?

- Is data protection a fixed/frequent or rare agenda item on meeting agendas at senior management level?

- How often is such training provided and is there ongoing refresher training?

- Are information security skills addressed in any of your organization's training programs?

- Are staff aware that unauthorized access to the personal data of customers is not allowed?

- How do you check that no internal unauthorized access to personal data has been undertaken?

- Are staff leaving employment aware that any customer data remain subject to confidentiality?

- Is there something to this effect built into the contract of employment?

- Can we have a copy of a typical staff contract?

☐ Marketing

(May or may not be relevant, depending on the type of organization.)

- Can you describe how a typical marketing campaign operates?

- What media do you use for marketing (e.g., online, mobile, Bluetooth, mailing, cold-calling)?

- Do you outsource marketing activities? If so, is there a contract in place? Does the contracted entity handle the personal data of your customers/clients? Does the contracted entity procure new customers for you?

☐ Customers

- How can customers opt out of such campaigns?

- How does a customer change his or her opt-out preference?

☐ Prospective Customers

- Do you purchase any third-party direct mail listings or commission tailored lists of prospective customers?

- If you engage in phone or e-mail marketing activities, can you show us how a National Directory Database (NDD) check is undertaken?

☐ Project Management Activities

- Are all new projects and initiatives that entail the processing of personal data "privacy-proofed" at the planning stage?

- Is a data protection impact assessment conducted at the development, testing, and delivery stage, that is, pre- and postimplementation?

☐ Information and Knowledge Management Practices

- Have you ever conducted an information and/or knowledge audit?

- Do you have a list or register of information assets for your organization?

- If so, can you distinguish personal data repositories from nonpersonal data within your organization?

☐ Contracts with Data Processors

- Do you outsource any processing of personal data?

- How are customers made aware that their personal data may be outsourced to a third party?

- Do you have contracts in place with such data processors?

- Can we see a couple of sample contracts?

- In relation to the transfer of data abroad, what type of data are involved?

☐ Access Requests

- How do you handle access requests received?

- What procedures are in place to amend inaccurate data when you are notified of same on foot of a request received?

- Are there procedures set out for handling such requests?

- How are staff made aware of these procedures and how is compliance with the procedures checked?

☐ Computer Systems and Security

Personal Computers of Employees

- Are passwords in use?

- How often are passwords changed?

- Who can change a password?

- Are there access level restrictions?

- Are documents sent externally by e-mail encrypted or password protected?

Removable Media

- Are ports such as compact disc and USB drives enabled? Are such drives capable of copying files?

- In relation to the use of laptops, under what circumstances are personal data held on these?

- Do laptops have remote access to company databases?

- Are laptops password protected and so on?

- Are laptops encrypted?

- Do staff have secure remote access to data when they are off-site so that personal data do not need to be stored elsewhere?

Network Security

- What type of backup system operates?

- Is there a set daily/weekly procedure?

- Where are backups kept?

- Is this a secure location?

- Are all entry routes to the server room/computer center subject to security checks?

- Do existing measures relating to computerized data ensure that data may only be accessed by persons whose remit it is to access such data?

- Is there a log created of access to data? Footprints? Audit trails?

- Are patterns of abnormal usage identifiable?

- What security measures are in place relating to facsimile transmissions?

Biometrics

- Are there any plans for a biometric time and attendance system to be put in place and do you understand the data protection implications of implementing such a system?

CCTV

- Is closed-circuit television (CCTV) in operation?

- Do you have a policy regarding the operation of CCTV?

- What is the retention period for CCTV footage?

- Are equipment and tapes/discs stored securely?

- Who has access to CCTV equipment?

- Is CCTV used for reasons other than security?

- Is there appropriate signage in relation to the uses made of CCTV?

- Are staff/customers aware of the purpose of CCTV?

Personal Data Inventory Tool

The EDPS provides an illustrative inventory tool in relation to (inward) processing activities and operations.

Inventory of Data Processing Operations (EDPS) (Inward Facing)

Category of Procedure		Processing Name	Contact Person	Processing Description	Notification to DPO	Prior Check	Status
Administrative procedures: Selection and recruitment	1	Recruit permanent staff					
	2	Recruit contract agents					
	3	Recruit temporary staff					
	4	Internal mobility					
	5	Recruit interim staff					
	6	Recruit trainees					
	7	Recruit seconded experts					
	8	Determination of rights and obligations					
Administrative procedures: Evaluation	9	Probationary reports					
	10	Staff evaluation					
	11	Promotion					
	12	Certification procedure					
	13	Attestation procedure					
Administrative procedures: Other	14	Retirement without reduction in pension rights					
	15	Staff training					
	16	Management of personal files					

(Continued)

Administrative procedures: Payroll and time management	17	Remuneration
	18	Social security benefits
	19	Pensions and allowances
	20	Leave and flexitime
	21	Teleworking
Administrative procedures: Discipline	22	Administrative enquiries
	23	Disciplinary procedures
Administrative procedures: Harassment	24	Antiharassment policy
Administrative procedures: Heath data	25	Preemployment medical examination
	26	Annual medical visits
	27	Specific medical checkups
	28	Medical files and certificates
Administrative procedures: Call for tender	29	Grants
	30	Procurement procedures
Core business	31	
	32	
	33	
Security procedures	34	Site security
	35	Video surveillance
	36	Access control

Inventory of Data Processing Operations (EDPS) (Inward Facing)

Category of Procedure		Processing Name	Contact Person	Processing Description	Notification to DPO	Prior Check	Status
Information technology (IT) procedures	37	E-mail services					
	38	Telephone systems					
	39	System logs					
	40	Active directory					
	41	Intranet					
	42	Software					
Support management	43	Site management					
	44	Contact management					
	45	Budget management					
	46	Document management					
	47	Event organization					
	48	Audit					

CHAPTER

Tools and Access Rights

☐ Access Right

The access right is referred to in Article 15 of the General Data Protection Regulation. It refers to the right of access for individual data subjects. Article 15(1) states that the data subject shall have the right to obtain from the controller confirmation of whether or not personal data concerning him or her are being processed and, where that is the case, access to the personal data and the following information:

• The purposes of the processing

• The categories of personal data concerned

• The recipients or categories of recipient to whom the personal data have been or will be disclosed, particularly recipients in third-party countries or international organizations

• Where possible, the envisaged period for which the personal data will be stored or, if not possible, the criteria used to determine that period

• The existence of the right to request from the controller rectification or erasure of personal data or restriction of processing of personal data concerning the data subject, or to object to such processing

- The right to lodge a complaint with a supervisory authority

- Where the personal data are not collected from the data subject, any available information as to their source

- The existence of automated decision-making, including profiling, referred to in Article 22(1) and (4) and, at least in those cases, meaningful information about the logic involved in, as well as the significance and the envisaged consequences of, such processing for the data subject*

☐ Confirmation Right Regarding Personal Data

Therefore, the data protection officer and organization must confirm to the data subject, upon request, whether personal data relating to him or her is being held and processed.

This requires procedures for

- Receiving data subject confirmation requests

- Identifying and reviewing data subject confirmation requests

- Identifying whether there are personal data relating to the data subject held by the organization

- Establishing a standard confirmation correspondence for communicating with data subjects in relation to such confirmation requests

- Sending a standard acknowledgment correspondence to the data subject advising of receipt and that the request is being dealt with

- Communicating with relevant departments in relation to the request and reviewing their replies

---

* The original Commission proposal for the General Data Protection Regulation (GDPR) referred to the purposes of the processing; the categories of personal data concerned; the recipients or categories of recipients to whom the personal data are to be or have been disclosed, particularly to recipients in third-party countries; the period for which the personal data will be stored; the existence of the right to request from the controller rectification or erasure of personal data concerning the data subject or to object to the processing of such personal data; the right to lodge a complaint to the supervisory authority and the contact details of the supervisory authority; communication of the personal data undergoing processing and of any available information as to their source; and the significance and envisaged consequences of such processing, at least in the case of the measures referred to in Article 20.

- Sending a standard reply correspondence to the data subject advising whether personal data relating to the requestor are held by the organization

☐ ACCESS RIGHTS REGARDING PERSONAL DATA

The controller shall provide a copy of the personal data undergoing processing. For any further copies requested by the data subject, the controller may charge a reasonable fee based on administrative costs. Where the data subject makes the request in electronic form, and unless otherwise requested by the data subject, the information shall be provided in an electronic form that is commonly used.

Therefore, upon request, the organization must provide a copy of the relevant personal data to the requestor.

This requires procedures for

- Receiving data subject access requests

- Identifying and reviewing data subject access requests

- Establishing a standard confirmation correspondence for communicating with data subjects in relation to such access requests

- Sending a standard acknowledgment correspondence to the data subject advising of receipt and that the request is being dealt with

- Communicating with relevant departments in relation to the request and reviewing their replies

- Identifying, receiving, and reviewing the personal data relating to the data subject held by the organization, the nature of same, and any particular issues arising

- Identifying whether any exemption issues arise

- Identifying whether any third-party data subject issues arise, such as third parties being included in or identified in the data

- Identifying if any redaction issues arise and how these issues should be dealt with in the particular circumstances

- Sending a standard reply correspondence to the data subject advising that personal data relating to the requestor are held by the organization and attaching same

- Ideally, also including a description and/or schedule of the personal data being furnished

It should be noted that it may no longer be possible to charge for the initial copy of the personal data furnished to the data subject.

☐ Considering an Access Request

One data protection supervisory authority states that, to make an access request the data subject must

- Apply in writing (which can include e-mail or other electronic form)

- Give any details that might be needed to help the organization identify him or her and locate all of the information the organization may keep about him or her, such as previous addresses and customer account numbers.

The data protection officer must therefore make assessments in relation to these issues when requests are received.

☐ Dealing with Access Requests

One commentary* refers to the advisability of having a processing system in place to deal with access requests. The main components referred to include:

- Data subject asks for personal data

- Data subject access request form issued

- Data subject access request form returned with appropriate fee (if requested)

---

* Morgan and Boardman, *Data Protection Strategy* (Sweet & Maxwell, 2003) 252.

- Personal data located by the legal department, data protection personnel, and so on

- Examination of same in relation to any third-party information, health data, or exempt data

- Data reviewed by the legal department

- Personal data copy issued to data subject

One data protection supervisory authority makes the following comments and suggestions for organizations in relation to access requests. On making an access request, any individual for whom personal data are kept is entitled to

- A copy of the personal data being held that relates to him or her

- The categories of their personal data and the purpose(s) for processing it

- The identity of those to whom the controller discloses the personal data

- The source of the personal data, unless it is contrary to public interest to reveal it

- The logic involved in automated decisions

- The data held in the form of opinions, except where such opinions were given in confidence and in such cases where the person's fundamental rights suggest that he or she should access the personal data in question

It is important that organizations have clear and *documented* processes and procedures in place to ensure that all relevant files and computers are checked for personal data in respect of which the access request is being made.

☐ Response to Access Request

In response to an access request, an organization must

- Supply the information to the individual data subject promptly and within the appropriate time limit of receiving the access request

- Provide the information in a form that will be clear to the ordinary person (e.g., any codes must be explained)

If the organization does not keep any information about the individual making the request, the organization should inform the individual within the period.

If the organization restricts the individual's right of access, that is, in accordance with one of the very limited restrictions (if any), the organization must notify the data subject in writing and it must include a statement of the reasons for refusal. The organization must also inform the individual of his or her entitlement to complain to the supervisory authority about the refusal.

One supervisory authority,* for example, provides the following guidance or checklist for data protection officers:

1 *Is this a subject access request?*
  No. Handle the query as part of your normal course of business.
  Yes. Go to 2.

2 *Do you have enough information to be sure of the requester's identity?*
  No. If you have good cause to doubt the requester's identity you can ask them to provide any evidence you reasonably need to confirm it. For example, you may ask for a piece of information held in your records that the person would be expected to know, such as membership details, or a witnessed copy of their signature. Once satisfied, go to 3.
  Yes. Go to 3.

3 *Do you need any other information to find the records they want?*
  No. Go to 4.
  Yes. You will need to ask the individual promptly for any other information you reasonably need to find the records they want. You might want to ask them to narrow down their request. For example, if you keep all your customers' information on one computer system and your suppliers' information on another, you could ask what relationship they had with you. Or, you could ask when they had dealings with you. However, they do have the right to ask for everything you have about them and this could mean a very wide search. You have [a time limit] to respond to a subject access request after receiving any further information you need and any fee you decide to charge. Go to 4.

4 *Are you going to charge a fee?*
  No. Go to 5.
  Yes. If you need a fee you must ask the individual promptly for one ... The [time limit] in which you must respond starts when you have

---

* *Data Protection Good Practice Note, Checklist for Handling Requests for Personal Information* (subject access requests), ICO, at http://www.ico.gov.uk/for_organisations/data_protection/subject_access_requests.aspx.

received the fee and all necessary information to help you find the records. Go to 5.

5 *Do you hold any information about the person?*

No. If you hold no personal information at all about the individual you must tell them this.

Yes. Go to 6.

6 *Will the information be changed between receiving the request and sending the response?*

No. Go to 7.

Yes. You can still make routine amendments and deletions to personal information after receiving a request. However, you must not make any changes to the records as a result of receiving the request, even if you find inaccurate or embarrassing information on the record. Go to 7.

7 *Does it include any information about other people?*

No. Go to 8.

Yes. You will not have to supply the information unless the other people mentioned have given their consent or it is reasonable to supply the information without their consent. Even when the other person's information should not be disclosed, you should still supply as much as possible by editing the references to other people. To help you on this point, we have published more detailed guidance on dealing with subject access requests involving other people's information.

Go to 8.

8 *Are you obliged to supply the information?*

No. If all the information you hold about the requester is exempt, then you can reply stating that you do not hold any of their personal information that you are required to reveal.

Yes. Go to 9.

9 *Does it include any complex terms or codes?*

No. Go to 10.

Yes. You must make sure that these are explained so that the information can be understood. Go to 10.

10 Prepare the response.

Data protection officers should always bear in mind that there can be some differences in national legislation, notwithstanding the common sources of Convention and EU law that include the new data protection regulation.

Records and Documentation Issues

☐ Records and Documentation

Article 30 of the General Data Protection Regulation (GDPR) requires controllers and processors, and their representatives, to maintain records in relation to their data processing activities and compliance.

Controller Documentation of Processing Activities (GDPR)

Records OF:	Documentation MUST contain:	BUT …
Controller and representative MUST maintain records of processing operations under its responsibility (i.e., including records held by the processor)	The name and contact details of the controller and, where applicable, the joint controller, representative, and data protection officer	Record obligations shall not apply to the following controllers and processors: enterprises or organizations employing fewer than 250 persons unless the processing carried out is likely to result in a risk to the rights and freedoms of data subjects, the processing is not occasional, or the processing includes special categories of data as referred to in Article 9(1) or personal data relating to criminal convictions and offenses referred to in Article 10	Shall make the documentation available to the supervisory authority on request
	The purposes of the processing		
	A description of the categories of data subjects and the categories of personal data		
	The categories of recipients to whom the personal data have been disclosed, including recipients in third-party countries or international organizations		

Where applicable, the transfers of personal data to a third-party country or an international organization, including the identification of that country or organization and, in the case of transfers referred to in the second subparagraph of Article 49(1), the documentation of appropriate safeguards

Where possible, the envisaged time limits for erasure of the different categories of data

Where possible, a general description of the technical and organizational security measures referred to in Article 32(1)

The above records MUST be in writing, including in electronic form

Processor Documentation of Processing Activities (GDPR)

Records OF:	Documentation MUST contain at least:	BUT ...	
The processor and representative MUST maintain records of all categories of processing activities carried out on behalf of a controller	The name and contact details of the processor or processors and of each controller on behalf of which the processor is acting, and, where applicable, of the controller's or the processor's representative and the Data Protection Officer	Record obligations shall not apply to the following controllers and processors: an enterprises or organizations employing fewer than 250 persons unless the processing carried out is likely to result in a risk to the rights and freedoms of data subjects, the processing is not occasional, or the processing includes special categories of data as referred to in Article 9(1) or personal data relating to criminal convictions and offenses referred to in Article 10	Shall make the documentation available to the supervisory authority on request
	The categories of processing carried out on behalf of each controller		

Where applicable, the transfers of personal data to a third-party country or an international organization, including the identification of that third-party country or international organization and, in the case of transfers referred to in the second subparagraph of Article 49(1), the documentation of suitable safeguards

Where possible, a general description of the technical and organizational security measures referred to in Article 32(1)

The above records MUST be in writing, including in electronic form

Engaging Processors

☐ Processors

The data protection officer must be aware of the need to ensure compliance in situations where processors are engaged and in managing the relationship with the processor. Article 28 refers to processor issues.

Engaging Processors	
Obligation	**Questions to Consider**
Controller MUST only use processors that provide sufficient guarantees of implementing appropriate technical and organizational measures in such a manner that the processing will meet the requirements of the General Data Protection Regulation (GDPR) and will ensure the protection of the rights of the data subject	Does the processor provide sufficient guarantees? Does the processor implement appropriate technical and organizational measures? Does the processor meet GDPR requirements? Does the processor ensure protection of data subject rights?

Subprocessors

Restriction on Subprocessing	Controller Written Authorization	Opportunity to Object	
The processor shall not engage another processor	Without prior specific or general written authorization from the controller	Where general written authorization has been given, the processor shall inform the controller of any intended changes concerning the addition or replacement of other processors, thereby giving the controller the opportunity to object to such changes	
In addition			
Where a processor engages another processor to carry out specific processing activities on behalf of the controller	The same data protection obligations, as set out in the contract or other legal act between the controller and the processor as referred to in paragraph 3, shall be imposed on that other processor by way of a contract or other legal act under Union or Member State law	In particular, to provide sufficient guarantees to implement appropriate technical and organizational measures in such a manner that the processing will meet the requirements of the regulation	Where the other processor fails to fulfill its data protection obligations, the initial processor shall remain fully liable to the controller for the performance of the other processor's obligations

Contract with the Processor

Contract	Binding	Sets Out
Processing by a processor shall be governed by a contract or other legal act under Union or Member State law	That is binding on the processor	With regard to the controller, and that sets out the subject matter and duration of the processing, the nature and purpose of the processing, the type of personal data and categories of data subjects, and the obligations and rights of the controller

Contract

Contract	Questions to Consider	
The contract shall stipulate, in particular, that the processor	Processes the personal data only on documented instruction from the controller, including with regard to transfers of personal data to a third-party country or an international organization, unless required to do so by Union or Member State law to which the processor is subject; in such a case, the processor shall inform the controller of that legal requirement before processing, unless that law prohibits such information on important grounds of public interest	Are there documented instructions separate to the contract? What are the contract, policy, and procedure requirements? Are transfers required?
	Ensure that persons authorized to process the personal data have committed themselves to confidentiality or are under an appropriate statutory obligation of confidentiality	Training? Contracts? Confidentiality?
	Takes all measures required, pursuant to Article 32	Measures required? Measures taken? Contract requirements? Procedure for same? Time and notice periods?

(Continued)

Respects the conditions referred to in paragraphs 2 and 4 for engaging another processor	Subprocessing? Permitted? Complaint?
Taking into account the nature of the processing, the processor assists the controller by taking appropriate technical and organizational measures, insofar as this is possible, for the fulfillment of the controller's obligation to respond to requests for exercising the data subject's rights as laid down in Chapter III	Considerations particular to the type of data?
Assists the controller in ensuring compliance with the obligations pursuant to Articles 32 to 36, taking into account the nature of processing and the information available to the processor	Compliance with obligations? Particular considerations?

Contract	Contract	Questions to Consider
	As determined by the controller, deletes or returns all personal data to the controller after the end of the provision of services relating to processing, and deletes existing copies unless Union or Member State law requires storage of the personal data	Contract requirements? Procedure for same? Time and notice periods?
	Makes available to the controller all information necessary to demonstrate compliance with the obligations laid down in this article and allows for (and contributes to) audits, including inspections, conducted by the controller or another auditor mandated by the controller. (With regard to point (h) of the first subparagraph, the processor shall immediately inform the controller if, in its opinion, an instruction infringes the regulation or other Union or Member State data protection provisions)	Contract requirements? Procedure for same? Time and notice periods? Documentation?

(Continued)

Contract	Questions to Consider
The contract shall stipulate, in particular, that the processor	Contract, policy, and procedure requirements
Acts only on instruction from the controller, particularly where the transfer of the personal data used is prohibited	Are documented instructions separate to the contract?
Employ only staff who have committed themselves to confidentiality or are under a statutory obligation of confidentiality	What obligation is passed to the processor regarding processor employees? Processor contactors?
Take all required measures, pursuant to Article 30	

Contract

Contract	Questions to Consider
Enlist another processor only with the prior permission of the controller	
Insofar as this is possible, given the nature of the processing, create in agreement with the controller the necessary technical and organizational requirements for the fulfillment of the controller's obligation to respond to requests for exercising the data subject's rights, as laid down in Chapter III	Contract requirements? Procedure for same? Time and notice periods?

Assist the controller in ensuring compliance with the obligations, pursuant to Articles 30–34	Contract requirements? Procedure for same? Time and notice periods?
Hand over all results to the controller after the end of the processing and not process the personal data	Contract requirements? Procedure for same? Time and notice periods?
Make available to the controller and the supervisory authority all information necessary to ensure compliance with the obligations laid down in this article	Contract requirements? Procedure for same? Time and notice periods? Attending processor and equipment on site?
The controller and the processor shall document in writing the controller's instructions and the processor's obligations referred to in paragraph 2	Controller consent? Contract requirements?

Adherence of a processor to an approved code of conduct or an approved certification mechanism may be used as an element to demonstrate sufficient guarantees as referred to in paragraphs 1 and 4 of this article.

The Commission may lay down standard contractual clauses for these matters and data protection officers should consult these as appropriate.

CHAPTER

Tools and Data Protection by Design and by Default

☐ Data Protection by Design and by Default

The Commission proposed a data protection requirement for the new data protection regime.* This new "approach ... [requires that] compliance is designed into systems holding information right from the start, rather than being bolted on afterwards or ignored."† Article 25 of the new General Data Protection Regulation (GDPR) specifies the new data protection by design and by default (DPbD) requirement. This is an increasingly important area of data protection.‡

Taking into account the state of the art, the cost of implementation, and the nature, scope, context, and purposes of processing as well

---

* See Spiekermann, "The Challenges of Privacy by Design," *Communications of the ACM* (2012)(55) 38; Spiekermann and Cranor, "Engineering Privacy," *IEEE Transactions on Software Engineering* (2009)(35) 67; Tielemans and Hildebrandt, "Data Protection by Design and Technology Neutral Law," *Computer Law and Security Review* (2013) (29:5) 509.
† ICO website, at http://www.ico.gov.uk/for_organisations/data_protection/topic_guides/privacy_by_design.aspx.
‡ Prior to the new GDPD, data protection supervisory authorities has issued recommendations in relation to data protection by design. The UK ICO for, example, issues it's Privacy Impact Assessment Code of Practice (i.e., Data Protection Impact Assessments). These now also need to be read in light of the General Data Protection Regulation changes.

as the risks of varying likelihood and severity for rights and freedoms of natural persons posed by the processing, the controller shall, both at the time of the determination of the means for processing and at the time of the processing itself, implement appropriate technical and organizational measures. Such measures include pseudonymization, which is designed to implement data protection principles such as data minimization in an effective manner, and to integrate the necessary safeguards into the processing in order to meet the requirements of the regulation and protect the rights of data subjects.*

The controller shall implement appropriate technical and organizational measures for ensuring that, by default, only personal data that are necessary for each specific purpose of the processing are processed. That obligation applies to the amount of personal data collected, the extent of their processing, the period of their storage, and their accessibility. In particular, such measures shall ensure that, by default, personal data are not made accessible to an indefinite number of natural persons without the individual's intervention.†

An approved certification mechanism may be used as an element to demonstrate compliance with the above requirements.

---

* GDPR Article 25(1).
† GDPR Article 25(2).

	Data Protection by Design (GDPR)			
Controller Shall Take Account of	Consider	Risks	Two Stages	Implement
Taking into account	The state of the art, cost of implementation, and nature, scope, context, and purposes of processing	As well as the risks of varying likelihood and severity of rights and freedoms of natural persons posed by the processing, the controller	Shall, both at the time of the determination of the means for processing and at the time of the processing itself	Implement appropriate technical and organizational measures, including pseudonymization, designed to implement data protection principles such as data minimization, in an effective manner and to integrate the necessary safeguards into the processing in order to meet the requirements of the regulation and protect the rights of data subjects

Data Protection by Default (GDPR)

Controller	Measures	Default	Obligations
The controller shall implement	Appropriate technical and organizational measures for ensuring that	By default	Only personal data that are necessary for each specific purpose of the processing are processed
			That obligation applies to the amount of personal data collected, the extent of their processing, the period of their storage, and their accessibility
			In particular, such measures shall ensure that, by default, personal data are not made accessible to an indefinite number of natural persons without the individual's intervention

Certification mechanisms may be used in accordance with the GDPR.

☐ Sample Tools

Various tools are available to data protection officers for the implantation of DPbD. These include, for example:

- Data protection by design report (i.e., DPbD)*

- Data protection by design implementation plan (i.e., DPbD)†

- Data protection impact assessment (DPIA) handbook (i.e., data protection impact assessments)‡

- Supervisory authority technical guidance note on privacy enhancing technologies (PETs)§

- Enterprise privacy group paper on PETs

- Homeland security, biometric identification, and personal detection ethics (HIDE)

- Glossary of privacy and data protection terms

- Data protection impact assessments: International study (Loughborough University) (i.e., DPIAs)

One supervisory authority report on privacy by design (PbD) notes that

---

* *Privacy by Design*, Information Commissioner's Office (2008). At http://www.ico. gov.uk/for_organisations/data_protection/topic_guides/privacy_by_design. aspx.

† At http://www.ico.gov.uk/upload/documents/pdb_report_html/pbd_ico_imple-mentation_plan.pdf.

‡ At http://www.ico.gov.uk/for_organisations/data_protection/topic_guides/pri-vacy_impact_assessment.aspx.

§ *Privacy by Design, An Overview of Privacy Enhancing Technologies*, 26 November 2008. At http://www.ico.gov.uk/for_organisations/data_protection/topic_guides/pri-vacy_by_design.aspx.

The capacity of organisations to acquire and use our personal details has increased dramatically since our data protection laws were first passed. There is an ever increasing amount of personal information collected and held about us as we go about our daily lives... we have seen a dramatic change in the capability of organisations to exploit modern technology that uses our information to deliver services, this has not been accompanied by a similar drive to develop new effective technical and procedural privacy safeguards. We have seen how vulnerable our most personal of details can be and these should not be put at risk.*

In the same report, it is stated that

This report is the first stage in bridging the current gap in the development and adoption of privacy-friendly solutions as part of modern information systems. It aims to address the current problems related to the handling of personal information and put into place a model for privacy by design that will ensure privacy achieves the same structured and professional recognition as information security has today.†

The report describes PbD as follows:

The purpose of privacy by design is to give due consideration to privacy needs prior to the development of new initiatives – in other words, to consider the impact of a system or process on individuals' privacy and to do this throughout the systems lifecycle, thus ensuring that appropriate controls are implemented and maintained.‡

The report refers to the various life cycles that arise in an organization.§ These can be products, services, systems, and processes, as described:

For a privacy by design approach to be effective, it must take into account the full lifecycle of any system or process, from the earliest stages of the system business case, through requirements gathering and design, to delivery, testing, operations, and out to the final decommissioning of the system.

This lifetime approach ensures that privacy controls are stronger, simpler and therefore cheaper to implement, harder to by-pass, and fully embedded in the system as part of its core functionality.

However, neither current design practices in the private and public sectors, nor existing tools tend to readily support such an approach. Current

---

* *Privacy by Design,* Information Commissioner's Office (2008). At http://www.ico. gov.uk/for_organisations/data_protection/topic_guides/privacy_by_design. aspx.
† Ibid 2.
‡ Ibid 7.
§ Ibid.

privacy practices and technologies are geared towards 'spot' implementations and "spot" verifications to confirm that privacy designs and practices are correct at a given moment within a given scope of inspection.*

Recommendations

An official supervisory authority report makes a number of recommendations in relation to DPbD practice.† These are set out as follows:

Working with industry bodies to build an *executive mandate for privacy by design*, supported by sample business cases for the costs, benefits and risks associated with the processing of personal information, and promotion of executive awareness of key privacy and identity concepts so that privacy is reflected in the business cases for new systems.

Encouraging widespread use of *privacy impact assessments* [data protection impact assessments (DPIAs)] *throughout the systems lifecycle*, and ensuring that these assessments are both maintained and published where appropriate to demonstrate transparency of privacy controls.

Supporting the development of *cross-sector standards for data sharing* both within and between organisations, so that privacy needs are harmonised with the pressures on public authorities and private organisations to share personal information.

Nurturing the development of *practical privacy standards* that will help organisations to turn the legal outcomes mandated under data protection laws into consistent, provable privacy implementations.

Promoting current and future research into PETs that deliver commercial products to manage consent and revocation, privacy-friendly identification and authentication, and prove the effectiveness of privacy controls.

Establishing more rigorous compliance and enforcement mechanisms by assigning responsibility for privacy management within organisations to nominated individuals, urging organisations to demonstrate greater clarity in their personal information processing, and empowering and providing the [supervisory authority] with the ability to investigate and enforce compliance where required.

The government, key industry representatives and academics, and the [supervisory authority] are urged to consider, prioritize and set in motion plans to deliver these recommendations and hence make privacy by design a reality.‡

---

* *Privacy by Design*, Information Commissioner's Office (2008). At http://www.ico. gov.uk/for_organisations/data_protection/topic_guides/privacy_by_design. aspx, at 7–8.

† Ibid, summarized at 3 and in detail at 22–31.

‡ Ibid, note emphasis in the original.

The report highlights the need and context for DPbD in relation to the many instances of data loss. It states that

> Consumer trust in the ability of public authorities and private organisations to manage personal information is at an all-time low ebb. A stream of high-profile privacy incidents … over the past year has shaken confidence in the data sharing agenda for government with associated impacts on high-profile data management programmes, and businesses are having to work that much harder to persuade customers to release personal information to them.*

DPbD is part of the solution whereby "the evolution of a new approach to the management of personal information that ingrains privacy principles into every part of every system in every organisation."†

Organizations need to address many key privacy and data protection issues, such as

> assessing information risks from the individual's perspective; adopting transparency and data minimisation principles; exploiting opportunities for differentiation through enhanced privacy practices; and ensuring that privacy needs influence their identity management agenda (since identity technologies are invariably needed to deliver effective privacy approaches).‡

---

* *Privacy by Design*, Information Commissioner's Office (2008). At http://www.ico.gov. uk/for_organisations/data_protection/topic_guides/privacy_by_design. aspx, at 6.
† Ibid.
‡ Ibid.

CHAPTER

Security and Data Breach Tools

☐ Data Breach

Organizations will need to assess the categories of personal data that may be involved in a data breach. They also need to assess the type of organization or sector that they are involved in. These factors may dictate how the data protection regime imposes time limits for respective notification of breaches.

☐ Notification Processes

Data protection officers and organizations need to develop and update, as appropriate, breach notification procedures. There needs to be an appropriate response plan for the different types of breach incidents, supervisory authorities, other regulators (if appropriate or required), data subjects, and other organizations, whether partners, processors, outsourced security, and so on.

Contracts and agreements should also be reviewed to ensure appropriate breach, notification, and security provisions.

Controller Breach Notification to Supervisory Authority (General Data Protection Regulation [GDPR])

Controller	Time	Notify	Unless	Content
In the case of a personal data breach, the controller shall	Without undue delay and, where feasible, not later than 72 hours after having become aware of it	Notify the personal data breach to the competent supervisory authority in accordance with Article 55	Unless the personal data breach is unlikely to result in a risk to the rights and freedoms of natural persons. Where the notification to the supervisory authority is not made within 72 hours, it shall be accompanied by an explanation for the delay	The notification shall, at least, describe the nature of the personal data breach including, where possible, the categories and approximate number of data subjects and personal data records concerned; communicate the name and contact details of the data protection officer or other contact point from whom more information can be obtained; describe the likely consequences of the personal data breach; describe the measures taken or proposed by the controller to address the personal data breach including, where appropriate, measures to mitigate its possible adverse effects

Where, and insofar as, it is not possible to provide all information at the same time, the information may be provided in phases without undue further delay.

The controller shall document any personal data breaches, including the facts relating to the personal data breach, its effects, and the remedial action taken. That documentation shall enable the supervisory authority to verify compliance with this article.

Controller Breach Notification to Data Subject (GDPR)

Controller	Time	Shall describe	Carve-out
Where the personal data breach is likely to result in a high risk to the rights and freedoms of natural persons, the controller shall communicate the personal data breach to the data subject	Without undue delay	Communication to the data subject shall describe, in clear and plain language, the nature of the personal data breach and shall contain at least the information and measures referred to in points (b), (c), and (d) of Article 33(3)	The communication shall not be required if any of the following conditions are met: The controller has implemented appropriate technical and organizational protection measures, and those measures were applied to the personal data affected by the personal data breach, in particular those that render the personal data unintelligible to any person who is not authorized to access it, such as encryption; the controller has taken subsequent measures to ensure that the high risk to the rights and freedoms of data subjects referred to in paragraph 1 is no longer likely to materialize; it would involve disproportionate effort. In such cases, there shall instead be a public communication or similar measure whereby the data subjects are informed in an equally effective manner

If the controller has not already communicated the personal data breach to the data subject, the supervisory authority, having considered the likelihood of the personal data breach resulting in a high risk, may require it to do so or may decide that any of the conditions referred to in paragraph 3 are met.

Taking into account the state of the art, the costs of implementation, and the nature, scope, context, and purposes of processing, as well as the risk of varying likelihood and severity to the rights and freedoms of natural persons, the controller and the processor shall implement appropriate technical and organizational measures to ensure a level of security appropriate to the risk, including *inter alia* implementation as appropriate:

- The pseudonymization and encryption of personal data

- The ability to ensure the ongoing confidentiality, integrity, availability, and resilience of processing systems and services

- The ability to restore the availability and access to personal data in a timely manner in the event of a physical or technical incident

- A process for regularly testing, assessing, and evaluating the effectiveness of technical and organizational measures for ensuring the security of processing*

In assessing the appropriate level of security, the risks that are presented by processing shall be accounted for, particularly the risk of accidental or unlawful destruction, loss, alteration, and unauthorized disclosure of or access to personal data transmitted, stored, or otherwise processed.†

Adherence to an approved code of conduct as referred to in Article 40 or to an approved certification mechanism as referred to in Article 42 may be used as an element by which to demonstrate compliance with the requirements set out in paragraph 1 of this article.‡

The controller and processor shall take steps to ensure that any natural person acting under the authority of the controller or the processor who has access to personal data does not process the data except on instruction from the controller, unless he or she is required to do so by Union or Member State law.§

☐ Security Standards

The requirement to comply with the new General Data Protection Regulation (GDPR) regime to maintain security and to prevent and deal with data breaches increasingly directs attention to detailed standards and implementation measures such as ISO 15408, ISO 27001, ISO 27005, ISO 31000, and BS10012:2009. Note also Regulation 45/2001 and Article 22 concerning the security of processing. One example is compliance with the ISO 27001 international standard for confidentiality and security. In particular, it refers to

- Security policies

- Organizational information security

---

* GDPR Article 31(1).
† GDPR Article 31(2).
‡ GDPR Article 31(3).
§ GDPR Article 31(4).

- Human resources (HR) security issues, including employees, families, and current and previous contractors

- Asset identification and control

- Encryption

- Physical and environmental security factors

- Operational security

- Communications security

- Acquisition, development, and maintenance of systems

- Supplier relations

- Security incident management

- Security issues and business continuity

- Compliance with internal policies and external issues such as a data protection regime and other laws

Also consider ISO 31000 on international risk management standards and BS10012:2009, a standard for personal information management systems.

Organizations, including processors, must implement appropriate security measures, by considering

- Data protection impact assessments

- Anonymizing data

- Deleting after use purpose

- Confidentiality

- Integrity

- Availability

- Access controls and restrictions

- Approved codes of conduct and certification

- Separating, segregating, and securing different data sets

- Encryption

Security thus requires a "systematic and holistic approach."*

☐ Incident Response

Some of the incident response and action points include (not in order of priority):

- Incident detection and reporting

- Incident notification to the organization (e.g., notifications or demands from hackers and online postings)

- Internal notification(s)

- Team notifications

- Risk assessment

- Data protection impact assessments

- Disciplinary action

- Hacker-related action

- Supervisory authority external breach notification

- Data subject breach notification

- Customer breach notification

---

* Guglielmetti, "Security Incidents Affecting Personal Data: An 'Exploratory Travel' from Technology to Law," DPO Meeting, 8 May 2015. Also note Santiago, "Risk Management and Data Protection," DPO Meeting, The EDPS Strategy, 2015–2019, Leading by Example, 8 May 2015.

☐ Breach and Security

Data breach issues should be considered in conjunction with the various risk reduction mechanisms referred to under the new GDPR regime, such as data protection impact assessments, data protection by design and by default, mandatory breach reporting, mandatory prior consultations with the supervisory authority in the case of identified high risks, codes of conduct, and certification mechanisms.

Data Protection Impact Assessment Tools

☐ Data Protection Impact Assessment Obligation

Article 35(1) of the new General Data Protection Regulation (GDPR) states that

> Where a type of processing in particular using new technologies, and taking into account the nature, scope, context and purposes of the processing, is likely to result in a high risk to the rights and freedoms of natural persons, the controller shall, prior to the processing, carry out an assessment of the impact of the envisaged processing operations on the protection of personal data. A single assessment may address a set of similar processing operations that present similar high risks.

The controller shall seek the advice of the data protection officer, where designated, when carrying out a data protection impact assessment.

Article 33(3) states that a data protection impact assessment shall particularly be required in the case of

- A systematic and extensive evaluation of personal aspects relating to natural persons that is based on automated processing, including profiling, and on which decisions are based that produce legal effects concerning the natural person, or similarly significantly affect the natural person

- Processing on a large scale of special categories of data referred to in Article 9(1), or of personal data relating to criminal convictions and offenses referred to in Article 10

- Systematic monitoring of a publicly accessible area on a large scale

The supervisory authority shall establish and make public a list of the kind of processing operations that are subject to the requirement for a data protection impact assessment and the kind of processing operations for which no data protection impact assessment is required.

The assessment shall at least contain

- A systematic description of the envisaged processing operations and the purposes of the processing, including, where applicable, the legitimate interest pursued by the controller

- An assessment of the necessity and proportionality of the processing operations in relation to the purposes

- An assessment of the risks to the rights and freedoms of data subjects as referred to in paragraph 1

- The measures envisaged to address the risks, including safeguards, security measures, and mechanisms to ensure the protection of personal data and to demonstrate compliance with the regulation, taking into account the rights and legitimate interests of data subjects and other persons concerned

☐ Identifying When to Undertake a Data Protection Impact Assessment

Article 35(1) requires that *"the controller … shall"* carry out a data protection impact assessment once the risk criteria are triggered. It is important to note that there does not need to be a real or actual risk present, but rather that there is or may be a risk; for example, where the processing "is likely to result in a high risk to the rights and freedoms of natural persons."

It is also the case that the net is cast reasonably wide in that the assessment of likelihood of risk is considered before the processing activity occurs. If this means considering *all and/or any* likelihood of risk, it is difficult for an organization or data protection officer to decide or conclude definitively in advance that there is no risk, no possibility of risk, a likelihood of there being no risk, or a likelihood or probability that no risk will arise. In addition, the provision refers to a risk factor, not that the risk will be followed through in actuality. Again, the assessment is in advance of go-live of the particular processing activity. Taking hacking as an example, it is not that there is a probable likelihood of a hack of particular data occurring, but rather that there is, in the circumstances, a likelihood of that risk arising or "a high risk *for* the rights and freedoms of individuals."

Example of Assessment Factors for Undertaking a Data Protection Impact Assessment (GDPR)

Does the processing nature	Likely result in high risk for rights and freedoms?	IF NO: No assessment IF YES: Must undertake data protection impact assessment
Does processing scope	Likely result in high risk for rights and freedoms?	IF NO: No assessment IF YES: Must undertake data protection impact assessment
Does processing context	Likely result in high risk for rights and freedoms?	IF NO: No assessment IF YES: Must undertake data protection impact assessment
Does processing purpose	Likely result in high risk for rights and freedoms?	IF NO: No assessment IF YES: Must undertake data protection impact assessment

(Continued)

Example of Assessment Factors for Undertaking a Data Protection Impact Assessment (GDPR)

Do new technologies	Likely result in high risk for rights and freedoms?	**IF NO:** No assessment	
		IF YES: Must undertake data protection impact assessment	
Does other processing	Likely result in high risk for rights and freedoms?	**IF NO:** No assessment	
		IF YES: Must undertake data protection impact assessment	
Does combination	Likely result in high risk for rights and freedoms?	**IF NO:** No assessment	
		IF YES: Must undertake data protection impact assessment	
		Impact assessment:	Assess impact of envisaged processing on personal data
			Consider if similar processing operations present similar high risks

Example of Assessment Factors for Undertaking a Data Protection Impact Assessment (GDPR)

IF	Systematic and extensive evaluation of personal aspects relating to natural persons that is based on automated processing, including profiling, and on which decisions are based that produce legal effects or significantly affect the natural person	MUST DO a data protection impact assessment
IF	Large-scale processing of special categories of data or data relating to criminal convictions and offenses data	MUST DO a data protection impact assessment
IF	Systematic monitoring of a publicly accessible area on a large scale	MUST DO a data protection impact assessment
	Other examples	MUST DO a data protection impact assessment

The data protection officer should also consult any list or materials published by the national supervisory authorities.

Example Content of Data Protection Impact Assessment (GDPR)

Must contain *at least*

Systematic description of envisaged
  processing operations

Processing purposes

Legitimate interest of controller

Assessment of necessity of processing
  operations in relation to purposes

Assessment of proportionality of processing
  operations in relation to purposes

Assessment of risks to rights and freedoms
  as described in paragraph 1

Measures to address the risks

Safeguards	To ensure the protection of personal data
	To demonstrate compliance with GDPR
Security	To ensure the protection of personal data
	To demonstrate compliance with GDPR
Mechanisms	To ensure the protection of personal data
	To demonstrate compliance with GDPR

Taking into account the rights and
  legitimate interests of data subjects and
  other persons concerned

Other content

Additional issues include

- Seeking the views of data subjects or their representatives (where appropriate)

- Whether a data protection impact assessment has already been made as part of a general impact assessment

- Whether there is a change in the risk represented by the processing operations

☐ Key Characteristics of Data Protection Impact Assessment

Understanding the many key characteristics and related documentation of data protection impact assessments will assist the data protection officer in assessing, implementing, assisting/leading, and reviewing the data protection impact assessment, both individually and in terms of a rolling process of ongoing and future assessments. Some key characteristics of data protection impact assessments include

- Statement of problem: Is government intervention both necessary and desirable?

- Definition of alternative remedies: These include different approaches such as the use of economic incentives or voluntary approaches.

- Determination of physical effects of each alternative, including potential unintended consequences: The net should be cast wide. Generally speaking, regulations or investments in many areas of public policy can have social, environmental, and other implications that must be kept in mind.

- Estimation of benefits and costs of each alternative: Benefits should be quantified and, where possible, monetized. Costs should be true opportunity costs and not simply expenditures.

- Assessment of other economic impacts including effects on competition, effects on small firms, and international trade implications.

- Identification of winners and losers, those in the community who stand to gain and lose from each alternative and, if possible, the extent of their gains and losses.

- Communication with the interested public, including the following activities: notification of intent to regulate, request for compliance costs and other data, public disclosure of regulatory proposals and supporting analysis, and consideration of and response to public comments.

- A clear choice of the preferred alternative, plus a statement defending that choice.

- Provision of a plan for ex-post analysis of regulatory outcomes: It is important to establish a benchmark against which to measure performance. Planning is needed to ensure that procedures are in place for the collection of data to permit such benchmarking.*

Some additional characteristics might include

- An assessment that focuses on a particular initiative or project

- An assessment that is performed in depth, through the project life cycle, and involves engagement with stakeholders

- An assessment that assesses a project against the needs, expectations, and concerns of all stakeholders, including but not limited to legal requirements

- An assessment that assesses all aspects of privacy and data protection

- An assessment that adopts a multiperspective approach, taking into account the costs and benefits as perceived by all stakeholders

- An assessment that adopts a multiperspective approach, taking into account the risks as perceived by all stakeholders

---

* OECD, "Regulatory Performance: Ex Post Evaluation of Regulatory Tools and Institutions," Working Party on Regulatory Management and Reform, Draft Report by the Secretariat, OECD, Paris (2004), 7; referred to in Parker, "(Regulatory) Impact Assessment and Better Regulation," in Wright and de Hert, eds, *Privacy Impact Assessment* (Springer, 2012) 80.

- An assessment as a process used to establish the undertakings that an organization needs to give

- An assessment as a process that identifies the problems and the solutions to them

- An assessment that is conducted before and in parallel with a project and that ensures that harmful and expensive problems that an audit would later expose are involved, and that unavoidable negative impacts on privacy are minimized and harms mitigated*

☐ Key Elements of Data Protection Impact Assessment Report

Some key elements of a data protection impact assessment report include

- The scope of the data protection impact assessment undertaken

- A summary of the consultative process undertaken

- The project background paper(s) provided to those consulted (appendices)

- Analysis of the data protection issues and risks arising from the data protection impact assessment

- The business case justifying privacy intrusion and implications, with the treatment or mitigating action and the time lines for implementation

- References to relevant laws, codes, and guidelines, including internal local group policies[†]

☐ Some Key Steps and Methodologies

Some of the key steps and methodologies in a data protection impact assessment include

---

* Clarke, "PIAs in Australia: A Work-In-Progress Report," in Wright and de Hert, eds, *Privacy Impact Assessment* (Springer, 2012) 121.
† Deadman and Chandler, above, 299.

- Identifying all of the personal data related to a program or service and looking at how it will be used

- Mapping where personal data are sent after collection

- Identifying privacy and data protection risks and the level of the risks

- Finding methods to eliminate or reduce the risks*

☐ Some Data Protection Impact Assessment Issues

Organizations and data protection officers might consider some of the potential issues that may arise, such as the following:

- Preparation

- Undertaking of the data protection impact assessment

- Timing of the data protection impact assessment

- Cost and resourcing the data protection impact assessment

- Who the report is for

- Issues and problems raised

- Independence of those undertaking the data protection impact assessment

- Any constraints

- Legal professional privilege and confidentiality

- After undertaking the data protection impact assessment, the *draft* data protection impact assessment report/comments/final report

---

* Office of the Privacy Commissioner of Canada, Fact Sheet on Privacy Impact Assessment. Also note the Office of the Information and Privacy Commissioner of Alberta, "Commissioner Accepts Privacy Impact assessment for the Alberta Security Screening Directive," press release, 16 January 2003.

- Whether the data protection impact assessment is a stand-alone or ongoing assessment in a (rolling) series

☐ Regular Monitoring

Recital 97 of the GDPR states that

> Where the processing is carried out by a public authority, except for courts or independent judicial authorities when acting in their judicial capacity, where, in the private sector, processing is carried out by a controller whose core activities consist of processing operations that require regular and systematic monitoring of the data subjects on a large scale, or where the core activities of the controller or the processor consist of processing on a large scale of special categories of personal data and data relating to criminal convictions and offenses, a person with expert knowledge of data protection law and practices should assist the controller or processor to monitor internal compliance with this Regulation. In the private sector, the core activities of a controller relate to its primary activities and do not relate to the processing of personal data as ancillary activities. The necessary level of expert knowledge should be determined in particular according to the data processing operations carried out and the protection required for the personal data processed by the controller or the processor. Such data protection officers, whether or not they are an employee of the controller, should be in a position to perform their duties and tasks in an independent manner.

Prior Consultation

Article 36 relates to prior consultation and states that the controller shall consult the supervisory authority prior to processing, where a data protection impact assessment indicates that the processing would result in a high risk in the absence of measures taken by the controller to mitigate the risk.

Prior Consultation Obligation (General Data Protection Regulation [GDPR])

The controller shall consult the supervisory authority	Prior to processing	Where a data protection impact assessment indicates that the processing would result in a high risk	In the absence of measures taken by the controller to mitigate the risk.

Prior Consultation Process (GDPR)

| The controller shall provide the supervisory authority with | where applicable, the respective responsibilities of the controller, joint controllers, and processors involved in the processing, in particular for processing within a group of undertakings; the purposes and means of the intended processing; the measures and safeguards provided to protect the rights and freedoms of data subjects pursuant to the regulation; where applicable, the contact details of the data protection officer; the data protection impact assessment provided for in Article 35; and any other information requested by the supervisory authority | Where the supervisory authority is of the opinion that the intended processing would infringe the regulation, in particular where the controller has insufficiently identified or mitigated the risk, the supervisory authority shall, within a period of up to 8 weeks of receipt of the request for consultation | Provide written advice to the controller and, where applicable, to the processor, and may use any of its powers. That period may be extended by 6 weeks, taking into account the complexity of the intended processing. The supervisory authority shall inform the controller and, where applicable, the processor, of any such extension within 1 month of receipt of the request for consultation, together with the reasons for the delay. Those periods may be suspended until the supervisory authority has obtained the information it has requested for the purposes of the consultation |

It remains to be seen what the meaning, standard, quality, and percentage of risk mitigation to likelihood of risk will be. If, for example, there are 10 potential risk mitigation measures available but the controller only takes 1 of these, it might be considered or argued that there is not sufficient or meaningful risk mitigation. If the one mitigation measure taken is the least meaningful of all the measures available, a likelihood of risk remains (or, potentially, remains relatively the same). Yet, a controller may argue that it has avoided the need to notify the supervisory authority by way of prior consultation. Controllers and data protection officers should be cautious in embarking upon a policy of aggressive compliance avoidance or compliance minimization. Such an approach could be counterproductive.

Data Breach

☐ Data Breaches

The issue of data breach has been increasing in importance for a number of years. Giving consideration to data breach and data breach preparedness will be one of the more significant tasks for the data protection officer. It will be considered both individually and also in conjunction with other stakeholders, from senior management to information technology (IT), security, incident response teams, and so on.

The data protection regime increasingly emphasizes preventative measures. While the data protection officer will be concerned with dealing with (and preparing to deal with) data breach incidents, a significant effort will be devoted to reducing and even eliminating as many data breach opportunities as possible.

Some of these pre-problem activities will include risk identification, risk minimization, risk elimination, security, security measures (both technical and nontechnical), reviews and observation, industry intelligence, and ongoing training. They will also involve some of the more explicit provisions addressed in the new data protection regime such as risk assessments, codes, certificates, data protection by design and by default, impact assessments, and consultations.

Significant technical resources, software, and related systems are provided by a number of third-party security and related vendors, which will be of assistance to organizations. Some of these resources may be directly applicable to the IT department but will also be relevant to the data protection officer.

The data protection officer will also be aware that the particular data that may be the target of a data breach are no longer limited to outward-facing personal data, but may also include inward-facing personal data. In the Sony "Interview" example, many personal e-mails, employee names, and other employee details were copies and were made public online. In the United States, many federal employees (some in the security sectors) were also the victims of having their personal details taken when official organizations were the subject of data breach.

One issue for data protection officers to also consider in relation to technical software and solutions is the balance between employee rights and the overly intrusive monitoring of employees. Just because monitoring is possible does not automatically mean that all such monitoring capabilities would be lawful under the data protection regime. Being as prepared as possible is highly recommended. Once a breach event occurs, it will be difficult to consider and deal with all issues if there is not a planned response plan in existence to be followed or to guide the organization.

Some of the particular phases and steps for the data protection officer to consider include

- Assessing breach risks

- Eliminating particular breach risks

- Reducing the potential of other breach risks

- Preparing for a breach incident

- Looking for the signals of a breach incident

- Discovering the breach

- Investigating the breach

- Assessing the breach

- Deciding the course of action

- Responding and implementing the action plan

- Resolving the breach

- Once a breach arises, contacting the internal response team members and/or teams and assembling them together

- Notifying the police (as applicable)

- Engaging third parties, whether as necessary or as part of the planned breach response plan, including forensic, data breach resolution, legal, public relations (PR) firm, technology, disaster recovery, and so on

- Notification stage, whereby the data breach (e.g., identity theft) is notified to the supervisory authority and affected data subjects are notified, including implementing the protection measures that the organization has taken for those affected and any steps that the organization recommends that those affected also take

- PR and public announcements

- Possibly, a dedicated breach notification webpage (or website)

- Call, e-mail, or postal notification of contacts (as appropriate)

- Responding to inquiries

- Resolution stage

- Resuming normal business, particularly where business or certain business activities were suspended

☐ Be Prepared

Being aware of the issues and preparing in advance is important, necessary, and brings many advantages. For example, preparing in advance

- Ensures that organizations can reduce the cost of the data breach incident

- Ensures the organization saves time and can deal with the issue immediately if the breach incident response plan is in place

- Helps in ensuring that defenses and responses are ready and in place

- Ensures that the main steps during the critical first 24 hours are already planned and available

- Ensures that those whom the organization needs to notify are pre-planned, from employees, officers, external agents and professionals, police and regulators, and of course customers

☐ Why Being Prepared and Aware Is Important

It is estimated that an average data breach incident in the United States can cost an organization 5.4 million dollars. Obviously, it can cost significantly more. In addition, such a breach can involve the personal data of millions of the organization's customers.

Data breach incidents can occur in any size of organization. Acting swiftly ensures that the risks can be minimized and responded to as quickly as possible. It is critical, therefore, to incorporate an appropriate security breach incident preparedness reaction plan.

Trying to identify all of the issues, involve the appropriate internal and external personnel required, and deal with the issue in a timely and appropriate manner will be almost impossible if the organization has not prepared for the occurrence of such an event and can follow a preplanned and documented procedure for effectively dealing with the issue.

This should involve senior management as well as being a recurring issue for review and update as appropriate.

☐ Team

The team will react to the issue and organize the responses according to the plan, ensuring others within the organization do likewise. The appropriate resources will be allocated to the issue and responses monitored in accordance with the plan.

☐ Lead Coordinator

The lead coordinator needs to be selected or appointed. He or she will usually be from an internal IT, legal, or privacy function and will

- Manage and coordinate the organization's overarching response effort and team activities.

- Act between senior management and individual team members and subgroups on advancing and reporting progress and issues.

- Identify the most important tasks and time critical issues, and document ongoing responses until conclusion.

- Deal with and monitor budget issues as regards the security breach response effort.

- Summarize the steps needed to assess the breach and deal with the particular breach.

- Ensure that all appropriate contact lists and details are kept up to date and distributed to those who need to have them.

- After the response and risk has dissipated, review the response, issues, and actions in order to better prepare for future potential incidents.

☐ Reporting

There should be an appropriate and communicated internal reporting structure in place so that directors and those on the response team are constantly and appropriately kept updated on events during the incident response cycle.

☐ Board Level Responsibility

As with data protection compliance and security issues, the issue of preparing, allocating, and resourcing the incident plan and reaction effort needs appropriate buy in and responsibility from an executive at board level.

☐ IT/IT Security

The IT and IT security teams and leads need to be involved, particularly in identifying breaches, being alert to breaches, and doing what may be needed to prevent or halt a breach once identified. They may also be involved in training other team members in issues such as safety; securing the organization's offices, equipment; evidence; preservation engaging and assisting external forensics; legal and PR expertise; and so on.

☐ Legal and Privacy

The organization should rely on internal and external legal, privacy, and data protection regulatory compliance input to the response to the breach incident and its implications. This can also help to minimize the risk of potential fines, litigation, and awards.

Factors to consider may include

- Whether to notify the affected persons, broadcasters and press, law enforcement, official agencies, or other third parties (e.g., banks and card issuers)

- Establishing relationships with expert external lawyers, early and prior to an incident arising and not after it happens

- Similarly so with external PR personnel

- Staying constantly up to date with national, European, and appropriate foreign data breach rules and regulations, and also industry-specific rules and standards

☐ Public Relations

Certain sizes of organizations and certain industry sectors may have specific requirements to notify the individuals affected. In some circumstances, the media may also need to be notified. Therefore, the response team and external and internal PR will need to consider doing the following:

- Choose the best notification routes and methods in advance of any issue arising.

- Deal with, warn, and prepare for information leaks, including monitoring such issues as they arise and tracing their source.

- Monitor and track media coverage.

- Monitor and track online media coverage.

- Monitor and track media coverage of press statements, releases, and comments.

☐ Customer Relations

Given that customers are potentially affected by a security breach incident, queries may arise. Therefore, an appropriate representative should be appointed to deal with these, either from within the team or liaising with the team.

Simulations and training in advance of any incident arising will apprise the representative of the issues that may be involved and how these may differ from other issues that they may have to deal with.

A plan should be put in place to have a telephone number or freephone number dedicated and available to customer queries if a breach incident occurs. It should be considered whether internal and/or external resources will be needed.

☐ Employees and Human Resources

Employees will also potentially be affected by a security breach incident and may have queries. Therefore, an appropriate HR representative should be appointed to deal with these, either from within the team or liaising with the team.

Simulations and training in advance of any incident arising will apprise the representative of the issues that may be involved and how these may differ from other issues that they may have to deal with. It should be considered whether internal and/or external resources will be needed.

☐ Police and Law Enforcement

The more severe the security breach, and whether data and confidential information have been accessed and taken, the more likely that the appropriate police and law enforcement will be notified and involved.

It is best to have all of the appropriate contact details in advance so that they are available and ready to hand if and when needed.

Identify which local and international police and law enforcement agencies could potentially be relevant, make appropriate contact, and document the appropriate contact details.

If police and law enforcement must be notified and involved, everyone on the team should be aware of this and of the appropriate legislation, regulations, and directives as well as the requirements that may be recommended to be followed by the police and law enforcement personnel, including requirements in terms of evidence, electronic evidence, preservation, and nondestruction or spoliation of such evidence.

☐ Providers of Breach Resolution Services

Consider appropriate vendors, rates, and so on in advance. This should be done well in advance of any potential breach issue arising to ensure availability, contacts, plans, and procedures are in place. It may be appropriate to have a response manager assigned and known in advance. He or she may also offer various escalations, tracking, reporting, protection, identifying of issues, responses, and so on.

☐ Training and Preparing for Breach Incidents

The organization should have organization-wide awareness procedures in place for its employees. Agents and contractors should also be made aware of security issues. Different units within the organization should have their own specific, tailored awareness and training policies.

Ideally, employees should be aware of security issues in their daily routines.

Protection measures should be in place and be appropriately reviewed and updated. This includes, for example, procedures, encryption, security software, and so on.

Rules, policies, and controls should be implemented to make sure that the risk of devices being brought onto the organization's premises and connecting to the organization's devices and equipment are limited. Access, if permitted, should be on a required basis only.

Employees should be aware of how to report suspicions and queries.

Training and updates for employees should be regularly scheduled. An organization's security is as strong as the weakest link. Therefore, employees are integral to ensuring and maintaining security.

The appropriate contacts within the organization should be regularly communicated to all employees, along with timely updates on risk topics.

Preparation and practice exercises should be organized regularly.

One of the key factors is to act quickly once an incident issue arises. Acting quickly helps to maintain security, preservation of assets and evidence, brand protection, and dealing with and resolving the security breach incident. All information regarding the incident should be recorded and documented, and the necessary reports should be made to the appropriate internal contact points, teams, and external assets such as legal and PR, as well as ensuring police and law enforcement engagement.

CHAPTER

Sample Data Protection
Officer Datasets

☐ Sample Data Protection Officer Datasets

The Data Protection Officer will variously consider the following potential types of documentation in terms of compliance, awareness building, training, and so on, namely:

- Policies

- Procedures

- Governance procedures

- Intranet

- Internet

- Charts and flows within the organization

- Role description within the organization

- Terms of reference and definitions

- Meeting notes

- Seminar notes and records

- Internal reports

- External reports

- Audits

- Audit reports

- Training presentations

- E-learning

- Electronic resources

- Training records

- Updating of training materials and documentation

- Updating records

- Access requests

- Data collection forms

- Fair processing notices

- Consent forms and notices

- Record management system

- Record management team, records, and procedures

- Information asset register

- Retention period classification

- Retention schedules and records

- Deletion, erasure, and destruction schedules

- Security standards, policies, and records

- Processor and outsourced security obligations and standards

- Incident logs and reports

- Contracts, terms, and clauses relating to security issues

- Off-site employee working issues, risks assessment and security protocols, and additional policies

- Data registers

- Electronic equipment registers

- Recording of structures, responsibilities, reporting, and contacts

- Key registers

- Audit reports

- Risk reports

- Testing reports

- Privacy by design and by default reports

- Consultation records and reports

- Data protection impact assessment reports

- Other audit reports

- Templates

- Data subject request records

- Data subject access request records

- Training materials and documentation

- Data protection performance reports and assessments

- Meeting minutes

- Records of responses to requests

- Records of raising data protection and risk issues

- Records of ongoing training throughout the year

- Agreements regarding transfers and sharing of data

- Rules for sharing and transfers

- System reviews

- Roles and responsibilities regarding data processors and outsourcing

- Data protection impact assessment templates

- Data protection by design and by default templates

- Employment descriptions

- Employment contracts

- Employment policies

- Team contacts, documentation, and procedures in relation to security breach incidents

- Rules, processes, procedures, and reporting templates in relation to data breach incidents

Model Tips and Guidelines
for the Role and Tasks

☐ Model Tips and Guidelines

Set out below are some suggested tips and guidelines that can be considered by Data Protection Officers and organizations:

- Detail an action plan for the *new* Data Protection Officer appointed to this new role.

- Detail an action plan for the *exiting* Data Protection Officer carrying over into the newly created, expanded, and mandated role of Data Protection Officer.

- Establish a period of a specific number of days as a Data Protection Officer action plan road map for the particular organization.

- Establish a clear, actionable, date-specific data protection road map for the organization.

- The road map (and ongoing compliance) will be particular to the organization, the business sector, the size of the organization, and the maturity of the organization.

- Take into account not only data protection compliance issues but also the security, operational, and personnel aspects of the challenges.

- Assess readiness, compliance, procedures, need for implementing and updating, training needs, consideration of specific issues, and challenges to the organization.

- Consider the role of the Data Protection Officer and the skills, knowledge, and experience expected.

- Examine the new data protection regime and its implications for the organization, including.

- Review the new and expanded obligations.

- Review the new and expanded rights of individual data subjects.

- Review the key features and responsibilities of the new Data Protection Officer role.

- Review the data protection impact assessments.

- Create and enforce data protection policies.

- Train staff and manage data protection teams.

- Data breach reporting processes and mitigation.

- Technological, legal, and compliance expertise required (both internal and external).

- Understand the importance of data protection law under the new data protection regime.

- Review the expanded role of the data protection supervisory authority.

- Understand the new role, functions, and powers of the supervisory authority.

- Review recent court decisions and their applicability to the organization.

- Understand and design the focused provision of information to the public, customer, and users.

- Review the new essential law, rules, and guidelines.

- Review how data protection regime applies to the organization.

- Review the key obligations imposed on data controllers in the public service (as applicable).

- Review what can and cannot be done with information under the organization's control.

- Review how data protection rules have been applied in practice in relevant cases.

- Review the requirements (and obligations) for sending personal data off site.

- Review the requirements (and obligations) for outsourcing personal data.

- Review the requirements and obligations for personal data management, life cycle, and destruction or deletion.

- Understand the origins of data protection law in the EU (and comparison and localization issues).

- Review the new expanded data protection principles.

- Review the new expanded lawful processing conditions and prior information disclosure.

- Review the cross-border data transfer regime.

- Review EU–US Privacy Shield issues.

- Review strengthened and new data subject rights.

- Review new issues for data subject access requests.

- Review information security issues and obligations.

- Implement a policy of risk identification and risk minimization.

- Review the new regime for data breach and notification of data breach obligations.

- Review electronic marketing and cookies issues.

- Develop good policies for handling personal data that are in compliance with the new data protection regime and are suitable to the organization's needs.

- Communicate internal data protection policies and processes to employees, customers, and members.

- Handle personal data-related queries or complaints.

- Alert the organization to any risks that might arise with regard to personal data.

- Liaise with the supervisory authority on data protection matters, if and when necessary.

- Map out the organization's personal data inventory.

- Review the organization's data management framework and processes.

- Align these with the new data protection regime.

- For example, determine how, when, and where the organization collects personal data and the purposes for the data collection, and ensure that consent has been obtained for the collection, use, and disclosure of the data.

- Develop policies to handle personal data in electronic or nonelectronic forms.

- Review the organization's personal data inventory to determine who has access to the personal data, how they are stored, and how long the personal data are kept for. Keep in mind the nine main obligations when doing so, specifically, the consent, purpose limitation, notification, access, rectification, accuracy, protection, retention limitation, transfer limitation, and openness and transparency obligations.

- For example, the consent obligation requires organizations to obtain an individual's consent before the collection, use, or disclosure of his/her personal data, unless an exception applies; while the notification obligation requires organizations to notify individuals of the purposes the personal data are being collected, used, or disclosed for.

- Be mindful not to over-collect personal data.

- Conduct a risk assessment exercise to flag any potential data protection risks and put in place data protection policies to mitigate those risks.

- Review data protection risks within the organization and come up with mitigating measures to address these issues.

- For example, the organization may wish to consider carrying out regular internal audits to ensure that its processes adhere to the new data protection regime.

- Where a breach occurs, the organization should also have processes and measures in place to respond to such situations.

- Keep employees informed of internal personal data protection processes and policies.

- Conduct a briefing to inform employees of the obligations under the new data protection regime.

- Ensure that employees are aware of any new developments as well as any existing laws and contracts that may affect the personal data under the organization's care.

- Employees should be aware of the internal policies and processes that the organization has put in place for the handling of personal data.

- Develop processes for handling queries or complaints from the public.

- Under the data access and rectification obligation, a member of the public may request access to their personal data in an organization's possession, or enquire about the ways that their personal data have been used over the past year.

- The organization should establish a formal procedure to handle such requests, such as identifying the person who is going to address the requests, the channel through which these requests will be addressed, and whether an administrative fee (if nationally applicable) should be imposed for such requests.

- The organization should develop a process to receive, investigate, and respond to complaints from the public, and so on.

- The data protection regime sets out an obligation for the business contact information (BCI) for the Data Protection Officer to be made available to the public.

- This person, or a team of persons, should be able to answer personal data-related queries and complaints on behalf of the organization.

- Educate the organization's customers on what the data protection regime means to them and how the organization will safeguard their personal data.

- Organizations should continually review their policies and maintain good data management practices to build trust with their customers in the long term.

- Advise senior management that data protection is no longer just a compliance or security issue.

- Ensure that senior management understands that it has become a strategic topic at boardroom level since significant changes to EU legislation have come into effect.

- Understand the applicable data protection legal framework as well as the interaction with different supervisory authorities.

- Analyze the potential impact of data protection requirements on the organization.

- Apply the legal theory in practice via a scenario-based, interactive approach.

- Understand what the main (current and upcoming) data protection obligations are, what the law requires, and how it is being enforced and applied in practice.

- Consider how a Data Protection Officer interacts with the rest of the organization.

- Consider how to "sell" data protection within the organization to senior management, employees, managers, and departments.

- Understand and connect the dots between the technical/operational and the people/management as well as the compliance side of data protection (e.g., security, information technology (IT) and technology, customer issues, employee issues, employee monitoring issues, etc.).

- Consider what you should know when engaging with IT, legal and compliance, IT security, sales and marketing, and human resources (HR) colleagues, and even with the board.

- Consider how to set up a realistic and manageable risk-based governance structure.

- Consider how to choose and start implementing a suitable (auditable) data protection program methodology for the organization.

- Consider how to effectively set up and monitor data protection compliance using tools such as data protection impact assessment, data mapping analysis, establishing an effective accountability framework, preparing for a data protection audit from a data protection supervisory authority, and so on.

- Plan to efficiently manage and achieve data protection compliance in a phased, structured, long-term manner.

- Develop a risk-based data protection management program.

- Develop actions in each phase of the program that will enhance effective data protection information gathering as well as its compliance with monitoring in practice.

- Develop skills and techniques that will ensure the ability to perform better in this complex and demanding role.

- Develop and promote the benefits of data protection, competitive advantage, and data protection return on investment (DP-ROI).

- Ensure an understanding of what the current challenges and opportunities are in the field of data protection.

- Consider, in advance, issues of (external or internal) audit and record scrutiny.

- Monitor the activities of all data users within the corporate group (e.g., HR, sales, marketing, and procurement functions).

- Liaise with relevant departments in respect to changes to processing activities, such as HR in relation to employees leaving, interviews and recruitment, new employees, and subcontractors.

- Provide advice to the organization, board, and employees on compliance.

- Manage data processors on behalf of the company.

- Monitor any outsourcing of data processing activities to third-party processors.

- Ensure third-party data processors enter into suitable contracts to ensure compliance with data protection regime.

- Define information security and data handling practices to be observed by third-party data processors.

- Raise awareness.

- Monitor implementation and applicability of the policies.

- Monitor implementation and applicability of the General Data Protection Regulation (GDPR).

- Ensure mandatory documentation is maintained.

- Monitor the documentation, notification, and communication of data breaches.

- Monitor data protection impact assessments and prior consultations.

- Monitor responses to the data protection supervisory authorities.

- Serve as the contact point for the data protection supervisory authorities.

- Inform employee representatives on employee data processing.

- Verify compliance with the GDPR.

- The Data Protection Officer will be a protected and ring-fenced employee.

- Constantly review future trends, issues, and problems, and consider pre-problem-solving solutions.

The above will assist, although particular organizations, and indeed particular sectors, will obviously require additional, nuanced solutions.

☐ Data Protection Officers: Preparing for the New GDPR Legal Regime

- Consider current reporting channels and any required amendments.

- Consider any amendments to contracts of employment.

- Consider changes required by and necessary to the current processes and procedures of the organization.

- Spread awareness and acceptance of the new data protection regime throughout the organization.

- Consider inward-facing data protection issues, employees, HR, and outward-facing issues affecting customers and users.

- Identify and consider the data held by the organization.

- Communicate the updated data protection policies and related information as appropriate within the organization, and to customers and users.

- Review the rights regime under the new GDPR and appropriate changes that are necessitated.

- Review current access requests and consider any amendments required to the process as well as the timeframe.

- Consider future deletion, takedown, forgetting, and erasure issues and requests.

- Review the personal data collected and aggregated, and the legal basis for processing such data.

- Issues of consent and recordal need to be reviewed in detail in light of the new data protection regime.

- Children are expressly referred to in the new data protection regime, and the organization needs to consider if, how, and why it may seek to collect the personal data of children.

- Data breach incidents are increasingly problematic and some of the considerations for dealing with the same are now encompassed in the new GDPR, including preparedness, risk, and reaction issues.

- Data protection by design and by default and data protection impact assessments need to be embraced within the organization and will need to have appropriate information disseminated as a result.

- Transfer and international issues will be important for certain organization and, when personal data are involved, particular additional considerations apply under the new data protection regime (in addition to issues such as the new EU–US Privacy Shield).

☐ New Data Protection Officers

- New Data Protection Officers may also wish to also consider the following.

- Ensure his or her contract is compliant with the new data protection regime.

- Ensure that he or she is reporting to the appropriate level of management in accordance with his or her duties, tasks, and function and in accordance with the new data protection regime.

- List or map out all departments within the organization.

- Identify the head or contact point within each department.

- Meet the head or contact point of each department.

- Pay particular attention to certain departments over others when they interact with personal data and data protection issues more than others.

- Identify and map the categories of personal data collected, used, and stored by the organization, by which departments and for what purposes, and where they are stored.

- Review current procedures and policies.

- Consider required amendments and updates.

- Review current access requests and other requests.

- Review data deletion policies and consider appropriateness and updating.

- Consider current issues and queries from other departments.

APPENDIX

☐ Data Protection Supervisory Authorities (EU)

Austria
Österreichische Datenschutzbehörde
Website: http://www.dsb.gv.at/

Belgium
Commission de la Protection de la Vie Privée
Website: http://www.privacycommission.be/

Bulgaria
Commission for Personal Data Protection
Website: http://www.cpdp.bg/

Croatia
Croatian Personal Data Protection Agency
Website: http://www.azop.hr/

Cyprus
Commissioner for Personal Data Protection
Website: http://www.dataprotection.gov.cy/

Czech Republic
The Office for Personal Data Protection
Website: http://www.uoou.cz/

Denmark
Datatilsynet
Website: http://www.datatilsynet.dk/

Estonia
Estonian Data Protection Inspectorate (Andmekaitse Inspektsioon)
Website: http://www.aki.ee/en

Finland
Office of the Data Protection Ombudsman
Website: http://www.tietosuoja.fi/en/

France
Commission Nationale de l'Informatique et des Libertés (CNIL)
Website: http://www.cnil.fr/

Germany
Der Bundesbeauftragte für den Datenschutz und die Informationsfreiheit
Website: http://www.bfdi.bund.de/

Greece
Hellenic Data Protection Authority
Website: http://www.dpa.gr/

Hungary
Data Protection Commissioner of Hungary
Website: http://www.naih.hu/

Ireland
Data Protection Commissioner
Website: http://www.dataprotection.ie/

Italy
Garante per la Protezione dei Dati Personali
Website: http://www.garanteprivacy.it/

Latvia Data Protection Supervisory Authority
Website: http://www.dvi.gov.lv/

Lithuania
State Data Protection
Website: http://www.ada.lt/

Luxembourg
Commission Nationale pour la Protection des Données
Website: http://www.cnpd.lu/

Malta
Office of the Data Protection Commissioner
Website: http://www.dataprotection.gov.mt/

The Netherlands
Autoriteit Persoonsgegevens
Website: https://autoriteitpersoonsgegevens.nl/nl

Poland
The Bureau of the Inspector General for the Protection of Personal Data
(GIODA)
Website: http://www.giodo.gov.pl/

Portugal
Comissão Nacional de Protecção de Dados (CNPD)
Website: http://www.cnpd.pt/

Romania
The National Supervisory Authority for Personal Data Processing
Website: http://www.dataprotection.ro/

Slovakia
Office for Personal Data Protection of the Slovak Republic
Website: http://www.dataprotection.gov.sk/

Slovenia
Information Commissioner
Website: http://www.ic-rs.si/

Spain
Agencia de Protección de Datos
Website: https://www.agpd.es/

Sweden
Datainspektionen
Website: http://www.datainspektionen.se/

United Kingdom
Information Commissioner's Office
Website: https://ico.org.uk

European Data Protection Supervisor
European Data Protection Supervisor
Website: http://www.edps.europa.eu/EDPSWEB/

☐ Data Protection Supervisory Authority (European Free Trade Area [EFTA])

Iceland
Icelandic Data Protection Agency
Website: http://www.personuvernd.is/

Liechtenstein
Data Protection Office
Website: http://www.llv.li/#/1758/datenschutzstelle

Norway
Datatilsynet
Website: https://www.datatilsynet.no/

Switzerland
Data Protection and Information Commissioner of Switzerland
Website: http://www.edoeb.admin.ch/

☐ Data Protection Supervisory Authority (EU Candidate Countries)

Former Yugoslav Republic of Macedonia
Directorate for Personal Data Protection
Website: http://www.privacy.mk/en

Montenegro
Agencija za Zaštitu Ličnih Podataka

Serbia
Poverenik za informacije od javnog značaja i zaštitu podataka o ličnosti
Website: www.poverenik.rs

☐ Data Protection Supervisory Authorities (Outside the EU)

Australia
Privacy Commissioner
Website: https://www.oaic.gov.au/

Canada
Privacy Commissioner of Canada
Website: https://www.priv.gc.ca/

Guernsey
Data Protection Commissioner
Website: http://www.gov.gg/ccm/navigation/home-department/data-protection-commissioner/

Hong Kong
Privacy Commissioner for Personal Data

Isle of Man
Information Commissioner

Israel
Israeli Law, Information, and Technology Authority (ILITA)
Website: http://www.justice.gov.il/en/pages/default.aspx

Japan
Government Information Protection Office
Website: http://www.soumu.go.jp/english/index.html

Jersey
Office of the Data Protection Commissioner
Website: https://dataci.je/

New Zealand
Privacy Commissioner
Website: https://www.privacy.org.nz/

South Korea
Personal Data Protection Center
Website: http://www.kisa.or.kr/english/

Taiwan
Bureau of Legal Affairs
Website: http://www.moj.gov.tw/mp095.html

Thailand
Official Information Commission's Office
Website: www.oic.thaigov.go.th/content_eng/default_eng.asp

United States
Federal Trade Commission
Website: https://www.ftc.gov/

☐ Data Protection Officer Associations

European Privacy Association

National Association of Data Protection and Freedom of Information Officers (NADPO) (UK)
Website: http://www.nadpo.co.uk/

Data Protection Forum (UK)
Website: www.dpforum.org.uk

Association of Data Protection Officers (Ireland)
Website: www.dpo.ie

Association of Compliance Officers in Ireland (Ireland)

German Association for Data Protection and Data Security (GDD)
Website: https://www.gdd.de/international/english

DPO Network Europe
Website: http://www.dponetwork.eu/

International Association of Privacy Professionals (IAPP)
Website: www.iapp.org

☐ Reference Links

EU Commission
Website: http://ec.europa.eu/justice/data-protection/index_en.htm

Working Party 29
Website: http://ec.europa.eu/justice/policies/privacy/working group/index_en.htm
This is being replaced by the European Data Protection Board.

Court of Justice
Website: http://europa.eu/about-eu/institutions-bodies/court-justice/index_en.htm

Court of Justice cases*
Website: http://curia.europa.eu/juris/recherche.jsf?language=en

ECHR
Website: http://www.echr.coe.int/ECHR/Homepage_En/

Irish Computer Society
Website: www.ics.ie

Irish Internet Association
Website: www.iia.ie

Society of Computers and Law
Website: www.scl.org

☐ Legislation Links

Data Protection Directive 1995:
http://eur-lex.europa.eu/LexUriServ/LexUriServ.do?uri=CELEX:31995
L0046:en:HTML

New General Data Protection Regulation
http://ec.europa.eu/justice/data-protection/reform/files/regulation_oj_
en.pdf

Proposed Data Protection Directive:
http://ec.europa.eu/home-affairs/doc_centre/police/docs/com_2012_
10_en.pdf

Proposed Data Protection Network and Information Security Directive:
http://ec.europa.eu/dgs/home-affairs/what-is-new/news/news/2013/
docs/1_directive_20130207_en.pdf

---

* Tzanou, "Balancing Fundamental Rights, United in Diversity? Some Reflections on
the Recent Case Law of the European Court of Justice on Data Protection," *CYELP*
(2010)(6) 53.

☐ European/International Legislation

Aarhus Convention on Access to Information, Public Participation in Decision-making, and Access to Justice in Environmental Matters 1998

Charter of Fundamental Rights of the European Union

CIS Convention on the Use of Information Technology for Customs Purposes 1995

Commission Decision 2004/91 of December 7, 2004, amending Decision 2001/497 as regards the introduction of an alternative set of standard clauses for transfer of personal data to third counties

Commission Decision 2004/535 on the adequate protection of personal data contained in PNRs of air passengers transferred to the United States Bureau of Customs and Border Protection

Convention for the Processing of Individuals with regard to the Automatic Processing of Personal Data 1981

Convention on Mutual Assistance Between Customs Administrations 1967

Convention on Mutual Assistance in Criminal Matters 2000

Council of Europe Convention 1981

Council Decision 2004/496 on the agreement between the European Community and the United States on the processing and transfer of passenger name record (PNR) data by air carriers to the US Department of Homeland Security, Bureau of Customs, and Border Protection

Council Directive 73/148 (Council Directive 73/148/EEC of 21 May 1973 on the abolition of restrictions on movement and residence within the Community for nationals of Member States with regard to establishment and the provision of services)

Council Directive 89/552 (Council Directive 89/552/EEC of 3 October 1989 on the coordination of certain provisions laid down by law, regulation, or administrative Action in Member States concerning the pursuit of television broadcasting activities)

Council Directive 95/46 (Directive 95/46/EC of the European Parliament and of the Council of 24 October 1995 on the protection of individuals with regard to the processing of personal data and on the free movement of such data) (DPD95)

Council Directive 1997/7/EC (Directive 97/7/EC of the European Parliament and of the Council of 20 May 1997 on the protection of consumers in respect of distance contracts—Statement by the Council and the Parliament re: Article 6[1]—Statement by the Commission re: Article 3[1], first indent) (Distance Selling Directive)

Council Directive 97/66 (Directive 97/66/EC of the European Parliament and of the Council of 15 December 1997 concerning the processing of personal data and the protection of privacy in the telecommunications sector) (Telecoms Data Protection Directive)

Council Directive 98/34 (Directive 98/34/EC of the European Parliament and of the Council of 22 June 1998 laying down a procedure for the provision of information in the field of technical standards and regulations and of rules on information society services)

Council Directive 98/48 (Directive 98/48/EC of the European Parliament and of the Council of 20 July 1998 amending Directive 98/34/EC laying down a procedure for the provision of information in the field of technical standards and regulations)

Council Directive 99/5 (Directive 1999/5/EC of the European Parliament and of the Council of 9 March 1999 on radio equipment and telecommunications terminal equipment and the mutual recognition of their conformity)

Council Directive 2000/31 (Directive 2000/31/EC of the European Parliament and of the Council of 8 June 2000 on certain legal aspects of information society services, in particular electronic commerce, in the internal market ("Directive on electronic commerce") (eCommerce Directive)

Council Directive 2002/21 Directive 2002/21/EC of the European Parliament and of the Council of 7 March 2002 on a common regulatory framework for electronic communications networks and services (Framework Directive)

Council Directive 2002/22 (Directive 2002/22/EC of the European Parliament and of the Council of 7 March 2002 on universal service and users' rights relating to electronic communications networks and services) (Universal Service Directive)

Council Directive 2002/58 (Directive 2002/58/EC of the European Parliament and of the Council of 12 July 2002 concerning the processing of personal data and the protection of privacy in the electronic communications sector [Directive on privacy and electronic communications]) (ePrivacy Directive)

Council Directive 2003/98 (Directive 2003/98/EC of the European Parliament and of the Council of 17 November 2003 on the reuse of public sector information)

Council Directive 2009/136/EC (Directive 2009/136/EC of the European Parliament and of the Council of 25 November 2009 amending Directive 2002/22/EC on universal service and users' rights relating to electronic communications networks and services; Directive 2002/58/EC concerning the processing of personal data and the protection of privacy in the electronic communications sector; and Regulation [EC] No. 2006/2004 on cooperation between national authorities responsible for the enforcement of consumer protection laws)

Council Regulation (EC) 2299/89 (Council Regulation [EEC] No. 2299/89 of 24 July 1989 on a code of conduct for computerized reservation systems)

Council Regulation 1035/97 (Council Regulation [EC] No. 1035/97 of 2 June 1997 establishing a European monitoring center on racism and xenophobia)

Council Regulation 2725/2000 (Council Regulation [EC] No. 2725/2000 of 11 December 2000 concerning the establishment of "Eurodac" for the comparison of fingerprints for the effective application of the Dublin Convention)

Council Regulation 2424/2001 (Council Regulation [EC] No. 2424/2001 of 6 December 2001 on the development of the second generation Schengen information system [SIS II])

Council Regulation 2580/2001 (Council Regulation [EC] No. 2580/2001 of 27 December 2001 on specific restrictive measures directed against certain persons and entities with a view to combating terrorism)

Council Regulation 45/2001 (Regulation [EC] 45/2001 of the European Parliament and of the Council of 18 December 2000 on the protection of individuals with regard to the processing of personal data by the Community institutions and bodies and on the free movement of such data)

Council Regulation 2252/2004 (Council Regulation [EC] No. 2252/2004 of 13 December 2004 on standards for security features and biometrics in passports and travel documents issued by Member States)

Council Regulation 871/2004 (Council Regulation [EC] No. 871/2004 of 29 April 2004 concerning the introduction of some new functions for the SIS, including in the fight against terrorism)

Cybercrime Convention

Decision 2001/497 of June 15, 2001 on standard contractual clauses for the transfer of personal data to third countries under Directive 95/46

Directive 95/46 on the protection of individuals with regard to the processing of personal data and on the free movement of the data

Directive 97/7 on the protection of consumers in respect of distance contracts

Directive 97/66 concerning the processing of personal data and the protection of privacy in the telecommunications sector (Telecommunications Directive)

Directive 98/48 amending Directive 98/34 (Directive 98/48/EC of the European Parliament and of the Council of 20 July 1998 amending Directive 98/34/EC laying down a procedure for the provision of information in the field of technical standards and regulations)

Directive 99/67 amending Directive 93/49 (Commission Directive 1999/67/EC of 28 June 1999 amending Directive 93/49/EEC setting out the schedule indicating the conditions to be met by ornamental plant propagating material and ornamental plants pursuant to Council Directive 91/682/EEC)

Directive 2002/19 on access to and interconnection of electronic communications networks and associated facilities

Directive 2002/21 on a common regulatory framework for electronic communications networks and services

Directive 2002/22 on universal service and users' rights relating to electronic communications networks and services

Directive 2002/58 concerning the processing of personal data and the protection of privacy in the electronic communications sector privacy and electronic communications directive

Directive 2002/96 on waste electrical and electronic equipment (WEEE)

Directive 2003/4 public access to environmental information

Directive 2005/18 on the retention of data generated or processed in connection with the provision of publicly available electronic communications services or of public communications networks

Directive 2006/24 on the retention of data generated or processed in connection with the provision of publicly available electronic communications services or of public communications networks and amending Directive 2002/58

Dublin Convention 1990 (convention determining the State responsible for examining applications for asylum lodged in one of the Member States of the European Communities—Dublin Convention)

EEA Agreement

EC Treaty

EU Charter of Fundamental Rights

Eurodac Convention 1996

Europol Convention on the Establishment of a European Police Force

European Convention for the Protection of Human Rights and Fundamental Freedoms 1950

Europol Convention

Lisbon Treaty

Mutual Assistance Convention

Nice Charter of Fundamental Rights 2000

Regulation 515/97 on mutual assistance between administrative authorities of the Member States

Regulation 45/2001 on the protection of individuals with regard to the processing of personal data by the Community institutions and bodies and on the free movement of such data

Regulation 343/2003 (Dublin II Regulation)

Regulation 1987/2006 (Schengen II/SIS II)

Rome EC Treaty 1957

Single European Act 1987

Strasbourg Convention

Treaty 108 of the Council of Europe Convention for the Protection of Individuals with regard to Automatic Processing of Personal Data 1981

Treaty of Amsterdam

Treaty on European Union

Treaty on European Union (consolidated)

UNCITRAL Model Law on Electronic Commerce

☐ EU Article 29 Working Party on Data Protection (WP29)

(Now Replaced by the European Data Protection Board [EDPB])

Update of Opinion 8/2010 on applicable law in light of the Court of Justice of the European Union (CJEU) judgment in Google Spain (WP 179 update), 16 December 2015

Statement on the implementation of the judgment of the CJEU of 6 October 2015 in the *Maximilian Schrems v Data Protection Commissioner* case (C-362-14)

Opinion 02/2015 on C-SIG code of conduct on cloud computing

Opinion 01/2015 on privacy and data protection issues relating to the utilization of drones

Explanatory document on the processor binding corporate rules, revised version, May 2015, WP 204

Cookie sweep combined analysis, 2015

Guidelines on the implementation of the CJEU judgment on *Google Spain and Inc v Agencia Española de Protección de Datos (AEPD) and Mario Costeja González*, c-131/121

Opinion 9/2014 on the application of Directive 2002/58/EC to device fingerprinting

Opinion 8/2014 on the recent developments on the Internet of things

Statement on Statement of the WP29 on the impact of the development of big data on the protection of individuals with regard to the processing of their personal data in the EU, 2014

Statement on the ruling of the CJEU which invalidates the Data Retention Directive, 2014

Statement on the role of a risk-based approach in data protection legal framework, 2014

Opinion 06/2014 on the "notion of legitimate interests of the data controller under Article 7 of Directive 95/46/EC"

Opinion 05/2014 on "anonymization techniques"

Working document 01/2014 on draft ad hoc contractual clauses "EU data processor to non-EU sub-processor"

Opinion 03/2014 on "personal data breach notification"

Opinion 02/2014 on a "referential for requirements for binding corporate rules submitted to national data protection authorities in the EU and cross-border privacy rules submitted to APEC CBPR accountability agents"

Opinion 07/2013 on the data protection impact assessment template for smart grid and smart metering systems ("DPIA template") prepared by Expert Group 2 of the Commission's Smart Grid Task Force

Working Document 02/2013 providing guidance on obtaining consent for cookies, 2013

Opinion 04/2013 on the data protection impact assessment template for smart grid and smart metering systems ("DPIA template") prepared by Expert Group 2 of the Commission's Smart Grid Task Force

Explanatory document on the processor binding corporate rules, WP 204 revised version, 2013

Opinion 03/2013 on purpose limitation

Opinion 02/2013 on apps on smart devices

Opinion 06/2012 on the draft Commission Decision on the measures applicable to the notification of personal data breaches under Directive 2002/58/EC on privacy and electronic communications

Opinion 05/2012 on cloud computing

Working Document 02/2012 setting up a table with the elements and principles to be found in processor binding corporate rules

Recommendation 1/2012 on the standard application form for approval of binding corporate rules for the transfer of personal data for processing activities

Opinion 04/2012 on cookie consent exemption

Opinion 03/2012 on developments in biometric technologies

Opinion 02/2012 on facial recognition in online and mobile services

Opinion 01/2012 on the data protection reform proposals

Opinion 16/2011 on EASA/IAB best practice recommendation on online behavioral advertising

Opinion 15/2011 on consent

Opinion 13/2011 on geolocation services on smart mobile devices

Working Document 01/2011 on the current EU personal data breach framework and recommendations for future policy developments

Opinion 12/2011 on smart metering

Opinion 9/2011 on the revised industry proposal for a privacy and data protection impact assessment framework for RFID applications (and annex: privacy and data protection impact assessment framework for RFID applications)

Opinion 8/2010 on applicable law (WP29 adds as follows: "In its judgment in Google Spain the Court of Justice of the European Union decided upon certain matters relating to the territorial scope of Directive 95/46/EC. The WP29 commenced an internal analysis of the potential implications of this judgment on applicable law and may provide further guidance on this issue during the course of 2015, including, possibly, additional examples.")

Opinion 5/2010 on the industry proposal for a privacy and data protection impact assessment framework for RFID applications

Opinion 4/2010 on the European code of conduct of FEDMA for the use of personal data in direct marketing

Opinion 3/2010 on the principle of accountability

Opinion 2/2010 on online behavioral advertising

Opinion 8/2001 on the processing of personal data in the employment context

Opinion 7/2003 on the reuse of public sector information and the protection of personal data

Opinion 4/2007 on the concept of personal data

Opinion 1/2010 on the concepts of "controller" and "processor"

Opinion 2/2010 on online behavioral advertising

Article 29: working party opinion on the processing of personal data in the employment context 8/2001

Opinion 3/2009 on the draft Commission decision on standard contractual clauses for the transfer of personal data to processors established in third countries, under Directive 95/46/EC (data controller to data processor)

Frequently asked questions in order to address some issues raised by the entry into force of the EU Commission Decision 2010/87/EU of 5 February 2010 on standard contractual clauses for the transfer of personal data to processors established in third countries under Directive 95/46/EC 2010

Opinion 3/2002 on the data protection provisions of a Commission proposal for a Directive on the harmonization of the laws, regulations and administrative provisions of the Member States concerning credit for consumers

Working document on the surveillance of electronic communications in the workplace 2002

Recommendation 1/2001 on employee evaluation data 2001

Recommendation 1/2007 on the standard application for approval of binding corporate rules for the transfer of personal data

The Future of Privacy joint contribution to the Consultation of the European Commission on the legal framework for the fundamental right to protection of personal data 2009

☐ Sample Cases to Consider

Europe

- *Asociación Nacional de Establecimientos Financieros de Crédito (ASNEF) (C-468/10), Federación de Comercio Electrónico y Marketing Directo (FECEMD) (C-469/10) v Administración del Estado, Court of Justice* (joined Cases C-468/10 and C-469/10), 24 November 2011

- *Bonnier Audio AB, Earbooks AB, Norstedts Förlagsgrupp AB, Piratförlaget AB, Storyside AB v Perfect Communication Sweden AB,* Court of Justice (C-461/10), 19 April 2012

- *ClientEarth and Pesticide Action Network Europe (PAN Europe) v European Food Safety Authority (EFSA)*, General Court (Sixth Chamber) (Case T-214/11), 13 September 2013

- *College van burgemeester en wethouders van Rotterdam v MEE Rijkeboer Netherlands*, Court of Justice (Case C-553/07), 7 May 2009

- *Commission v Hungary*, Court of Justice (Grand Chamber) (Case C-288/12), 8 April 2014

- *Dennekamp v Parliament*, Court of Justice (Case T-82/09), 23 November 2011

- *Digital Rights Ireland (C-293/12) v Minister for Communications, Marine and Natural Resources, Minister for Justice, Equality and Law Reform, Commissioner of the Garda Síochána, Ireland, The Attorney General, and Kärntner Landesregierung (C-594/12), Michael Seitlinger, Christof Tschohl and others*, Court of Justice (Grand Chamber) (joined cases C-293/12 and C-594/12), 8 April 2014

- *Egan and Hackett v Parliament*, Court of Justice (Case T-190/10), 28 March 2012

- *European Commission v Republic of Austria*, Court of Justice (Case C-614/10), 16 October 2012)

- *European Commission v The Bavarian Lager Co Ltd, European Data Protection Supervisor*, Court of Justice (Case C-28/08 P), 29 June 2010)

- *European Commission supported by European Data Protection Supervisor v Federal Republic of Germany*, Court of Justice (Case C-518/07), 9 March 2010

- *European Parliament v Council of the European Union*, Court of Justice (joined Cases C-317/04 and C-318/04), 30 May 2006

- *Google Spain SL and Google Inc v Agencia Española de Protección de Datos (AEPD) and Mario Costeja González*, Court of Justice (Grand Chamber) (Case C-131/12), 13 May 2014

- *Heinz Huber v Bundesrepublik Germany*, Court of Justice (Case C-524/06), 16 December 2008

- *Institut professionnel des agents immobiliers (IPI) v Geoffrey Englebert and Others*, Court of Justice (Third Chamber) (Case C-473/12), 7 November 2013

- *Lindqvist v Kammaraklagaren,* Court of Justice (Case C-101/01), 6 November 2013; [2004] 1 CMLR 0 (ECJ)

- *Nikolaou v Commission,* Court of First Instance (Case T-259/03), 12 September 2007

- *Pharmacontinente—Saúde e Higiene SA and Others v Autoridade Para As Condições do Trabalho (ACT),* Court of Justice (Eighth Chamber) (Case C-683/13), 19 June 2014

- *Probst v nexnet GmbH,* Court of Justice (Case C-119/12), 22 November 2012

- *Scarlet Extended SA v Société belge des auteurs, compositeurs et éditeurs SCRL (SABAM),* Court of Justice (Case C-70/10), 24 November 2011

- *Schrems v Commissioner,* Court of Justice (Grand Chamber) (Case C-362/14), 6 October 2015

- *Schwarz v Stadt Bochum,* Court of Justice (Fourth Chamber) (Case C-291/12), 17 October 2013

- Reference for a preliminary ruling from the *Juzgado de lo Mercantil No 5 de Madrid - Spain/Productores de Música de España (Promusicae) v Telefónica de España SAU,* Court of Justice (Case C-275/06), 29 January 2008

- Reference for a preliminary ruling from the *Oberster Gerichtshof (Austria),* Court of Justice (Case C-557/07), 19 February 2009

- Reference for a preliminary ruling from the *Verfassungsgerichtshof and Oberster Gerichtshof: Rechnungshof (C-465/00) v Österreichischer Rundfunk and Others and between Christa Neukomm (C-138/01), Joseph Lauermann (C-139/01) and Österreichischer Rundfunk,* Court of Justice (joined Cases C-465/00, C-138/01 and C-139/01), 20 May 2003

- *Tietosuojavaltuutettu v Satakunnan Markkinapörssi Oy, Satamedia Oy,* Court of Justice (Case C-73/07), 16 December 2008

- *Volker und Markus Schecke GbR (C-92/09), Hartmut Eifert (C-93/09) v Land Hessen,* Court of Justice (Case C-92/09 and C-93/09), 9 November 2010

- *Worten—Equipamentos para o Lar SA v Autoridade para as Condições de Trabalho (ACT),* Court of Justice (Third Chamber) (Case C-342/12), 30 May 2013

- *X*, Court of Justice, (Case C-486/12 – X), 12 December 2013

- YS (C-141/12) v Minister voor Immigratie, Integratie en Asiel and Minister voor Immigratie, Integratie en Asiel (C-372/12) v M and S, Court of Justice (joined cases C-141/12 and C-372/12), 17 July 2014

Cases

Supervisory authority complaints, cases, and case studies that may be useful for organizations to consider:

- *Prudential*

- *Microsoft v Paul Martin McDonald*

- *McCall v Facebook*

- *Information Commissioners Office (ICO) v Niebel, ICO v McNeish*

- *Rugby Football Union v Viagogo Limited*

- *Durham County Council v Dunn*

- *British Gas*

- *Brian Reed Beetson Robertson*

- *Campbell v Mirror Group Newspapers (MGN)*

- *CCN Systems v Data Protection Registrar*

- *Lindqvist v Kammaraklagaren*

- *Commission v Bavarian Lager*

- *Common Services Agency v Scottish Information Commissioner*

- *Douglas v Hello!*

- *Halford v United Kingdom*

- *Von Hannover*

- *Mosley*

- *Motion Picture Association v British Telecom (BT)*

- *WP29 (now EDPB) and Data Protection Authorities/Google* (re: Google policy change and breaches)

- Barclays/Lara Davies prosecution

- Sony

- *Facebook Beacon* case (United States)

- *Digital Rights Ireland* and *Seitlinger and Others*

- *Schrems v Commissioner*

- *Tamiz v Google*

- *Google v Vidal-Hall*

- *Mosley v Google*

- *Google Spain SL Google Inc v Agencia Española de Protección de Datos, Mario Costeja González*

- *Weltimmo v Nemzeti Adatvédelmi és Információszabadság Hatóság*

- *Bărbulescu v Romania*

Ireland

- *Data Protection Commissioner/Facebook*, audit by the Data Protection Commissioner (2011 and 2012)

- *Dublin Bus v Data Protection Commissioner* (2012) IEHC 339 8/8/2012

- *EMI v Eircom* (2005) IEHC 233, (2005) 4 IR 148

- *EMI v Eircom* (2010) IEHC 108 16/4/2010

- *EMI v UPC* (2010) IEHC 377 11/10/2010

- *EMI v Data Protection Commissioner* (2012) IEHC 264 27/6/2012

- *Realm Communications v Data Protection Commissioner* (2009) IEHC 1 9/1/2009

- *Shelly-Morris v Dublin Bus* (2003) 1 IR 232

- *EU Article 29 Working Party on Data Protection and Data Protection Authorities/Google*, privacy policy change (2012)

United Kingdom

- *A v B* (2002) 3 WLR 452

- *Amp v Utilux* (1972) RPC 103

- *Asda v Thompson* (2004) IRLR 598

- *Attorney General v Guardian Newspapers (No. 2)* (1990) 1 AC 109

- *Baker v Secretary of State for the Home Office (Information Tribunal)* (2001) UKHRR 1275

- *Brian Reid Beetson Robertson v Wakefield Metropolitan Council, Secretary of State for the Home Department* (2001) EWHC Admin 915

- *British Gas v Data Protection Registrar* (1998) UKIT DA98-3492 (4 March 1998)

- *Campbell v MGN* (2002) EWHC 299

- *Campbell v MGN* (2003) EMLR 2 (CA)

- *Campbell v MGN* (2004) UKHL 22

- *CCN Systems v Data Protection Registrar* (1991) Case DA/90 5/49/19, Data Protection Tribunal

- *Charleston v News Group Newspapers* (1995) 2 AC 65

- *Clark v Associated Newspapers* (1998) RPC 261

- *Coco v AN Clark (Engineers)* (1968) FSR 415

- *Common Services Agency v Scottish Information Commissioner* (2008) UKHL 47

- *Community Charge Registration Officer of Rhondda Borough Council v Data Protection Registrar* (DA/90 25/49/2)

- *Community Charge Registration officers of Runnymede Borough Council, South Northamptonshire District Council and Harrow Borough Council v Data Protection Registrar* (DA/90 4/49/3)

- *Credit and Data Marketing Services v Data Protection Registrar* (Case 1991 DA/90 25/49/10, Data Protection Tribunal)

- *Denco v Joinson* (1991) ICR 172

- *Douglas and Jones v Hello* (2003) UKHC 786

- *Douglas and Jones v Hello* (No. 2) (2003) UKHC 55; (2003) 1 AER 1087

- *Douglas and Jones v Hello* UKSC (2005).

- *Douglas and Jones v Hello* (2005) UKSC available at http://www.bailii.org/ew/cases/EWCA/Civ/2005/595.html

- *Durant v Financial Services Authority* (2003) EWCA Civ 1746; B2/2002/2636 (A) 20 March 2002

- *Equifax Europe v Data Protection Registrar* (28 February 1992, Case DA/90/5/49/7) Data Protection Tribunal

- *Ezsias v Welsh Ministers* (2007) EWHC B15 (QB); [2007] AER (D) 65

- *Gaskin v United Kingdom* (A/160) (1990) 1 FLR 167; [1990] 12 EHRR 36

- *Godfrey v Demon Internet* (2001) QB 201

- *Halford v United Kingdom* (1997) IRLR 471; [1997] 24 EHRR 523

- *Innovations (Mail Order) v Data Protection Registrar* (DA92 31/49/1, 1992)

- *Johnson v Medical Union* (2004) EWHC 347

- *Johnson v Medical Union* (2007) EWCA Civ 262

- *Law Society v Kordowski* (2011) EWHC 3185

- *Leander v Sweden* (A/116) (1987) 9 EHRR 433

- *Lion Laboratories v Evans* (1984) AER 414

- *Midlands Electrical v Data Information Registrar* (1999) UKIT DA99-B1 7 May 1999; (1999) Info TLR 217

- *MG v United Kingdom* (1999) (application no. 44657/98) *Times*, 3 February 2003, ECHR

- *Microsoft Corp v McDonald (t/s Bizads)* (2006) EWHC 3410

- *Murray v Big Pictures (UK) Ltd* (2008) EWCA Civ 446 (07 May 2008), ([2008] 2 FLR 599, [2008] 3 FCR 661, [2008] 3 WLR 1360, [2008] ECDR 12, [2008] EMLR 12, [2008] EWCA Civ 446, [2008] Fam Law 732, [2008] HRLR 33, [2008] UKHRR 736, [2009] Ch 481); From England and Wales Court of Appeal (Civil Division) Decisions

- *O'Flynn v Airlinks* (2002) EAT 10269/01

- *P v Wozencroft* (2002) EWHC 1724

- *Pennwell v Isles* (2007) IRLR 700

- *R v Rooney* (2006) EWCA Crim 1841

- *R v Secretary of State for the Home Department ex p Lord* (2003) EWHC 2073

- *R (on the application of Addinell) v Sheffield City Council* (2001) ACD 61, QBD (Admin Ct)

- *R (on the application of S) v Plymouth City Council* (2002) EWCA Civ 388; (2002) 1 FLR 1177; (2002) 1 WLR 2583, CA

- *R (on the application of Robertson) v Wakefield MDC sub nom R (on the application of Robertson) v Electoral Registration Officer* (2001) EWHC 1760 (Admin)

- *Ramsbro B239-00*, Sweden Supreme Court (unofficial translation shc-campsite.mdlf.org/look/download/English/rj_pdf)

- *Runnymede BC v Data Protection Registrar* (1990)

- *Secretary of State for the Home Department v Wainwright, sub nom Wainwright v Secretary for the Home Department* (2001) EWCA Civ 2081

- *Smith v Lloyd TSB Bank* (2005) EWHC 246

- *Soering v United Kingdom* (1989) 1 EHRR 439

- *Spring v Guardian Assurance* (1995) AC

- *Sunderland Housing Company v Baines* (2006) EWHC 2359

- *Totalise v Motley Fool* [2002] 1 WLR 1233 (CA); (2002) AER 872

- *Tournier v National Provincial and Union Bank of England* (1924) 1 KB 461

Australia

- *Milorad Trkulja v Google*, Supreme Court of Victoria, Melbourne, (2012) VSC 533, 12 November 2012

- *Trkulja v Yahoo! Inc & Anor* (2012) VSC 88

New Zealand

- *A v Google*, HC AK CIV: 2011-404-002780, 5 March 2012

Decisions

Decision C (2001) 1539 of 15 June 2001 on the standard contractual clauses for the transfer of personal data to third countries, under Directive 95/46/EC

Commission Decision of 19 October 2010 pursuant to Directive 95/46/EC of the European Parliament and of the Council on the adequate protection of personal data in Andorra

Commission Decision of 30/06/2003 pursuant to Directive 95/46/EC of the European Parliament and of the Council on the adequate protection of personal data in Argentina

Council Decision 2008/651/CFSP/JHA of 30 June 2008 on the signing, on behalf of the European Union, of an agreement between the European Union and Australia on the processing and transfer of European Union-sourced PNR data by air carriers to the Australian Customs Service

Council Decision of 18 July 2005 on the conclusion of an agreement between the European Community and the Government of Canada on the processing of API/PNR data (2006/230/EC)

Commission Decision of 6 September 2005 on the adequate protection of personal data contained in the PNRs of air passengers transferred to the Canada Border Services Agency

Commission Decision of 20 December 2001 pursuant to Directive 95/46/EC of the European Parliament and of the Council on the adequate protection of personal data provided by the Canadian Personal Information Protection and Electronic Documents Act

Commission Decision of 26 July 2000 pursuant to Directive 95/46/EC of the European Parliament and of the Council on the adequate protection of personal data provided in Switzerland

Commission Decision of 5 March 2010 pursuant to Directive 95/46/EC of the European Parliament and of the Council on the adequate protection provided by the Faeroese Act on processing of personal data

Commission Decision of 21 November 2003 on the adequate protection of personal data in Guernsey

Commission Decision 2011/61/EU of 31 January 2011 pursuant to Directive 95/46/EC of the European Parliament and of the Council on the adequate protection of personal data by the State of Israel with regard to automated processing of personal data

Commission Decision 2004/411/EC of 28.4.2004 on the adequate protection of personal data in the Isle of Man

Commission Decision of 8 May 2008 pursuant to Directive 95/46/EC of the European Parliament and of the Council on the adequate protection of personal data in Jersey

Decisions on Transfer of PNR Data to the United States

Commission Staff Working Paper: The application of Commission Decision 520/2000/EC of 26 July 2000 pursuant to Directive 95/46 of the European Parliament and of the Council on the adequate protection of personal data provided by the Safe Harbor Privacy Principles and related frequently asked questions issued by the US Department of Commerce

Commission Decision of 26 July 2000 pursuant to Directive 95/46/EC of the European Parliament and of the Council on the adequacy of the protection provided by the Safe Harbor privacy principles and related frequently asked questions issued by the US Department of Commerce

☐ Reference Text

Austria

Atluri and Pernul, eds, *Data and Applications Security and Privacy XXVIII: 28th Annual IFIP WG 11.3 Working Conference, DBSec 2014*, Vienna, Austria, July 14–16, 2014. Proceedings (Berlin: Springer, 2014).

Chalton, Gaskill and Sterling, *Encyclopedia of Data Protection* (Sweet and Maxwell, 1992).

Foresti, *Security and Trust Management: 11th International Workshop, STM 2015*, Vienna, Austria, September 21–22, 2015 (Springer 2015).

Szydlo, Principles underlying independence of national data protection authorities: *Commission v Austria, Common Market Law Review* (2013) (50:6) 1809.

Belgium

Belgium's Data Protection Bill: the Impact on Your Operations (Business International, 1986).

Challenges of Privacy and Data Protection Law: Perspectives of European and North American Law (Bruylant, 2008).

Chalton, Gaskill and Sterling, *Encyclopedia of Data Protection* (Sweet and Maxwell, 1992).

Daem, Fraudedetectie en Veiligheidsvrijwaring: Een Privacyrechtelijke Analyse Van de Toelaatbaarheidsgronden Voor Data Profilering (KU Leuven. Faculteit Rechtsgeleerdheid, 2015).

De Bot, *Verwerking van Persoonsgegevens* (Kluwer, 2001).

Dumortier, ed, *Recent Developments in Data Privacy Law: Belgium's Data Protection Bill and the European Draft Directive* (Leuven University Press, 1992).

Fuster, *Emergence of Personal Data Protection as a Fundamental Right of the EU* (Springer, 2014).

Fuster, The right to the protection of personal data and EU law, *Law, Governance and Technology Series* (2014)(16) 213.

Hijmans and Kranenborg, eds, *Data Protection Anno 2014: Contributions in Honour of Peter Hustinx, European Data Protection Supervisor (2004–2014)* (Intersentia, 2014).

Hildebrandt and Tielemans, Data protection by design and technology neutral law, *Computer Law & Security Review: The International Journal of Technology Law and Practice* (2013)(29:5) 509.

Kengen, *The Right to Be Forgotten v Freedom of Expression: How to Balance These Rights while Taking the Internet Environment into Account?* (KU Leuven. Faculteit Rechtsgeleerdheid, 2015).

Kindt, *Privacy and Data Protection Issues of Biometric Applications: A Comparative Legal Analysis* (Springer, 2013).

Kuschewsky, *Data Protection & Privacy: Jurisdictional Comparisons* (Thomson Reuters, 2012).

Pérez Asinari and Palazzi, eds, *Défis du Droit à la Protection de la Vie Privée: Perspectives du Droit Européen et Nord-Américain.*

Bulgaria

Chalton, Gaskill and Sterling, *Encyclopedia of Data Protection* (Sweet and Maxwell, 1992).

Data Protection Laws of the World Handbook: Second Edition - Bulgaria (Mondaq, 2013).

Croatia

Blythe, Croatia's computer laws: Promotion of growth in e-commerce via greater cyber-security, *European Journal of Law and Economics* (2008) (26:1) 75.

Brezak, *Nakladni Zavod Matice Hrvatske* (1998) (translated title: *Right to Personality: Legal Protection of Personal Data from Abuse*).

Chalton, Gaskill and Sterling, *Encyclopedia of Data Protection* (Sweet and Maxwell, 1992).

Dragičević and Gumzej, Cloud computing data protection aspects under Croatian and European Union law, in *Software, Telecommunications and Computer Networks (SoftCOM), 22nd International Conference on Software, Telecommunications and Computer Networks*, 17, 19.9.2014., Split, IEEE, (2014) 192.

Dragičević and Gumzej, Privatnost I Zaštita Osobnih Podataka U Digitalnom Okruženju, in Dragičević, (ed.) *Pravna Informatika I Pravo Informacijskih Tehnologija* (Narodne Novine, 2015). (Title of chapter translated as: "Privacy and Personal Data Protection in the Digital Environment").

Gumzej, Data protection for the digital age: Comprehensive effects of the evolving law of accountability, *Juridical Tribune* (2012)(2:2) 82.

Gumzej, Evolving challenges and legal safeguards in processing user data in electronic communications, in: *Proceedings of 12th International Conference on Telecommunications*, Zagreb, 26, 28.6.2013, IEEE (2013) 271.

Gumzej, *Zaštita Podataka U Elektroničkim Komunikacijama, Pravni Fakultet U Zagrebu*, PhD dissertation (2011) See details at: https://bib.irb.hr/prikazi-rad?&rad=721849.

Gumzej and Dragičević, Convergence in communications and e-privacy regulatory challenges, with a local perspective, in: *Proceedings of 13th International Conference on Telecommunications, ConTEL 2015*, Graz, Austria, Graz University of Technology Institute of Microwave and Photonic Engineering/IEEE (2015) 1.

Gumzej and Grgić, ePrivacy rules and data processing in Users' terminal equipment: A Croatian experience, in: *Proceedings of the 36th International Convention on Information & Communication Technology Electronics & Microelectronics 2013* (Rijeka, 2013) 1501.

Gumzej, Selected aspects of proposed new EU general data protection legal framework and the croatian perspective, *Juridical Tribune* (2013) (3:2) Editura ASE, Bucharest, 178.

Schepman, Koren, Horvat, Kurtovic and Hebrang Grgic, Anonymity of library users in the Netherlands and Croatia, *New Library World* (2008) (109:9/10) 407.

Cyprus

Chalton, Gaskill and Sterling, *Encyclopedia of Data Protection* (Sweet and Maxwell, 1992).

Czech Republic

Chalton, Gaskill and Sterling, *Encyclopedia of Data Protection* (Sweet and Maxwell, 1992).

Majtényi, Ensuring data protection in east-central Europe, *Social Research* (2002) (69:1) 151.

Matejka, *Internet Jako Objekt Práva: Hledání Rovnováhy Autonomie a Soukromí. 1. Vydání* (Prague: CZ.NIC, 2013).

Polčák, *Internet a Proměny Práva 1 vyd* (Prague: Auditorium, 2012) 388.

Polčák, Čermák, Loebl, Gřivna, Matejka, Schlossberger. Cyber law in the Czech Republic, *Encyclopaedia of Laws/Cyberlaw* (Alpen aan den Rijn: Kluwer Law International, 2015) (2) 228.

Denmark

Bing, *Transnational Data Flows and the Scandinavian Data Protection Legislation* (Stockholm Institute for Scandinavian Law, 1980).

Blume, *Data Beskyttelses Ret* (2016).

Cameron and Blume, *Data Protection Laws in the United Kingdom and Denmark* (1988).

Chalton, Gaskill and Sterling, *Encyclopedia of Data Protection* (Sweet and Maxwell, 1992).

Kuner, Google Spain in the EU and international context, *Maastricht Journal of European and Comparative Law* (2015) (22:1) 158.

Kuner, The court of justice of the EU judgment on data protection and internet search engines, LSE Law, Society, and Economy Working Paper Series, ed., London School of Economics and Political Science (2015) 1.

Kuner, *Transborder Data Flows and Data Privacy Law* (Oxford University Press, 2013).

Tranberg, Proportionality and data protection in the case law of the European court of justice, *International Data Privacy Law* (2011)(1:4) 239.

Estonia

Anthes, Estonia: A model for e-government, Communications of the ACM (05/2015).

Chalton, Gaskill and Sterling, *Encyclopedia of Data Protection* (Sweet and Maxwell, 1992).

Hansen, Case law of the European Court of Human Rights and the Supreme Court of Estonia in disclosing personal data in court judgments, *Juridica International* (2015)(23) 17.

König and Hug, New Media Usage and Privacy Policies of Newspaper Websites of the Baltic States/Nauju Ziniasklaidos Priemoniu Panaudojimas Baltijos Valstybiu Laikrasciu Tinklalapiuose ir ju Privatumo Politika, *Current Issues of Business and Law* (2012)(7:1) 27.

Männiko, *Õigus Privaatsusele Ja Andmekaitse* (2011).

Tikk and Nõmper, *Informatsioon Ja Õigus* (2007).

Finland

Blume, *Nordic Data Protection Law* (Djoef, 2001).

Chalton, Gaskill and Sterling, *Encyclopedia of Data Protection* (Sweet and Maxwell, 1992-).

Pitkänen, Warma and Tiilikka, *Henkilötietojen Suoja* (Sidottu, Talentum, 2013).

Raento, The data subject's right of access and to be informed in Finland: An experimental study, *International Journal of Law and Information Technology* (2006) (14:3).

Saarenpaa, Data protection: In pursuit of information. Some background to, and implementations of, data protection in Finland, *International Review of Law, Computers & Technology* (1997) (11:1).

France

Chalton, Gaskill and Sterling, *Encyclopedia of Data Protection* (Sweet and Maxwell, 1992).

Fenoll-Trousseau and Haas, *Internet et Protection des Données Personelles* (Litec, 2000).

Flaherty, *Protecting Privacy in Surveillance Societies: The Federal Republic of Germany, Sweden, France, Canada, and the United States* (University of North Carolina Press, 2014).

Frayssinet and Fauvet, *Informatique Fichiers et Liberté: Les Règles, Les Sanctions, La Doctrine de la CNIL* (Litec, 1992).

Lucas, *Le Droit de l'informatique* (PUF, 1987).

Moatti, *La Communication Informatique en Toute Liberté: Histoire et éthique de L'information Numériqu* (Association des Publications de la Faculté des Lettres de Nice, 1998).

Nugter, *Transborder Flow of Personal Data Within the EC: A Comparative Analysis of the Privacy Statutes of the Federal Republic of Germany, France, the United Kingdom and The Netherlands and Their Impact on the Private Sector* (Kluwer, 1990).

Untersinger, *Anonymat Sur internet: Comprendre Pour Protéger Sa Vie Privée* (Eyrolles, 2013).

Germany

Chalton, Gaskill and Sterling, *Encyclopedia of Data Protection* (Sweet and Maxwell, 1992).

Eckert, Katsikas and Pernul, eds, Trust, *Privacy, and Security in Digital Business: 11th International Conference, TrustBus 2014,* Munich, Germany, September 2–3, 2014. Proceedings (Springer, 2014).

Flaherty, *Protecting Privacy in Surveillance Societies: The Federal Republic of Germany, Sweden, France, Canada, and the United States* (University of North Carolina Press, 2014).

Gutiérrez Zarza, *Exchange of Information and Data Protection in Cross-border Criminal Proceedings in Europe* (Berlin: Springer, 2014).

Horstkotte, *Data Protection in Germany* (IN-Press, Goethe-Institut Inter Nationes, 2001).

Ismail, *Beyond Data Protection: Strategic Case Studies and Practical Guidance* (Berlin: Springer, 2013).

Knyrim, and Trieb, Smart metering under EU data protection law, *International Data Privacy Law* (2011) (1:2) 121.

Kodde, Germany's "Right to be forgotten": Between the freedom of expression and the right to informational self-determination, *International Review of Law, Computers & Technology* (23 February 2016) 1.

Lee and Duttge, *The Law in the Information and Risk Society* (Universitätsverlag Göttingen, 2011).

Louis, *Grundzüge des Datenschutzrechts* (Heymann, 1981).

Nugter, *Transborder Flow of Personal Data Within the EC: A Comparative Analysis of the Privacy Statutes of the Federal Republic of Germany, France, the United Kingdom and The Netherlands and Their Impact on the Private Sector* (Kluwer, 1990).

Pahud de Mortanges, ed, *Staatliches Datenschutzrecht und Kirchen* (Universitätsverl, 1999).

Sunyaev, *Health-Care Telematics in Germany: Design and Application of a Security Analysis Method* (Wiesbaden, 2011).

Tinnefeld and Tubies, *Datenschutzrecht* (Oldenbourg, 1989).

Greece

Chalton, Gaskill and Sterling, *Encyclopedia of Data Protection* (Sweet and Maxwell, 1992).

Preneel and Ikonomou, eds, *Privacy Technologies and Policy: Second Annual Privacy Forum, APF 2014, Athens, Greece, May 20–21, 2014. Proceedings.*

Vlachos, Minou, Assimakopouos, Toska, The Landscape of Cybercrime in Greece, *Information Management & Computer Security* (2011) (19:2).

Hungary

Chalton, Gaskill and Sterling, *Encyclopedia of Data Protection* (Sweet and Maxwell, 1992).

Majtényi, Ensuring data protection in east-central Europe, *Social Research* (2002) (69:1) 151.

Misiunaite-Kamarauskiene, Recent case-law of the court of justice of the European Union regarding the fundamental rights to respect for private and family life and to protection of personal data, *Jurisprudencija* (2014)(21:4).

Ireland

Carey, *Data Protection: A Practical Guide to Irish and EU Law* (Thomson Round Hall, 2010).

Chalton, Gaskill and Sterling, *Encyclopedia of Data Protection* (Sweet and Maxwell, 1992).

Clark, *Data Protection Law in Ireland* (Round Hall Press, 1990).

Delany, Carolan and Murphy, *The Right to Privacy: A Doctrinal and Comparative Analysis* (Thomson Round Hall, 2008).

Goodbody, *A Practical Guide to Data Protection Law in Ireland* (Thomson Round Hall, 2003).

Kelleher, *Privacy and Data Protection Law in Ireland* (Bloomsbury, 2015).

Lambert, *Data Protection Law in Ireland: Sources and Issues* (Clarus Press, 2016).

Italy

Bendin, *Impresa e Comunicazione: Dalla Privacy al Web* (Mercato e Mass Media) (1999).

Chalton, Gaskill and Sterling, *Encyclopedia of Data Protection* (Sweet and Maxwell, 1992).

Resta, Systematic government access to private-sector data in Italy, *International Data Privacy Law* (2014)(4:1) 139.

Ziccardi, *Cyber Law in Italy* (Kluwer, 2013).

Latvia

Chalton, Gaskill and Sterling, *Encyclopedia of Data Protection* (Sweet and Maxwell, 1992).

König and Hug, New Media Usage and Privacy Policies of Newspaper Websites of the Baltic States/Nauju Ziniasklaidos Priemoniu Panaudojimas Baltijos Valstybiu Laikrasciu Tinklalapiuose ir ju Privatumo Politika, *Current Issues of Business and Law* (2012)(7:1) 27.

Lithuania

Chalton, Gaskill and Sterling, *Encyclopedia of Data Protection* (Sweet and Maxwell, 1992).

König and Hug, New Media Usage and Privacy Policies of Newspaper Websites of the Baltic States/Nauju Ziniasklaidos Priemoniu Panaudojimas Baltijos Valstybiu Laikrasciu Tinklalapiuose ir ju Privatumo Politika, *Current Issues of Business and Law* (2012)(7:1) 27.

Tatjana Bileviciene; Egle Bileviciute, Dynamics of crimes against the security of electronic data and information systems and its influence on the development of electronic business in Lithuania, *Jurisprudencija* (2011)(18:2) 2019.

Trofimovs, Lithuania, *Certain Aspects of Personal Data Protection, Legislation* (Sorainen, 2013).

Šmite, Ethics and law on the electronic frontier, *Informatics in Education: An International Journal* (2004) 91.

Luxembourg

Berendt, Engel, Ikonomou and Métayer, Privacy Technologies and Policy: Third Annual Privacy Forum, APF 2015, Luxembourg, Luxembourg, October 7–8, 2015, Selected Papers.

Chalton, Gaskill and Sterling, *Encyclopedia of Data Protection* (Sweet and Maxwell, 1992).

Data Protection Laws of the World Handbook: Second Edition - Luxembourg (Mondaq, 2013).

Kosta, The Way to Luxemburg: National Court Decisions on the Compatibility of the Data Retention Directive with the Rights to Privacy and Data Protection (15 October 2013).

Pierre-Beausse, *La Protection Des Données Personnelles* (European Schl Bks, 2005).

Malta

Cannataci, *Privacy and Data Protection Law: International Development and Maltese Perspectives* (Norwegian University Press, 1986).

Cannataci and Mifsud-Bonnici, Data protection comes of age: The data protection clauses in the European constitutional treaty, *Information & Communications Technology Law* (2005)(14:1) 5.

Chalton, Gaskill and Sterling, *Encyclopedia of Data Protection* (Sweet and Maxwell, 1992).

Privacy and Data Protection Laws in Malta, *Computer Law and Security Review: The International Journal of Technology and Practice* (1996)(12:4) 235.

Weitzenboeck, Information law reform: Malta, *Computer Law and Security Review: The International Journal of Technology and Practice* (2001)(17:1) 45.

The Netherlands

Balthasar, Complete Independence of National Data Protection Supervisory Authorities Second Try: Comments on the Judgment of the CJEU of 16 October 2012,C-614/10, with Due Regard to its Previous Judgment of 9 March 2010,C-518/07, *Utrecht Law Review* (2013)(9:3) 26.

Barendrecht, Giesen and Schellekens, *Overheidsaansprakelijkheid Voor Informatieverstrekking: Nederlands Recht, Rechtsvergelijking en de Aansprakelijkheid van Particuliere Informatieverstrekkers* (Boom Juridische Uitgevers, 2002).

Bokler, *A fair and Just weighing? Data Protection and Medical Research: A Comparison Between the Netherlands and Germany* (Leuven: sn, 2000).

Chalton, Gaskill and Sterling, *Encyclopedia of Data Protection* (Sweet and Maxwell, 1992).

Cristofaro and Murdoch, eds, *Privacy Enhancing Technologies in Proceedings of 14th International Symposium, PETS 2014, Amsterdam, The Netherlands, July 16–18, 2014* (Springer, 2014).

Cuijpers and Koops, Smart metering and privacy in Europe: Lessons from the Dutch case, in Gutwirth, Leenes, de Hert and Poullet, *European Data Protection: Coming of Age* (Springer, 2013).

Galetta and de Hert, The Proceduralisation of Data Protection Remedies Under EU Data Protection Law: Towards a More Effective and Data Subject-Oriented Remedial System? Review of European Administrative Law (2015)(8:1) 125.

Gutwirth, *European Data Protection: Coming of Age* (Springer, 2012).

Gutwirth, Leenes, de Hert and Poullet, eds, European Data Protection: Coming of Age (Springer, 2013).

Gutwirth, *Leenes and De Hert, Reloading Data Protection: Multidisciplinary Insights and Contemporary Challenges* (Springer Netherlands, 2014).

Gutwirth, Poullet and De Hert, *Data Protection in a Profiled World* (Springer Netherlands, 2010).

Gutwirth, *Reforming European Data Protection Law* (Springer Netherlands, 2014).

Holvast, *Het Gebruik van Persoonlijkheidsprofielen in de Publieke Sector* (Sdu, 2001).

Hondius, *Emerging Data Protection in Europe* (North-Holland, 1975).

Hooghiemstra and Nouwt, *Sdu Commentaar Wet Bescherming Persoonsgegevens (abonnement) online/boek* (Sdu, annual publication).

Kilian, Rechtsfragen der Medizinischen Forschung mit Patientendaten: Datenschutz und Forschungsfreiheit im Konflikt (Toeche-Mittler, 1983).

Moerel, *Big Data Protection: How to Make the Draft EU Regulation on Data Protection Future Proof* (Tilburg University, 2014).

Muijen, *Handleiding Politie en Privacy: de Betekenis van de Wet Persoonsregistraties en de Wet Politieregisters Voor de Politiepraktijk* ('s-Gravenhage: VUGA, 1995).

Nugter, *Transborder Flow of Personal Data Within the EC: A Comparative Analysis of the Privacy Statutes of the Federal Republic of Germany, France, the United Kingdom and The Netherlands and Their Impact on the Private Sector* (Kluwer, 1990).

Overkleeft-Verburg, *De Wet Persoonsregistraties: Norm, Toepassing en Evaluatie* (Tjeenk-Willink, 1995).

Prins, Cuijpers, Broeders, *Wetenschappelijke Raad Voor Het Regeringsbeleid, De staat van Informative* (Amsterdam University Press, 2011).

Prins and Berkvens, *Privacyregulering in Theorie en Praktijk* (Kluwer, 2007).

Purtova, Private law solutions in European data protection: Relationship to privacy, and waiver of data protection rights, *Netherlands Quarterly of Human Rights* (2010)(28:2) 179.

Wheeler and Winburn, *Cloud Storage Security: A Practical Guide* (Elsevier: 2015).

Poland

Chalton, Gaskill and Sterling, *Encyclopedia of Data Protection* (Sweet and Maxwell, 1992).

Galewska, *Cyber Law in Poland* (Kluwer, 2011).

Kutyłowski and Vaidya, eds, *Computer Security: ESORICS 2014: 19th European Symposium on Research in Computer Security, Wroclaw, Poland, September 7–11, 2014. Proceedings, Part II* (Springer International Publishing, 2014).

Majtényi, Ensuring data protection in east-central Europe, *Social Research* (2002)(69:1) 151.

Podkowik, Privacy in the digital era: Polish electronic surveillance law declared partially unconstitutional: Judgment of the constitutional tribunal of Poland of 30 July 2014, K 23/11, *European Constitutional Law Review* (2015)(11:3) 577.

Ziuziański and Furmankiewicz, E-health artificial intelligence system implementation: Case study of knowledge management dashboard of epidemiological data in Poland, *Journal of Biology* (2014).

Portugal

Chalton, Gaskill and Sterling, *Encyclopedia of Data Protection* (Sweet and Maxwell, 1992).

Data Protection Laws of the World Handbook: Second Edition - Portugal (Mondaq, 2013).

Romania

Chalton, Gaskill and Sterling, *Encyclopedia of Data Protection* (Sweet and Maxwell, 1992).

Cîrstea, Implications of electronic commerce law in Romania, *Perspectives of Business Law Journal* (2014)(3:1) 139.

Data Protection Laws of the World Handbook: Second Edition—Romania (Mondaq, 2013).

Zanfir, Protectia Datelor Personale. Drepturile Persoanei Vizate (Praxis, 2014).

Slovakia

Chalton, Gaskill and Sterling, *Encyclopedia of Data Protection* (Sweet and Maxwell, 1992).

Majtényi, Ensuring data protection in east-central Europe, *Social Research* (2002)(69:1) 151.

Slovenia

Boštjan, and Carlisle, Investigating the legal protection of data, information and knowledge under the EU data protection regime, *International Review of Law Computers & Technology* (2009)(23:3) 189.

Boštjan, SPAM na Sodišču, Nove Tehnologije za Poslovni svet (2006).

Boštjan and Carlisle, Compiling medical data into national medical databases: Legitimate practice or data protection concern? *Ethical, Legal, and Social Issues in Medical Informatics* (2008) 228.

Boštjan and Carlisle, Data protection and database theory [Elektronski vir]: Applying database design principles to personal data identification, *British & Irish Law, Education and Technology Association* (2007).

Chalton, Gaskill and Sterling, *Encyclopedia of Data Protection* (Sweet and Maxwell, 1992).

Custers and Uršič, Big data and data reuse [Elektronski vir]: A taxonomy of data reuse for balancing big data benefits and personal data protection, *International Data Privacy Law* (2016)(5).

Fuchs, Boersma, Albrechtslund, and Sandoval, eds, Toward a critique of surveillance in the age of the internet [Elektronski vir]: A reflection on the internet and surveillance, *Nasl. z nasl. Zaslona, TI*=TripleC [*Elektronski vir*] (2012)(10:1) 92.

Hudoklin, Security problems in electronic data interchange systems, *Electronic Data Interchange: Proceedings* (1990) 186.

Macová and Vrabko Zákon, č 122/2013 ZzO Ochrane Osobných Údajov, S Komentárom (Eurokódex, 2013).

Markelj and Bernik, Information security related to the use of mobile devices in Slovene enterprises, *Varstvoslovje* (2014)(16:2) 154.

Markelj and Zgaga, Comprehension of cyber threats and their consequences in Slovenia, *Computer Law & Security Review* (2016).

Mičo, *Zmeny v Ochrane Osobných Údajo* (Kluwer, 2014).

Recher, Budak and Rajh, Eye in the Sky: Contextualizing Development with Online Privacy Concern in Western Balkan Countries, *Radni Materijali EIZ-a = EIZ working papers* (2015).

Selinšek, Veliko Podatkovje v Pravu in Ekonomiji: Veliki Izzivi Ali Velike Težave? = Big Data in Law and Economy: Big Challenges or Big Troubles? *Lexonomica: Revija za Pravo in Ekonomijo = Journal of Law and Economics* (2015) 161.

Valková, Dudáš and Palúš, *Zákon O Ochrane Osobných Údajov* (DMJ Projekt, 2014).

Spain

Chalton, Gaskill and Sterling, *Encyclopedia of Data Protection* (Sweet and Maxwell, 1992).

Chen, The EU data protection law reform: Challenges for service trade liberalization and possible approaches for harmonizing privacy standards into the context of GATS, *Spanish Yearbook of International Law* (2015)(19).

González, Emergence of Personal Data Protection as a Fundamental Right of the EU (Springer, 2014).

Leiva, Data protection law in Spain and Latin America: Survey of legal approaches, *International Law News* (09/2012) 16.

Lynskey, Control over personal data in a digital age: Google Spain v AEPD and Mario Costeja Gonzalez, *The Modern Law Review* (2015)(78:3) 522.

Pradillo, Fighting against cybercrime in Europe: The admissibility of remote searches in Spain, *European Journal of Crime, Criminal Law and Criminal Justice* (2011)(19:4) 363.

Sweden

Chalton, Gaskill and Sterling, *Encyclopedia of Data Protection* (Sweet and Maxwell, 1992).

Flaherty, *Protecting Privacy in Surveillance Societies: The Federal Republic of Germany, Sweden, France, Canada, and the United States* (University of North Carolina Press, 2014).

Öman and Lindblom, *Personuppgiftslagen, En kommentar*, 4th edition (Norstedts Gula Bibliotek).

United Kingdom

Chalton, Gaskill and Sterling, *Encyclopedia of Data Protection* (Sweet and Maxwell, 1992-).

Jay, *Data Protection: Law and Practice* (Sweet and Maxwell, 2012).

Jay, *Data Protection Law and Practice* (First Supplement, 2014).

Lambert, *A Users Guide to Data Protection* (Bloomsbury, 2016).

Lloyd, *A Guide to the Data Protection Act 1998* (Butterworths, 1998).

Nugter, *Transborder Flow of Personal Data within the EC: A Comparative Analysis of the Privacy Statutes of the Federal Republic of Germany, France, the United Kingdom and The Netherlands and Their Impact on the Private Sector* (Kluwer Law, 1990).

☐ General Texts

Some general data protection related legal texts include:

Asscher and Hoogcarspel, *Regulating Spam: A European Perspective after the Adoption of the E-Privacy Directive* (TMC Asser; Cambridge: Cambridge University Press, 2006).

Bainbridge, *Introduction to Information Technology Law* (Pearson Longman, 2008, updates in 2010).

Beyleveld, Townend and Wright, *Research Ethics Committees, Data Protection and Medical Research in European Countries* (Ashgate, 2005).

Beyleveld et al., *Implementation of the Data Protection Directive in Relation to Medical Research in Europe* (Ashgate, 2005).

Birkinshaw and Varney, *Government and Information: The Law Relating to Access, Disclosure and their Regulation* (Bloomsbury, 2012).

Buffington, *Data Protection for Virtual Data Centers* (Wiley, 2010).

Burnett, *Outsourcing: The Legal Contract* (Faculty of Information Technology of the Institute of Chartered Accountants, 2005).

Burnett, *Outsourcing IT: The Legal Aspects: Planning, Contracting, Managing and the Law* (Gower, 2009).

Butler, ed., *E-Commerce and Convergence: A Guide to the Law of Digital Media* (Tottel, 2012).

Bygrave, *Data Protection Law: Approaching its Rationale, Logic and Limits* (Kluwer, 2002).

Büllesbach et al., *Concise European IT Law* (Wolters Kluwer, 2010).

Calder, *A Business Guide to Information Security: How to Protect Your Company's IT Assets, Reduce Risks and Understand the Law* (Kogan, 2005).

Carey, *Data Protection: A Practical Guide to UK and EU Law* (Oxford University Press, 2015).

Conradi, ed., *Communications Law Handbook* (Bloomsbury, 2009).

Corrigan, *Data Protection for Photographers: A Guide to Storing and Protecting Your Valuable Digital Assets* (Rocky Nook, 2014).

Datta and Datta, *Face Detection and Recognition: Theory and Practice* (CRC Press, 2015).

Diffie and Landau, *Privacy on the Line, The Politics of Wiretapping and Encryption* (Cambridge, MA; London: MIT, 2007).

Earle, *Data Protection in the NHS* (Informa, 2003).

Edwards, ed., *The New Legal Framework for E-Commerce in Europe* (Hart, 2005).

Edwards and Waelde, eds, *Law and the Internet* (Hart, 2009) (Chapters 14–21).

Encyclopedia of Data Protection.

Engineering Employers' Federation, *Data Protection: A Practical for Employers* (Engineering Employers' Federation, 2005).

Fawke and Townsend, *Data Protection & the Pensions Industry: Implications of the Data Protection Act* (Masons, 2002).

First Report on the Implementation of the Data Protection Directive (95/46/EC) (i.e., DPD95).

Fuster, *The Emergence of Personal Data Protection as a Fundamental Right of the EU* (Springer, 2014).

Gough, ed., *Data Protection for Financial Firms: A Practical Guide to Managing Privacy and Information Risk* (Risk Books, 2009).

Gutwirth and Leenes, *Data Protection on the Move: Current Developments in ICT and Privacy/Data Protection* (Springer, 2015).

Gutwirth and Leenes, *Reforming European Data Protection Law* (Law, Governance and Technology Series/Issues in Privacy and Data Protection) (2014).

Hess, *Protecting Privacy in Private International and Procedural Law and by Data Protection: European and American Developments* (Ashgate, 2015).

Jay, *Data Protection: Law and Practice* (Sweet and Maxwell, 2012).

Jay, *Data Protection Law and Practice* (First Supplement, 2014).

Jay and Clarke, *Data Protection Compliance in the UK: A Pocket Guide* (IT Governance Publishing, 2008).

Jay and Hamilton, *Data Protection: Law and Practice* (Bainbridge, *Data Protection Law* (XPL, 2005).

Kuner, *European Data Protection Law: Corporate Compliance and Regulation* (Oxford University Press, 2007).

Kuner, *European Data Protection Law: Corporate Regulation and Compliance* (Oxford University Press, 2007).

Kuschewsky, *Data Protection & Privacy: Jurisdictional Comparisons* (Thomson Reuters, 2012).

Lambert, *A Users Guide to Data Protection* (Bloomsbury, 2016).

Lambert, *International Handbook of Social Media Laws* (Bloomsbury, 2014).

Lambert, *Social Networking: Law, Rights and Policy* (Clarus, 2014).

Lloyd, *Information Technology Law* (Oxford University Press, 2014).

Lynskey, *The Foundations of EU Data Protection Law* (OUP, 2015).

Macdonald, *Data Protection: Legal Compliance and Good Practice for Employers* (Tottel, 2008).

Mario Viola de Azevedo Cunha, *Market Integration Through Data Protection: An Analysis of the Insurance and Financial Industries in the EU (Law, Governance and Technology Series)* (Springer, 2015).

Matthews, *Data Protection Toolkit* (2014).

Morgan and Boardman, *Data Protection Strategy, Implementing Data Protection Compliance* (Sweet & Maxwell, 2012).

Murray, *Information Technology Law: The Law and Society* (Oxford University Press, 2013) (Chapters 18, 19).

Purtova, *Property Rights in Personal Data, A European Perspective* (Kluwer, 2012).

Reed, *Computer Law* (Oxford University Press, 2011) (Chapters 10, 11).

Room, *Data Protection and Compliance in Context* (British Computer Society, 2007).

Rowland and Kohl, *Information Technology Law* (Routledge, 2016).

Ryan, *The EU Regulatory Framework for Electronic Communications Handbook* (Bloomsbury, 2010).

Schachter, *Information and Decisional Privacy* (Carolina Academic Press, 2003).

Schmidt and Payton, *Privacy in the Age of Big Data: Recognizing Threats, Defending Your Rights, and Protecting Your Family* (Rowman, 2015).

Singleton, *Data Protection and Employment Practices* (LexisNexis/Tolley, 2005).

Smith, *Internet Law and Regulation* (Sweet & Maxwell, 2016) (Chapter 7).

Smith and Moseley, *The New Data Protection Liabilities & Risks for Direct Marketers: Handbook* (Forum Business Media, 2005).

Ticher, *Data Protection and the Cloud: Are the Risks Too Great?* (Ticher, 2015).

Ticher, *Data Protection for Voluntary Organisations* (Directory of Social Change in association with Bates, Wells & Braithwaite, 2009).

Webster, *Data Protection in the Financial Services Industry* (Gower, 2006).

Webster, *Effective Data Protection: Managing Information in an Era of Change* (ICSA Information & Training, 2011).

INDEX

A

Access requests
    considerations, 236
    dealing with, 236–237
    and implicit required tasks, 191–192
    and personal data, 226–227
    response to, 237–239
Access rights
    overview, 233–234
    and personal data, 235–236
        confirmation regarding, 234–235
Advisory function, 199–200
Awareness-raising and information
        function, 199

B

BCI. *see* Business contact
        information (BCI)
Biometrics, 228
Business contact information (BCI), 308

C

Compliance monitoring, 201
Computer systems and security
    biometrics, 228
    network security, 228
    personal computers of employees, 227
    removable media, 227
Conflict/nondirection function, 203
Controllers
    awareness-raising of, 126
    compliance with rights of data
            subjects, 165
    implicit required tasks compliance
            with rights of

codes of conduct and certification,
        183–185
communication of personal data
        breach to data subject, 172–174
data protection impact assessments,
        174–182
data protection officer, 183
notification of personal data breach,
        171–172
prior consultation, 182–183
security of processing, 170–171
inform and advise of data protection
        obligations, 119–120
training of, 127
    employees involved in processing
            operations, 127
Cooperation function, 200–201

D

Data breach, 265
    board level responsibility, 293
    communication to data subject,
            172–174
    customer relations, 295
    employees and human resources,
            173–174, 295
    incident response, 270
    IT/IT security, 293–294
    lead coordinator, 292–293
    legal and privacy, 294
    notification of, 171–172, 265–268
    overview, 289–291
    police and law enforcement, 295–296
    preparing in advance, 291–292
        importance, 292
    public relations, 294–295
    reporting, 293